Foundations,
Private Giving, and
Public Policy

Foundations, Private Giving, and Public Policy

Report and Recommendations of the Commission on Foundations and Private Philanthropy

THE UNIVERSITY OF CHICAGO PRESS
CHICAGO AND LONDON

International Standard Book Number: 0–226–66286–1
Library of Congress Catalog Card Number: 78–139831

THE UNIVERSITY OF CHICAGO PRESS, CHICAGO 60637
THE UNIVERSITY OF CHICAGO PRESS, LTD., LONDON

Contents

Biographical Notes on Commission Members and Staff — vii
A Personal Preface, by Peter G. Peterson — xi
Acknowledgments — xxi

1. In the Beginning — 1

PART ONE. PRIVATE PHILANTHROPY

2. The Role of Philanthropy in a Changing Society — 11
3. Financial Needs of Charitable Organizations — 21
4. Tax Incentives and Philanthropy — 30

PART TWO. FOUNDATIONS

5. Foundations: Their Characteristics and Work — 39
6. Financial Abuses of Foundations — 54
7. Politics and Public Concern over Foundations — 63
8. Foundation Funds: Sources, Investment Performance,
   and Amount of Payout — 72
9. How Foundations Have Spent Their Money — 77
10. Management of Foundation Grants — 87
11. Foundation Achievements: An Overview — 93
12. Other Views of Foundation Achievements — 112
13. The Commission's Assessment of Foundations — 117

PART THREE. RECOMMENDATIONS

14. Angle of Vision   123
15. Recommendations to Foundations   126
16. Recommendations to Government I: Tax Policy and
    Tax Administration   145
17. Recommendations to Government II: Regulation of
    Foundations—Payout, Reporting, and
    Administrative Expenditures   147
18. Recommendations to Government III: The New Law—
    Legislative Activities of Foundations and the Birth Rate of
    New Foundations   160
19. Federal Regulation of Foundations: Further Considerations
    and Summary   169
20. For the Future: An Advisory Board on Philanthropic Policy   121

APPENDIXES

  I. Description of Surveys   191
 II. Findings of the Survey of Distinguished Citizens   201
III. Findings of the Survey of Chicago Philanthropic
     Organizations   227
 IV. Tables Summarizing the Survey of Foundations   241
  V. Philanthropy and the Economy, by Mary Hamilton   256
 VI. Enlightened Self-interest and Corporate Philanthropy,
     by William J. Baumol   262

Index   279

Biographical Notes on Commission Members and Staff

Chairman

PETER G. PETERSON. Chairman and Chief Executive Officer, Bell and Howell Company, Chicago

Members

J. PAUL AUSTIN. Chairman, President, and Chief Executive Officer, The Coca-Cola Company, Atlanta

DANIEL BELL. Professor of Sociology, Harvard University; author; Chairman, Commission on the Year 2000 of the American Academy of Arts and Sciences; member, President's Commission on Technology, Automation, and Economic Progress

DANIEL P. BRYANT. Chairman and Chief Executive Officer, Bekins Van and Storage Company, Los Angeles; lawyer; Director and Past President, Los Angeles Area Chamber of Commerce

JAMES CHAMBERS. President and Publisher, *Dallas Times-Herald*; author

SHELDON S. COHEN. Cohen and Uretz; former Commissioner of Internal Revenue, U.S. Treasury Department

THOMAS B. CURTIS. Vice-president and General Counsel, Encyclopaedia Britannica; former U.S. Representative from Second Congressional District, Missouri, and member of House Ways and Means Committee, Joint Economic Committee

PAUL A. FREUND. Professor, Harvard University Law School; expert in constitutional law; author; editor-in-chief of multivolume *History of the Supreme Court*, now in preparation, commissioned by the U.S. Congress; Past President, American Academy of Arts and Sciences

MARTIN FRIEDMAN. Director, Walker Art Center, Minneapolis; American Fine Arts Commissioner, São Paulo Bienal; member, National Collection of Fine Arts Commission; author and lecturer on contemporary international art

PATRICIA ROBERTS HARRIS. Strasser, Spiegelberg, Fried, Frank, and Kampelman; member, National Commission on the Causes and Prevention of Violence; former Dean and Professor, Howard University Law School; former U.S. Ambassador to Luxembourg

A. LEON HIGGINBOTHAM, JR. U.S. District Court Judge, Eastern District of Pennsylvania; Vice-chairman, National Commission on the Causes and Prevention of Violence; former commissioner, Federal Trade Commission; member, White House Conference to Fulfill These Rights; member, Commission on Reform of U.S. Criminal Law

LANE KIRKLAND. Secretary-Treasurer, American Federation of Labor and Congress of Industrial Organizations

PHILIP R. LEE, M.D. Chancellor, University of California, San Francisco; former Assistant Secretary, U.S. Department of Health, Education, and Welfare

EDWARD H. LEVI. President, University of Chicago; former law professor, Dean of the Law School; past member, White House Task Force on Education, White House Central Group in Domestic Affairs; author

FRANKLIN A. LONG. Director for Program on Science, Technology, and Society, Cornell University; former member, President's Science Advisory Committee; former assistant director, U.S. Arms Control and Disarmament Agency

A. S. MIKE MONRONEY. Consultant, Aviation and Transportation; former U.S. Senator and U.S. Representative from Oklahoma; former chairman, Senate Post Office and Civil Service Committee, and member, Senate Appropriations Committee

Executive Director
EVERETT L. HOLLIS. Partner, Mayer, Brown, and Platt, Chicago; former General Counsel, Atomic Energy Commission

Associate Director
FRITZ HEIMANN. Associate Corporate Counsel, General Electric Company

Associate Director
WALTER J. BLUM. Professor, University of Chicago Law School

Assistant Director
 WILLIAM A. WINEBERG. Associate, Mayer, Brown, and Platt, Chicago
Assistant Director
 JOHN R. LABOVITZ, J.D., University of Chicago Law School, 1969
Chairman, Finance Committee
 HERMON DUNLAP SMITH. Chairman, Finance Committee, Marlennan
 Corporation

A Personal Preface

We live in a period of contradictory protests in America. Many people who protest against "the power of the Establishment" also protest that the Establishment alone can set things right but refuses to use its power to that end. Many other people who protest the failure of the government to redress their personal grievances also protest that the government has made unwarranted invasions into those spheres of life which should be preserved for private decisions. In this confused atmosphere it is not entirely surprising that American philanthropy should also be viewed in a contradictory light.

In one view of philanthropy, Americans focus on the great range of private, nonprofit institutions which depend in whole or in part on philanthropic support. They particularly favor this kind of support for the "traditional" objects of charity—churches, universities, hospitals, libraries, museums, symphony orchestras, Community Chest groups. Many also acclaim social innovation, when stated in the abstract, as a universal virtue; some of these same voices, however, express the wistful hope for change without controversy when it impinges on their special domains. In general, though, Americans give philanthropic institutions high marks.

In another view, many of the same Americans tend to become sharply critical when they focus on the philanthropic donors themselves; so much so that, in a reversal of the biblical injunction, it may seem better to receive than to give.

The criticism of private philanthropy has had its roots in many causes. There was a handful of specific cases in the public prints where the agents or agencies of private philanthropy were accused of bad judgment bordering on folly, or of an outright abuse of privilege. A substantial part of the hostility sprang directly from members of the Congress. A sizable number were convinced foundations had become partisan political instruments instead of agencies to promote the general welfare—that they were promoting extreme ideologies both of the left and, to a lesser degree, of the right. A passionate element was added to this charge by individual members of Congress who saw an electioneering item in a handful of well publicized foundation grants. To put the matter plainly, they felt these grants were explicitly designed to defeat incumbent Congressmen in the districts where the projects were carried on. All in all, then, the inference was drawn that foundations were as involved in politics as in "charity."

Available tools of auditing and public reporting, however, had not been used to make known the actual frequency and the types of such abuses. In consequence, an air of the illicit enveloped philanthropy in general and the charitable foundations in particular. Even the worthiest of these suffered a loss of public trust.

For another thing, the foundations themselves had previously looked with nonseeing eyes at the warning signs of the troubles they faced. Many ignored the obligations of public accountability and neglected to take timely measures of necessary self-correction. And, in any case, they failed to discharge a duty incumbent upon all institutions in a democracy—a duty to explain themselves to the public.

Why this? The Commission on Foundations and Philanthropy sensed that philanthropy and the foundations assumed that they were so well thought of by the community at large that they could dispense with the need to monitor themselves or to accumulate evidence about the nature and quality of their performance. The high costs of this illusion could be seen in 1969 when the Congress dealt with what became the Tax Reform Act of 1969. The Congress was strongly disposed initially— and often through misinformation and misconceptions—to give a punitive cast to the provisions of the act that dealt with private philanthropy and in particular with the foundations.

By remaining a kind of closed society in an era when openness is a byword, the foundations excited public suspicion that they were engaged, not in a great range of activities that promoted the general welfare, but in secret things done in a dark corner. By their reluctance to discuss publicly their failures as well as their successes, the foundations foreclosed the right to their own fragile humanity. They became instead symbols of secret wealth which mysteriously used the levers of power to promote obscure, devious, or even sinister purposes.

To cap this burden of suspicion, many irrepressible and unexplored questions posed their own challenges to private philanthropy and the foundations—questions which had a common root in this fact: that the traditional areas of philanthropy such as higher education, health, and scientific research had come to feel the imprint of the growing, necessary, and often dominant role of government.

Total foundation grants in 1968, for example, were only three-fourths of 1 percent of the federal budget. Figures of this kind, duplicated in many aspects of the general welfare, forced many people to ask numerous questions. For example, did tax benefits to foundations waste the very funds the government itself urgently needed to pay for comprehensive public programs which could come to grips with acute social problems? Should the allocation of national resources for the general welfare be made in a democracy by a decision of the people as a whole acting through their elected governmental representatives? Did the foundations, by their own nature, violate this fundamental democratic principle? Did they represent a case where a handful of wealthy men in control of the foundations could do what they pleased with billions of dollars of tax benefits, yet were not called to public account for their decisions?

And still more questions: Was there any useful role that the foundations could play in the future? If foundations only duplicated on a small scale what the government was already doing on an immense scale, would they not lose one of the key reasons for their existence? On the other hand, was it possible for foundations to do a number of things differently and better than governmental agencies? If so, would not this point to the merit of maintaining a dual system of private giving and government funding as a means for allocating resources for the general welfare?

A full account of the evolution of the Commission on Foundations and Philanthropy is to be found in the first chapter of this volume. Yet it should be stressed at this point that the commission is not a governmental agency, nor was it created to have an ongoing life.

The commission is an outgrowth of the American instinct for private associations noted by Alexis de Tocqueville 130 years ago. It is composed of a private group of citizens not associated with foundations and was formed for the purpose of preparing this report on other private associations representing American institutions of philanthropy. The life span of the commission was limited to the time necessary and available to complete its task; and it depended on the financial contributions of private individuals and organizations other than foundations to cover its expenses.

This report, therefore, is in no sense an official document, though hopefully it has something to say to government officials, to the officers of the institutions of private philanthropy, and still more to the public at large. Its power to persuade or convince, however, is limited to the credibility of the evidence presented in the body of the report and to the logic of the policy conclusions drawn from the evidence. The aim of the report is to make an objective appraisal of philanthropic foundations in America and, beyond this, to recommend long-range policies which might require new lines of action either by various agencies of government or by American philanthropic institutions and individuals.

It is beyond the scope of this personal preface to summarize all the findings of fact and policy recommendations that are set forth in the body of the commission's report. Something will be gained, however, if a reader in a hurry is alerted to several key conclusions reached by the commission and amplified in the report.

The commission concluded, first of all, that the public interest is best served through a strong dual system of private giving and government funding as a means for allocating resources for the general welfare. Given the acute and growing financial problems that face private charitable organizations, such a system will require more money rather than simply more rhetoric. Legislative and executive leaders must decide whether they wish to encourage more private giving as a strategy for the solution of our social problems or to rely more heavily on public funding. I do not believe this question has been answered or even conscientiously (or perhaps even consciously) reviewed.

No government agency, however vigorously led, can readily break the crust of ingrained bureaucratic habits which can lead to the mechanical performance of old things in the old ways—though the old ways may have been rendered obsolete by new conditions. No government agency, however enlightened, can hold the entire nation in a single vision or can move quickly enough to do all the things a pluralistic society demands. None, however courageous, is at liberty to undertake the high-risk ventures that are inherent in social innovations—ventures which are as likely to end in an instructive failure as in a singular success. The very bigness of Big Government, with its generalizing rules, makes it a seemingly remote monolith, unresponsive either to urgent and unique local needs or to emergent new opportunities for imaginative social action.

Private philanthropy, if served by free, dedicated individuals, receives more from them than money. It receives part of their own person, their direct concern with the fate of other people, their determination to do something to cleanse and ennoble human life. Aside from this decisive personal element, private philanthropic institutions are structurally equipped to act in constructive ways not readily available even to the best agencies of government. They can experiment with diverse approaches to social problems, without fear of being voted out of office if any particular program undertaken in good faith and with careful preparation nonetheless fails in the end. They can make their own failures a source of knowledge to government itself about what it would be wise to *avoid* in its policies—just as they can provide government with a model of a successful social test that can be written for the nation as a whole. They can apply their sophistication and independence to the legitimate demand for healthy criticism of America's institutions—government and nongovernment alike.

It seems to me that private philanthropy and the foundations can serve the general welfare in the same way that innovative businessmen, at the head of small-scale enterprises, often lead the great breakthroughs in the technological realm—breakthroughs which the great corporations either fail to foresee or cannot venture for internal reasons.

Indeed, just as we need the decentralized, small-scale business enterprise that can perform these works of economic and technological progress, we need the venturesome work of private philanthropy as an instrument for decentralizing the decision-making process in the realm of social policy. We need it to keep open the avenues to a multiplicity of choices, to a freedom of options, to ardent competition among proposed solutions to common problems until the marketplace itself decides which particular solutions make the most sense.

This system of private philanthropy and foundations has against its record some follies and excesses that were avoidable. They must be guarded against in the future, since a handful of dramatic abuses have brought this system as a whole under a cloud of suspicion. Yet, even if *all* the follies, excesses, inequities, and abuses charged against private philanthropy were factually true, would anything be gained if private philanthropy were "legislated out of existence"? When we consider the alternative of an American life in which private philanthropy no longer played a key role, the picture that looms up is a bleak one.

It is my strong impression that in the past few years even those individuals who are among the most socially compassionate of American
citizens and the most enthusiastic advocates of public funding for general welfare programs have been forced by the evidence of their own
senses to reduce the scale of the social gains they anticipated from government programs alone. They have been forced increasingly to recognize some of the inherent limitations of such programs and to look more
to the private sector and local forces as alternative sources of initiatives
bearing on the general welfare.

On the same grounds, the commission concluded that the nation
would be the ultimate loser if government agencies placed unnecessary
restrictions on the freedom of private philanthropy to sponsor the kind
of programs which it alone is in a position to do. The commission also
concluded that private philanthropy would not repay the public for the
tax benefits it receives if it adhered solely to the "safe" routine of established charitable activities and failed to live up to its full potentialities by risking itself in the causes of social invention and the search for
excellence.

At the same time, the commission agreed that past instances of individual sources of private philanthropy having abused their tax privileges are not mere figments of overwrought imaginations. Such abuses
have been real enough, not in a great sweep of cases, but in enough
cases to lead the commission to support a policy of government regulation of certain financial aspects of private philanthropy.

Many foundations seem to be the victims of a self-induced amnesia
in the sense that they have forgotten the basic reason for the granting
of their tax-favored status—that they could add to the general welfare
by their own charitable works. Having forgotten this truth, many foundations show a low payout rate to charity, some hanging on to "their"
assets in order to control corporations. Still others are obviously more
interested in increasing the market value of their assets than in enlarging
the scope of their charitable activities.

The commission was aware that its support of governmental regulation of high payout rates would not win universal acclaim from the
foundations themselves. Yet a candid examination of the facts of the
matter, including the growing financial crises of charitable organizations,
led the commission to recommend that government regulation of foundations to insure a high payout rate was not only necessary and proper
but should be a first principle of the governmental regulatory machinery.

At the same time, the commission strongly resisted invasion by the route of government regulation that would restrict the right of the foundations to be active in the field of public affairs. This does not mean the commission looked with favor upon tax exemptions that would allow foundations to interfere with the political process. Far from it. The commission recognized that in some of the instances of abuse charged against specific foundations—to the detriment of all—foundations did use their resources in dubious ways to serve the interests of persons prominently identified with partisan politics. The commission believed that the criticism these actions invited was fully warranted, regardless of the motives behind the decisions of the foundations in question.

The commission is in full agreement with those who insist that, in the field of public affairs, *education* and not political pressure is the one and only proper aim for foundation activities. Yet the commission was no less fearful that overzealous governmental legislation and regulation (rationalized in the name of "curbing improper political operations" of the foundations) could prove an ambassador of death to legitimate educational activities undertaken by the foundations—activities that would help create a healthier climate in which public policy questions could be decided by the political process.

Many people expressed the hope that the commission would formulate a foolproof set of guidelines to determine when a grant is charitable or noncharitable, partisan or nonpartisan, for education or for "political propaganda." If this expression of hope was in its own way a note of confidence in the wisdom of the commission, it was perhaps as unrealistic as a project to build mountains without valleys.

The commission was convinced that it could not, nor could anyone else, formulate the kind of guidelines that would govern all cases and controversies. The most the commission felt it could do was to suggest some criteria and processes that might help draw the line between the "permissible" and "nonpermissible" in the realm of public affairs.

In sum, government policing and public reporting are necessary to minimize financial and other abuses. Government involvement in program, however, can easily go counter to the basic principle of private philanthropy and put the government in the anomalous position of dominating a group of organizations that have, as a chief reason for being, the fact they are *not* governmental.

One across-the-board recommendation made by the commission merits a special mention. It is the proposal for the creation of an Advisory Board on Philanthropic Policy. A private body of this sort, though set up under public auspices, could have a continuing influence on every aspect of American philanthropy. It would be an ongoing mechanism and would stay abreast of changing circumstances, of unresolved and emergent questions, of new concepts of philanthropy's function in society. It would extend into the future the kind of studies and recommendations made by this commission, but would do so under conditions which promised a more thoroughgoing analysis and a continual reevaluation.

We recognize that so brief a study as ours can by no means meet the country's needs. Without presuming to claim for our commission the virtues we have proposed for the new board, we hope that there will be such a board and trust we may, in effect, pass on to them the work which we began.

Though the financial resources of the commission were on the bare-boned side, and only a small staff could be engaged to direct and coordinate the field work, the staff offset in dedication and competence what it lacked in financial muscle and manpower. My fellow commissioners and I will always be grateful to them personally and to the firm of Mayer, Brown, and Platt and to General Electric Company for making staff members available to us. We are also grateful to Mr. Hermon D. Smith for assuming the onerous burden of raising funds from private sources for the support of the commission's work. At the time of this writing, Mr. Smith is still heroically trying to persuade donors—who by now are less affluent—that they should help reduce the impressive deficit of our commission. Specific thanks are also due to Sidney Hyman, who, in a race against the absolute of time, made a major contribution to the architecture, style, and editing of the final manuscript.

In the course of its efforts, the commission was gratified to receive hospitable access to decision makers in government and to present to them new lines of thought for their consideration. Congressional leaders such as Representative Wilbur Mills of the House Ways and Means Committee and Senator Russell Long of the Senate Finance Committee, as well as ranking officials in the Treasury Department, gave thoughtful and detailed consideration to the preliminary findings of the commission. They were also a source of helpful initial suggestions about ways in which the commission might formulate various lines of its inquiry. In all this, we have tried to do a piece of research and analysis untainted by biases of either advocacy or antagonism.

The individuals listed in the Acknowledgments are only a few of those who have also contributed to the work of the commission in a variety of ways—testifying before the commission, submitting papers, conducting surveys, criticizing drafts, discussing ideas. They provided an invaluable resource as a sounding board for conclusions which emerged from the commission's study. In most cases, their time was contributed voluntarily outside of business hours and without compensation. The commission is in their debt.

PETER G. PETERSON

Acknowledgments

The commission is grateful to the following individuals, and many others, for their help:

Bernard R. Berelson, President, The Population Council

Norman Bradburn, Director, National Opinion Research Center

Kingman Brewster, Jr., President, Yale University

McGeorge Bundy, President, The Ford Foundation

Edwin Cohen, Assistant Secretary for Tax Policy, U.S. Treasury Department

Norman Cousins, Editor, *The Saturday Review*

Merrimon Cuninggim, President, Danforth Foundation

Adrian W. DeWind, Paul, Weiss, Goldberg, Rifkind, Wharton, and Garrison

Douglas Dillon, Former U. S. Secretary of the Treasury

Stuart Duhl, D'Ancona, Pflaum, Wyatt, and Riskind

Carmel P. Ebb, Associate Editor, *Review of Securities Regulation*

William T. Finley, Jr., Sharon, Pierson, and Semmes

David F. Freeman, President, Council on Foundations

Marion Fremont-Smith, Choate, Hall, and Stewart; Former Assistant Attorney General and Director of Public Charities, Commonwealth of Massachusetts

Kermit Gordon, President, The Brookings Institution

Julius Greenfield, Assistant Attorney General for Charitable Foundations, State of New York

Mary T. Hamilton, Graduate School of Business, University of Chicago

David K. Hardin, President, Market Facts, Inc.

Arnold Harberger, Chairman, Department of Economics, University of Chicago

David R. Hunter, Executive Director, Stern Family Fund

Lemuel Hunter, Retired Vice-president, Inland Steel Company

Sidney Hyman, Adlai Stevenson Institute

Morris Janowitz, Chairman, Department of Sociology, University of Chicago

John Jeuck, Professor, Graduate School of Business, University of Chicago.

Vernon Jordan, Director, Voter Education Project, Southern Regional Council, Inc.

Carl Kaysen, Director, Institute for Advanced Study

Francis Keppel, Chairman, General Learning Corporation; former Assistant Secretary, U.S. Department of Health, Education, and Welfare

James Killian, Chairman, Massachusetts Institute of Technology

William A. W. Krebs, Vice-president, Arthur D. Little, Inc.

Robert N. Kreidler, Executive Vice-president, Alfred P. Sloan Foundation

Edwin H. Land, Chairman and President, Polaroid Corporation

Russell Long, U.S. Senator, Arkansas; Chairman, Senate Finance Committee

James Lorie, Professor, Graduate School of Business, University of Chicago

John Martin, Chief Counsel, U.S. House Ways and Means Committee

John Mendenhall, Arthur Andersen and Company

Wilbur D. Mills, U.S. Representative, Second District, Arkansas; Chairman, House Ways and Means Committee

Lloyd N. Morrisett, President, Markle Foundation

Morton Moskin, White and Case

Norman Nie, Senior Study Director, National Opinion Research Center

James A. Norton, Director, Cleveland Foundation

Frederick H. Osborn, Jr., Executive Secretary, Smith, Kline, and French Foundation

Acknowledgments xxiii

Manning M. Pattillo, Jr., President, The Foundation Center
Joseph Pechman, The Brookings Institution
Alan Pifer, President, Carnegie Corporation
Daniel Robinson, Peat, Marwick, Mitchell, and Company
Mitchell Rogovin, Arnold and Porter
Oscar Ruebhausen, Debevoise, Plimpton, Lyons, and Gates
John M. Russell, Former President, Markle Foundation
John Schwartz, Executive Vice-president, American Association of
Fund Raising Counsel, Inc.
Edward Shils, Professor, Department of Sociology, University of
Chicago
John Simon, Professor, Yale University Law School; President,
Taconic Foundation
Datus C. Smith, Jr., Vice-president of JDR III Fund
Norman A. Sugarman, Baker, Hostetler, and Patterson
Stanley Surrey, Professor, Harvard University Law School; Former
Assistant Secretary for Tax Policy, U.S. Treasury Department
Robert L. Sutherland, Executive Director, The Hogg Foundation for
Mental Health; President, Southwestern Conference of Foundations
Michael Taussig, Professor, Rutgers University
Randolph Thrower, Commissioner of Internal Revenue, U.S. Treasury
Department
Thomas Troyer, Caplin and Drysdale
Ralph Tyler, Director Emeritus, Center for Advanced Study in the
Behavioral Sciences
Thomas Vail, Chief Counsel, Senate Finance Committee
Charls E. Walker, Undersecretary of the Treasury
Robert C. Weaver, President, The Bernard M. Baruch College;
former U.S. Secretary of Housing and Urban Development
Lloyd Williams, Associate Director of Industrial Marketing, Market
Facts, Inc.
Bernard Wolfman, Professor, University of Pennsylvania Law School
Laurence N. Woodworth, Chief of Staff, Joint Committee on Internal
Revenue Taxation, U.S. Congress
Frank H. Woods, Jr., Secretary-Treasurer, Woods Charitable Fund,
Inc.

Staff Associates

Richard H. Chandler, Robert Ciricillo, John Gelb, Phillips W. Goodell, William R. Hansen, John Johnston, Ruth Moore, John Ozag, Thomas Parrish, William Wing

In addition, the commission would like to thank the staffs of the following organizations:

Internal Revenue Service, The Foundation Center, U.S. Treasury Department, Senate Finance Committee, House Ways and Means Committee, American Association of Fund Raising Counsel, Arthur Andersen and Company, Market Facts, Inc., National Opinion Research Center

Americans of all ages, all conditions, and all dispositions constantly form associations. They have not only commercial and manufacturing companies, in which all take part, but associations of a thousand other kinds, religious, moral, serious, futile, general or restricted, enormous or diminutive. The Americans make associations to give entertainments, to found seminaries, to build inns, to construct churches, to diffuse books, to send missionaries to the Antipodes; in this manner they found hospitals, prisons, and schools. If it is proposed to inculcate some truth or foster some feeling by the encouragement of a great example, they form a society. Wherever at the head of some new undertaking you see the government in France, or a man of rank in England, in the United States you will be sure to find an association. . . .

Nothing, in my opinion, is more deserving of our attention than the intellectual and moral associations of America. The political and industrial associations of that country strike us forcibly; but the others elude our observation, or if we discover them, we understand them imperfectly because we have hardly ever seen anything of the kind. It must be acknowledged, however, that they are as necessary to the American people as the former, and perhaps more so. In democratic countries the science of association is the mother of science; the progress of all the rest depends upon the progress it has made.

—Alexis de Tocqueville
Democracy in America   (1840)

1

In the Beginning

When Henry David Thoreau wrote an essay about philanthropy more than a century ago, he set two truths in opposition to each other. "Philanthropy," said he, "is the only virtue which is sufficiently appreciated by mankind." But, said he, when the integrity of philanthropy is marred from any cause, then "there is no odor as bad as that which rises from goodness tainted."

In twentieth-century America, the cross-pull between these same truths appears in the many arguments about philanthropy that have flared in government forums and in the broad reaches of American society. The immediate issues and the lineup of adversaries have changed from one case to the next, and there have also been times of truce among them. Sooner or later, however, a new dispute has led to a new clash among a new set of adversaries.

This has been particularly true in the last few decades along the front of philanthropy occupied by the foundations.

If the outcome of the issues in dispute turned *only* on a clash between external statistics, then a particular set of statistics would now call for a directed verdict in favor of American philanthropy and the foundations. Leaving unreported gifts to one side, reported American philanthropic giving in 1969 alone amounted to 17.6 billion[1]—a sum exceeding in size the combined gross national products of Bolivia, Burma, Cambodia, Ceylon, Greece, and Thailand. At the same time, the distribution picture of this sum, viewed from the standpoint of beneficiaries and the

---

1. The figures cited are based on data compiled by the American Association of Fund-Raising Counsel, Inc. and are published in *Giving USA* 1970. These statistics are necessarily based on estimates and can include some duplications.

percentage of the total each received, looked like this: religion—8.0 billion or 45 percent; health and hospitals—2.8 billion or 16 percent; education—2.9 billion or 17 percent; human resources—1.2 billion or 7 percent; civic and cultural—0.8 billion or 4 percent; other beneficiaries—1.9 billion or 11 percent.

This is not the kind of philanthropy that results from a costume charity ball. In quantity and quality, it stands on a distinctive plane of its own, not remotely approached in any other nation—and especially not, when one takes into account the main sources of the reported philanthropic gifts in 1969. Living individuals who were donors in that year gave 12.6 billion or 77 percent of the total; individual bequests accounted for 1.5 billion or 9 percent; the foundations contributed 1.6 billion or 9 percent, and the corporations 0.9 billion, or 5 percent.[2] Nor is this all. An estimated fifty-five to sixty million individual Americans—or more than one-fourth of the total population—currently do volunteer work for philanthropies; in the case of American businessmen alone, the annual monetary value of their volunteer services for philanthropies was recently put by *Fortune* magazine at around $5 billion.

Still, perhaps because of their importance, American philanthropy generally and the foundations specifically have come under heavy siege in recent years. Their inner life and their external effects have been investigated by four congressional committees, analyzed in a study by the Treasury Department, and frontally attacked by individual critics respected for their professional competence in law or finance. Able men have also come to the defense of philanthropy. Yet even when the best of the defenders have directly joined the issue with the best of the critics, the result has not always been a gain in public understanding. More often than not, the self-centered advocacy of each side has served only to cloud the public's view of the dynamics of American philanthropy.

In late 1968, in response to these conditions, John D. Rockefeller III brought together other concerned people for a series of meetings focused

2. The growth of corporate giving reflects the view of an increasing number of corporations that they have a clear stake in the conditions of social health—and not just because it is "good public relations." It is apparently because they have decided the strength of corporations is indivisible with the strength of the society around them. If the society is sick, then its contagions, sooner or later, will afflict the corporations. If society is healthy, then the corporations themselves will draw strength from that health. See appendix VI for fuller discussion in paper entitled "Enlightened Self-Interest and Corporate Philanthropy," by W. J. Baumol.

on two main questions. Was it possible to secure an independent appraisal of American philanthropy? What should be the long-range role of philanthropy and foundations in American life? At one point in the discussions, a suggestion made by Alan Pifer, president of the Carnegie Corporation, was endorsed by the other participants: that an independent commission be formed to study all relevant matters bearing on foundations and private philanthropy and to issue a report containing long-range policy recommendations with respect to them.

Subsequently, in February 1969, Mr. Rockefeller invited Peter G. Peterson, chairman of the board of Bell and Howell, to form the proposed commission. Mr. Peterson accepted, subject to conditions which were eventually adopted by the commission as a whole and released to the press. It was agreed that legislative and executive leaders in government would be consulted in order to determine whether, in their view, the proposed commission could serve a useful purpose. It was agreed further that the commission would be a *private* group of citizens whose members and staff would be chosen by Mr. Peterson. It was agreed that the main criterion for choosing the members and staff would be the need to safeguard the independence of the commission and to have it embrace the broadest possible range of representative viewpoints. Hence, it was also agreed that the commission would seek to raise its own funds from a diversity of nonfoundation sources such as individuals, corporations, and unions.

The first law of life is the law of surprise. So it was in the case of the Commission on Foundations and Private Philanthropy. It began its work with confidence that its primary task would be to formulate judgments on the principal policy questions raised by the role of foundations in our society, not to collect facts. A work outline adopted by the commission on 14 April 1969—an early date in its life—noted that "the commission does not expect to engage in any extensive fact-gathering activities." The reason: "It is assumed that necessary data about foundations and their activities are available from both public and private sources."

The shock of disillusion was not long in coming. Some of the data on hand were quite extensive, but available statistics were not responsive to certain questions central to the commission's inquiry.

The pain of this discovery was increased by an event which intersected with it. This was the time when serious charges against foundations reverberated in the House of Representatives as it moved to enact its version of the 1969 tax reform bill. Among other things it was charged (1) that many or most of the foundations were nothing but tax dodges for millionaires; (2) that many foundations represented great concentration of money and power, controlled by a self-appointed, self-perpetuating "Ivy League" establishment; (3) that the foundations were heavily involved in politics, not charity; (4) that the foundations often used their money to further extreme ideologies, whether of the left or the right; (5) that the foundations squandered on high salaries and lavish expense accounts the money that ought to go to charity; (6) that the foundations hoarded money as though it were their own when, in fact, the money belongs to the public and should be spent on charity.

All this called for a very careful examination by the commission, and for reasons apart from the effect such examination might have on the specific tax measures before the Congress. Yet when the commission cast about for relevant data, there was very little hard evidence on hand which either refuted or supported the allegations made.

The commission asked questions, for example, about the frequency of the alleged abuses by foundations, classifying these abuses according to specific types. The answers it got came in one of two forms. In one form, it was said that no relevant studies existed. In the other, an anecdote was told, but with no clear indication whether the anecdote was true, or, if true, whether it was part of a persistent pattern or merely an eccentric spore.

So it went when the commission asked other questions. It was claimed, for example, that there were approximately 22,000 foundations[3] in the United States. But was there an agreed-upon definition of a foundation? There was not. Every man was his own dictionary, with the result that another source put the number of foundations at 45,000.[4] It was also frequently asserted that the foundations had assets of $20.5 billion. Yet this figure, when touched, had no solid feel. It was inherently vague because the assets which foundations report to the Internal Revenue Service (Form 990-A) are sometimes computed at what they originally cost or on some basis other than their market value. If so, the $20.5 billion reported as the total of all foundation assets was in all probability low.

3. Foundation Center 1968 annual report. The Foundation Center is located in New York City and collects and publishes information on foundations and provides other services to foundations such as consulting help.
4. Representative Wright Patman's estimate.

Information gaps of every kind abounded. The commission, therefore, was forced to mount fact-finding expeditions of its own before it could begin to identify long-range policy questions in the realm of philanthropy and to formulate recommendations with respect to them.[5] The necessary information retrieval entailed many hearings, extensive interviews with leaders in different spheres of American life and with officials of charitable organizations. It also entailed special surveys of accountants across the nation, studies of foundation reports filed with the Internal Revenue Service, and detailed questionnaires framed to get at information that was not otherwise available. Part of the actual work was done directly by the commission and its staff. Part was done by outside agencies such as Arthur Andersen and Company, an accounting firm, and Market Facts, Inc., a market research organization, with the National Opinion Research Center at the University of Chicago acting in the capacity of consultants.

The commission, as we have indicated, began its work in a year when the institution of the foundation, and charitable giving in general, were under scrutiny by Congress in connection with the Tax Reform Act of 1969. Commission studies, even in "first draft," showed that the version of the tax measure as approved by the House would have an inhibiting effect on the scope of private philanthropy; the studies in turn underlay the testimony which the chairman of the commission presented before the Senate Finance Committee when that committee was considering the tax reform act. In the course of the legislative process, some of the provisions most harmful to philanthropy were eased or eliminated in the final version of the bill as enacted. Yet the experience as a whole raised an uneasy question: Who spoke for philanthropy when the chips were down?

The executive branch of the government apparently was not in a position to provide top policy guidance with respect to philanthropy. Nineteen sixty-nine was the first year of a new administration in Washington. It had to staff and organize itself as an executive. It had to deal with the urgent problem of war and peace. And in the competition for its time and attention, the claims posed by philanthropic issues were understandably overlooked. Yet, in the absence of its own top policy guidance with respect to philanthropy, it is quite possible that key tax decisions having major effects on philanthropy are being made inadvertently; or, lacking direction from above, bill-drafting technicians at

5. An account of the methods used to collect necessary data appears in appendix I.

the staff level are in effect making the decisions. Some of the voices at
the staff level are not friendly to private giving. A chance choice of
technical advisers may influence the ways in which philanthropy's needs
are considered or ignored.

That possibility has been heightened by the fact that, when the Congress was enacting the Tax Reform Act of 1969, philanthropy generally
and the foundations specifically seemed to lack the active support of a
broad based public constituency. The vocal part of the public seemed far
more ready to decry the faults of some foundations than the silent part
was ready to come to the support of what was worth preserving in
others. Why?

The question—and the clarity that comes with crisis—enabled the
commission to see its own purpose with fresh eyes. Its fact finding
was obviously necessary. Yet it was not enough for the commission
merely to gather facts for use in analyzing the common allegations
about foundations. Nor was it enough for the commission merely to
focus on foundation-related matters which were on the congressional
agenda—or should be on it. Many long-range issues and answers bearing on philanthropy in general and on the foundations in particular
lay outside a legislative frame. The commission, then, recognized the
need to focus its deliberations and recommendations on a range of
matters that it grouped under the following five heads:

The role of philanthropy in a changing society. Since the government
now supports on a massive scale many of the educational, scientific, and
social projects that private philanthropy pioneered, is there still an
important role for private philanthropy? What is the rationale in today's scheme of things for "private" charitable institutions supported
largely by public funds? From the standpoint of final results affecting
the quality of American life, does it really make any difference whether
funds flow from public sources alone, from private sources alone, or
from public *and* private sources concurrently?

The needs of America's charitable organizations. What are the likely
financial needs of charitable organizations in the years ahead? If we
want these private charitable organizations to continue to function, can
we assume that existing sources of support will probably be adequate
to their needs? Do these needs indicate any role for the foundations?

Tax incentives for philanthropy. Are tax incentives essential if necessary private funds are to become available for charitable purposes? Are
current tax incentives fair and efficient? To meet tomorrow's needs, are
new and better tax incentives for philanthropy necessary?

The "taint" in philanthropy and foundations. What are the kinds of abuses of private giving in general and some of the specific abuses of foundations? Are they so pervasive as to cast serious doubts on the propriety and effectiveness of incentives for private giving or for giving through foundations? What should be done to minimize the actual abuses and to clear the critical atmosphere that surrounds philanthropy and the foundations?

Foundations as an institution. To what extent is a "philanthropic middleman," such as a foundation, necessary if the public interest is to be served? Is it clear that the same programs would not be carried out if we depended on public funding or on direct giving by individuals? What can foundations do to improve the quantity and quality of their contributions to American society? In view of the way massive government funding has changed the setting in which foundations operate, what are appropriate future roles for the foundations? And in all of this, what should be done to increase public understanding of the role of foundations and public confidence that the role will be faithfully discharged?

In appraising our own work, the commission makes no claim either that our data is definitive or that we have fully and decisively answered all major questions that must be asked about the foundations and philanthropy. The constraints of time and resources limited the scope and refinement of our data. Yet, in view of the scarcity of previously existing information, the kind of studies we undertook were essential to the commission's work. It is our hope that the evidence we have gathered puts our recommendations on a far firmer footing than the usual reliance on hearsay when judgments are made about philanthropy and the foundations.

Part 1
Private
Philanthropy

2

The Role of
Philanthropy in a
Changing Society

In America these days, nothing stands still in one place for very long. Old systems of thought are unhinged. The legitimacy of most forms of authority is being questioned. People with unredressed grievances and with hopes deferred too long have become impatient with patience. In this strained atmosphere the institutions of philanthropy, like almost all other institutions, face a rising demand that they justify their inner life and their external effects.

The first question asked about them is this: Are the dynamics at American philanthropic institutions congruous with America's highest interest? If that first question is ignored, or if it cannot be convincingly answered in the affirmative, then the fate in store for philanthropy could resemble that of the man in the fable who was so abstracted from his own life that he scarcely knew he existed until one fine morning he awoke and found himself dead.

There are some who may agree "in principle" with the worth of private philanthropy, but, when a crunch is on, they view philanthropy as Lord Melbourne, prime minister of England in the early years of Queen Victoria's reign, viewed religion. "I have," said he, "as much respect for religion as the next person. But things have come to a pretty pass when religion is allowed to interfere with England's interests."

Critics who assert that American philanthropy actually goes against the grain of America's highest interest advance several lines of argument in support of their conclusions.

They say first that philanthropy in America is hardly "pure" in motive, nor is it an evangelical expression of human fraternity. It is tied at the hip bone to tax deductions and, as such, is a self-serving instrument of greater use to the wealthy than to the average taxpayer. Why? Because under existing tax laws, persons in the lower income brackets have little incentive to contribute to charity. But, as a taxpayer with rising income moves into higher tax brackets, the more do deductions for charity increase in importance; the higher his income, the less each dollar he contributes costs him in after-tax income, or, to put it another way, the more these charitable contributions cost the government. Further, only the wealthy, and not people of modest means, are likely to be in a position to gain substantial added tax benefits by giving appreciated property instead of cash to philanthropic institutions. Present tax laws, therefore, foster a concentration of philanthropic giving (especially for nonreligious purposes) in the hands of the rich.

This in turn, so it is argued, means that tax incentives for charitable giving serve the process of "elitism" instead of the cause of "democratic pluralism." It serves that process because wealthy people are free to use billions of dollars to support their eccentricities and hobbies— billions of dollars which would otherwise be absorbed into the pool of government funds for uses approved by a vote of the representatives of the people. No similar freedom or subsidy is available for the less well-to-do. Even when the latter deduct their charitable contributions from taxable income, their margin of freedom is confined to their choice of the organizations which will receive their donations. They will, however, have little say about what is done with the money they contribute. Board members of charitable organizations are more likely to be the larger donors to it.

Second, say the critics, it is wrong to take at face value the claims of philanthropic organizations that, since they are private, they are a more efficient instrument of action than the government, and that there is a commitment behind private dollars which government dollars lack. There may be more important goals and more efficient means to attain them, and in any case there is no guarantee that the private commitment is actually in the public interest. The freedom of private philanthropic organizations to choose their own goals can lead to redundant or wasteful disbursement, the scattering of seeds that produce only a harvest of dead leaves, and a diversion—into the high costs of public relations and advertising incident to fund raising—of money meant for charitable causes.

The critics then ask a passionate question. When funds are desperately needed to support massive governmental efforts to solve acute social problems, why should tax dollars be lost in the form of charitable deductions for privately selected purposes? After all, the very existence of the tax incentive for philanthropy plainly means that charitable expenditures are not purely private expenditures. They are made partly with dollars which, were it not for charitable deductions allowed by tax laws, would have become public funds to be allocated through the governmental process under the controlling power of the electorate as a whole. Thus, say the critics, in place of a democratic allocation of resources, we have a market place for philanthropy dominated by a plutocracy that can do what it pleases without being called to public account for what it does.

Is there an answer to these lines of argument? The commission is convinced that there is. At the same time, in formulating its own answering argument, the commission has taken care to bypass the ambush of three assumptions. It does not assume that private philanthropy is a perfect system that has no need for further, and perhaps substantial, improvement. It does not assume that the system will never have any entries in its record of some follies, excesses, redundancy—and, above all, of some of the failures that are inherent in pioneering, high risk ventures. Least of all does the commission assume that the system can make a "perfect allocation" of its resources, "accountable in full" to the public—a concept, incidentally, which cannot even be defined precisely, let alone attained.

The heart of the commission's position, expressed in shorthand form, comes to this. Despite the claims made about how governmental decisions are less "elitist," more "democratic," and "more accountable to the public," the test of practical experience clearly makes a strong *dual* system of private giving *and* government funding a better way to allocate resources for the general welfare than the alternative of relying solely on governmental allocations.

Stated more fully, the commission's judgment of such a dual system of private giving and public funding, rests on the following propositions transposed into the form of beliefs:

1. We believe that the improvement of the material and moral condition of the individual human being is central to our society's outlook.

2. We believe that just as the health of a muscle depends on its being exercised, the individual braces his freedom and enlarges his perceptions through actions on behalf of others which he initiates voluntarily and for which he is willing to assume personal responsibility.

3. We believe that a society which encourages a sense among its

citizens that they have a reciprocal responsibility for themselves and for others strengthens its own fabric—whereas a society which spurs every man to live in and for himself alone weakens the society by weakening the bonds of fraternity.

4. We believe that government is destined to play an ever-increasing and indispensable role in areas that have traditionally been served by private philanthropic activity. While a government limited in power to the work of a policeman on the beat was adequate for a society whose frontier ran parallel to the land, it is not adequate for a society whose frontier runs perpendicular to the land in the form of our giant industrial complexes and our great urban areas. Unless the power of government is brought to bear on the salient problems of our highly urbanized and industrialized civilization, the problems will increase, not diminish. It is worth recalling that at the onset of the Great Depression of the 1930s, there were people who felt that the economic collapse would right itself through the curative power of "natural causes" and that private philanthropy in the meantime could take care of people in acute distress. Nothing of the sort was in fact possible, and the reluctance—on doctrinaire grounds—to invoke the power of government in order to revive the economy served only to make the economic distress more acute.

5. At the same time, we believe that government should not venture to do those things which private citizens and private institutions can do as well or better. Government by its nature must generalize, and it moves toward its decisions slowly. Human life itself, however, is infinitely varied in its nuances, in its perceptions, in the directions in which it moves, and in the pace at which it moves. Our society, therefore, is in obvious need of private philanthropic institutions standing outside the frame of government but in support of the public interest—just as scouts move in advance of a main body of troops to probe what lies ahead. We need philanthropic institutions which can spot emergent problems, diagnose them, and test alternative ways to deal with them.

This is not to say that private philanthropic funds should merely provide an increment—even though a relatively small one—to what government is doing. A narrow view of that kind would weaken any justification for the existence of philanthropy as an island of autonomy alongside a system of government funding. It would weaken any justification for the diversion of money that would otherwise become funds in the public treasury. Such diversion—exclusive of the realm of religion, from which the government is constitutionally excluded—is most strongly justified when private philanthropic money is used, not as a substitute for tax dollars, but as a supplement of a special kind that serves the public interest in ways in which the government itself is under various operational constraints.

A major case in point turns on the question of whether social change in our day will be a product of the blind play of accident and force or whether it will result from rational reflection and deliberate choice. If we want it to be a result of rational reflection and deliberate choice, then we need social laboratories where new ideas and social innovations can be tested in actual practice. This work of peaceful social innovation is extremely important—at least as important as technological innovation—and probably even more difficult and less understood. In an era of unprecedented technological innovations, social innovation lags seriously. Yet, there is a suggestive analogy between the way new things are born in the commercial sector and the way the support by private philanthropy for laboratory tests of social innovations can lead to an impressive payoff.

In the commercial sector, success usually starts with a vision, often very personal, of what tomorrow's consumers will want, and whether there are technological possibilities of meeting it. The mere bigness of a large industrial establishment, however, is no guarantee that it will have that kind of vision or will have it exclusively. Large industrial establishments can be the captive of a self-generated consensus which says with great force that a proposed new technology is not workable or that the market does not want it or need it. But this is not always the last word about the matter. An entrepreneur, often small, new, and from an unlikely background, arrives on the commercial scene. He is committed to a vision of how a proposed new technology *is* workable and why consumers of tomorrow will want it and need it. He manages to get access to venture capital—a crucial need. He subjects his judgment to a practical test in the formidable world of real things.

In the social realm as well, the consensus mechanism of the large, established institutions of government are not always the best and are certainly not the only way to innovate measures that lead to orderly social change. In statist societies, governments held in thrall by ideologies and dogmas have irrevocably committed the lives of millions of people to large-scale social experiments—such as farm collectivization—with cruel and costly consequences. Even governments of democratic societies have initiated massive programs on the basis of untested theories. Great expectations were aroused by the claimed benefits of what these programs would lead to. But the expectations eventually collapsed, and the result served only to increase public cynicism about the whole of the political process.

The moral of the story is clear. Just as the technological realm and the commercial realm need the innovative individual and the small firm, so does our social realm need them. It needs the person or the single, small institution to have a new vision of what should and can be done. But who will "sponsor" the necessary experiment with "venture capital"? The innovators must be in a position to choose from among alternative sponsors. If their range of choice is confined only to the sponsorship of the federal government, then the innovative process is bound to suffer a loss of the mobility, diversity, pluralism, and decentralization that are prerequisites of orderly social change. There would be this loss, first, because the inner life of government is strained to the limit in merely trying to find the resources that can meet today's massive and pressing needs. Government is not inclined to focus on the long tomorrow. An administration tends to concentrate its thoughts and efforts to the hard enough task of merely staying afloat in today's storms. It has little reserve strength for any major planning and developmental initiatives bearing on a future in which a new administration will have the responsibilities of power.

It is true that individual states in the American union can be laboratories for social experiments. They are places where "pilot projects" can be put to the test of practice, and successful social inventions can then become, by adoption, the common property of the nation. This, indeed, is a root source of strength for our federal system of government. Yet the problems besetting our society are so many and so complex that we need many different kinds of laboratories where social experiments can be conducted. Private philanthropy can help fill this need.

We have also reached an hour in American history when no institution can cultivate its own garden without thought of events on the move outside the garden wall. Walls of privacy have been breached by the daily shocks and eruptions that have swept across American life. The spirit of dissent has spread its contagion across our student population and from there to other sectors of American life. And we deceive ourselves if we think the signs and sounds of distress are limited to an anarchistic handful of young people. If they are not to reach their climax in a war of all against all, we are summoned by this turmoil carefully to consider the ways in which we can convert dissent into a force for constructive action and civil peace.

We must evolve more responsive processes through which our young and disenfranchised can secure a fair piece of the social action, whether or not they can acquire a piece of our affluent *economic* action.

Indeed, perhaps it is fair to say that part of the unrest in our society is due to the paradoxical fact that nothing fails like success—that the more successful we have been in assuring the citizen his physical needs will be met, the more sensitive he becomes to other cravings of his soul and mind, as he yearns to realize his potentialities as a human being. In this yearning, he becomes all the more aware of institutional structures, with their inertia and congealed ideologies. He feels that all these stand between him and his vision of an elevated condition of life.

In this seemingly chaotic and clearly diverse and demanding setting, it is perhaps true that only a pluralistic society can become a responsive one. Philanthropy, we believe, must bring a fresh understanding of what pluralism can mean in American life.

We have said a pluralistic society must be one in which multiple options and multiple initiatives are open to its members. Multiple options more than ever will require a mature understanding of majority and minority approaches, living side by side. Responsive pluralism requires the majority be willing to place itself under a self-denying ordinance *not* to use the weight of its larger numbers to crush the minority's claim for equitable consideration and coexistence. It means conversely that the minority is willing to place itself under a self-denying ordinance not to use for frivolous and vengeful reasons any veto power it has over the desires of the majority.

This delicate balance cannot be legislated. It is a habit of the heart which reminds the citizen that today's majority might well be tomorrow's minority and, of course, that today's minority might well be tomorrow's majority.

Nor is this delicate balance likely to be funded by a majoritarian political process alone. We believe private sector philanthropy must be a major source of support for the multiple options our society offers.

Philanthropy, then, must have sufficient funds, and in particular sufficient *uncommitted and mobile* funds, so that it can respond to unmet and still unseen needs of society. Yet, if a Declaration of Independence does not by itself make a people free, neither will more funds by itself insure philanthropy a defensible and relevant place in American life. To ensure such a place for itself, philanthropy must be independent and must use freedom in responsible and courageous ways. It will ensure nothing if it simply enjoys an easy popularity by applying its weight to the end of having everything stand still.

While we believe that the system of strong dual funding is based on sound theoretical principles, we also believe that it offers pragmatic advantages measurable in dollars and cents. In this connection, two points should be made about the relative "costs" to society of a private charity dollar compared to that of a governmental social dollar. First, the donor contributes part of the gift out of *his own net* worth—even after the tax deduction. Second, any review of cost effectiveness of the private charitable sector must also take into account a factor previously noted—namely, the value of the labor represented by volunteer work on behalf of philanthropies.

In 71 percent of the fifty-odd Chicago charitable organizations we interviewed, the number of volunteer workers exceeded the number of paid employees. If the modest value of three dollars per hour is placed on volunteer labor, then the dollar value of volunteer labor in one out of five Chicago charitable organizations exceeds the total payroll costs. This includes such organizations as the Chicago YMCA, Red Cross, United Cerebral Palsy, and Girl Scouts. A manpower survey recently completed by the Welfare Council of Metropolitan Chicago shows that Chicago agencies received more than a million hours per month of volunteer work for everything from the delivery of services to fund raising. Short of a concrete test, it is hard to say how many of the people involved in the delivery of services would reduce their voluntary work if functions now discharged by private charitable enterprises became a governmental monopoly. It seems fair to guess, however, that there would be a sharp falloff in the quantity and quality of their efforts.

Values in dollars are not the only means for judging the worth of volunteer work in private philanthropy. Society also gains from the way the individual who voluntarily participates in philanthropic efforts builds up an immunity to a malaise common to our day. It is the malaise of the man who stands frustrated in the face of a thousand things he sees should be done. He wants to help make events become what they ought to be—to repair the broken connections between talk and being heard, between pain experienced and a remedy, between urgent needs and their solution. Yet, in the shadow of a big government he may feel powerless to do any of this by himself. Recoiling, he migrates psychologically out of society. He becomes indifferent alike to any good or evil befalling it and withdraws ever deeper into his private self.

It is otherwise with many individuals who volunteer for the work of private philanthropy. The more they concern themselves with the welfare of other people, the more alive they feel through having absorbed within themselves the throb of the society around them. The individual volunteer cannot do everything he would like to do. Yet when he does with all his might that which lies closest at hand, he is less frustrated because he is rewarded with a sense of his own identity—rewarded because he can see his identity stamped on the face of things he helped turn for the better through his personal efforts. He and society are jointly the gainers, whereas both would be the losers if private philanthropy was foreclosed, and its non-dollar values were also wiped out.

The commission, in arriving at its conclusions about the merits of maintaining a dual system of public funding and private support for socially desirable projects, found it instructive to listen closely to a lesson taught by Europe's experiences with philanthropy.

It is enough to say here that, after the secular authorities in European nation-states for various reasons curbed the economic capacity of ecclesiastical organizations to engage in extensive philanthropic activities, the long-range consequences were fourfold. First, the sense of personal responsibility by the individual for the welfare of his neighbor was hobbled. Second, the government staked out a monopoly of decision and initiative in areas which, in American experience, were retained as a preserve for private philanthropic efforts. Third, in contrast to America, where private charitable institutions were often the prime innovators and experimenters in social, scientific, cultural, and educational fields, European society depended for its general welfare almost totally on the decisions of government itself. Fourth, this habit of dependence fostered in Europe the kind of stultifying attitudes and values which, in the archetype case of France, were recently excoriated by no less a person than the premier, Jacques Chaban-Delmas. Said he:

An octopus, and an inefficient one! That is what—we all know it—the State is becoming, despite the fact that there is a corps of generally efficient, at times outstanding, civil servants. An octopus, I say, for, by indefinitely extending its responsibilities it has gradually put our entire French society under its paternalism. . . .

The distribution of social subsidies is governed by a narrow legal concept of equality that leads to inequality. On the pretext of not distinguishing between beneficiaries, identically the same assistance is being given to those who have the greatest need of it, those who have only a moderate need of it, and those who have no need of it at all. Result: the initial aims are not achieved.

. . . [A]s de Tocqueville demonstrated—and this continues to be true—there is a deep-lying connection between the omnipotence of the State and the weakness of community life in our country.

As a result of this situation, each social or occupational group, or rather their representatives, not feeling secure enough to be able to negotiate directly and responsibly with other groups, fall back on the practice of submitting their claims to the State, often complicating their claims with a somewhat veiled rivalry. Thus, all too often a real social dialogue is replaced with an appeal to the State for protection, which only strengthens even further the State's control over the life of the people and, at the same time, places an excessively heavy burden on the entire economy.

In addition to what the commission learned from European experience, sources lying closer to home stressed the worth of maintaining a dual system of public funding and private support for socially desirable projects. The commission put a specific question to fifty Chicago charitable organizations which have had intimate experience with various kinds of financial support. Would they favor government support for the work done by their own organizations being increased to a point at which there was little or no room for private effort? Almost all replies strongly opposed any such total reliance on public funding to the exclusion of private support. It was observed that, under such an arrangement, social efforts would be affected by every turn in the political winds, by every accident flowing from a change of administration, and by every political scramble for government funds. Further, as the power of day-to-day decisions gravitated to the governmental bureaucracy, an all-too familiar consequence would start to unfold. The realities of local conditions—whether on the side of danger or of opportunity—either would not be seen or might be forced to fit a bureaucratic Procrustean bed.

Autonomous islands of private philanthropy existing side by side with a system for public funding provide indispensable initiatives to change. In the realm of social efforts, such an arrangement corresponds to what we have evolved in the realm of economic efforts—a "mixed economy" arrangement that serves as a model to the world.

3

Financial Needs of Charitable Organizations

The word "charity" comes from the Latin *caritas*. It means heartfelt love, natural affection, or spontaneous goodness for the benefit of others. In this root sense of the word, "charitable" organizations are not limited to the relief of poverty and distress. They include a great range of institutions—schools, colleges, universities, hospitals, museums, symphonies, libraries—which are operated on a private, non-profit basis to perform socially beneficial functions, often on a *continuing* basis.

The independence of charitable organizations to pursue their own "natural affection" and "spontaneous goodness" depends in the final analysis on the nature and extent of their financial support. This being so, there is a question to be asked. Is that support adequate to their needs? It is not. Even as things stand right now, many philanthropic institutions are already living with an acute financial crisis, and if things go on as they are without a remedy, the crisis will become all the more acute in the future.

It is true, of course, that the task of gauging the future needs of charitable organizations involves more than the usual risks that accompany any effort to try to lip-read history. It is hard, for example, to distinguish between tangible needs and the desire of organizations to grow bigger, or to separate objective requirements from the fund-raising instincts natural to any charitable organization.

The commission, for its part, was aware of these grounds for a miscarriage of judgment. As a safety measure, we pursued several lines of inquiry and used the findings they led to as a basis for our own projections about the present and future needs of charitable organizations. Thus, we examined their financial records and discussed them with their executives and boards of directors. We asked noted specialists in medicine, education, arts, welfare, and so on to trace the trends of actual expenditures in their own fields and what the likely needs would be in 1975. We asked other specialists to trace the patterns of philanthropic giving and the amount of dollar giving that might reasonably be expected in 1975.

From these projections, two cross-currents soon surfaced into clear view. On the one side, private giving has at best followed the trend of the gross national product and may have fallen behind it in recent years. On the other, the needs of charitable organizations are now growing and will grow at a rate significantly faster than the growth of the GNP. In consequence, if we intend to maintain the private sector's contribution to the nation's charitable accounts, and, further, if private giving follows past trends, there will be an estimated multibillion dollar deficit in private giving by 1975.

This general conclusion was particularized when the commission surveyed the income and expenditures of thirty-nine charitable organizations in Chicago in the five years between 1963 and 1968. The results showed that in this period the growth of their expenditures exceeded by more than 15 percent the growth of the GNP. In 1968, 54 percent of these Chicago organizations expended more than their income from all sources. In their case, there is nothing contingent about the crisis of a budget deficit. The crisis is here and now.

Meanwhile, the difficulty existing organizations face in raising funds to meet their needs has been increased by the emergence of new charitable organizations which assert their own competitive claims on the private philanthropic dollar. The new organizations vary in character. Some supplement the work of traditional institutions. Some have been formed in order to introduce new approaches in areas such as education and social welfare. Some were born in consequence of government programs in community services, housing for low-income families and the aged, research in the natural and social sciences, and other fields. They may be heavily subsidized by the government, especially in their initial stages, yet they often require private financing either to match government funding or to permit the expansion of their activities. Still other new organizations, such as those devoted to public policy issues, have been created independently of any government initiative and rely solely on private sources to support their work.

Against this general background of more claimants for the private philanthropic dollar, a number of specific causes for the current financial bite felt by charitable organizations became clear to the commission in its inquiry.

First, the business of charity, by its very nature, cannot be automated. It is a business in which people concern themselves with the needs of other people. To describe it in economic terms: the philanthropic sector is "labor intensive"—in contrast to manufacturing enterprises, which are often "capital intensive." Its financial condition is thus particularly vulnerable to increases in the costs of the labor it employs—again in contrast to manufacturing enterprises, which can materially offset increases in labor rates by using new technologies which increase productivity. The extent of this difference can be seen by glancing at the percentage of total operating expenses which went into the salaries and related personnel expenses of fifty Chicago philanthropic institutions between 1963 and 1968 and at the way that percentage looked in the case of United States manufacturing establishments as a whole:[1]

	1963	1968
Chicago philanthropic institutions	58%	66%
US manufacturing establishments	23%	24%

Wages and salaries, which have increased more rapidly than other costs throughout the economy, are the major portion of the budget of costs of these charitable organizations. For many of them, moreover, wage and salary costs have risen significantly more than in other sectors of the economy. One reason is the raising of professional standards in some fields such as social services. Another is that there has been a change in attitude about the compensation of full-time employees of most charitable institutions. It is no longer possible to pay them at scales well below those of industry and government and expect sufficient numbers of dedicated, full-time workers with no other source of income to contribute part of their services as a free gift, particularly since there is already a shortage of skilled personnel for many types of charitable organizations.

Salary increases for employees of Chicago charitable organizations are dramatically illustrated in chart 1.

Another major cause for the financial crisis of charitable organizations strikes the naked eye. There has been an increasing social demand for the services of these organizations due to population growth and

1. Source for U.S. figures: U.S. Department of Commerce, *Statistical Abstract, 1969.* See appendixes I and III for description and fuller report on the Survey of Chicago Philanthropic Organizations.

CHART 1

SALARY INCREASES: EMPLOYEES OF CHICAGO CHARITABLE ORGANIZATIONS
VERSUS U.S. PRODUCTION WORKERS

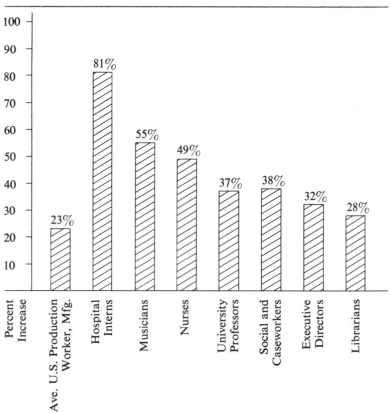

Source: United States Department of Commerce.

urbanization, technological advances, affluence, and the changing values
of society, but, in many instances, fees and user charges have lagged
behind costs. Some institutions have been reluctant to charge any direct
fees. Others feel that the true cost of the services is much more than the
public should or could pay—and, indeed, that those who are most in
need of the services are often the very people who can least afford to
pay for them.

There are also institutions—such as museums, hospitals, or universities—which indirectly benefit an entire community, not just the people who make direct use of their services. Many of these, it turns out, have increased their fees, often with great boldness when compared with price increases in general. In the Chicago institutions studied by the commission, the extent of these increases is indicated in chart 2.

CHART 2
INCREASING FEES FOR SERVICES FOR SELECTED INSTITUTIONS, 1963–68

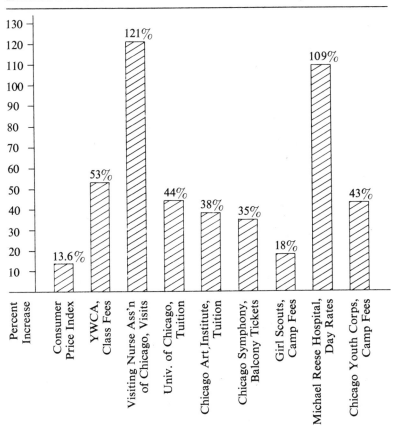

Still, since the costs of these institutions continue to increase faster than the revenues collected from the increased fees charged the people who directly use their services, increased amounts must be collected from the indirect beneficiaries in the community. It is hard to do this, however, through the mechanism of the market.

Meanwhile, the new stress on social, economic, and racial justice has worked in two ways to increase costs for charitable institutions: (1) Many charitable institutions have been trying to improve the delivery of their services to residents of the urban ghettos; and this has meant, not only new approaches, but new programs by institutions which never before deliberately sought out particular groups in the community with an offering of services. (2) While charity has traditionally sought to relieve poverty and human suffering, it now places a greater emphasis than ever before on the more difficult and—over the short term, at least —the more costly treatment of the causes of social and economic instability.

This leads to many new pressures. In the case of colleges and universities, even as they face a need to broaden their curricula in order to keep pace with the knowledge explosion, they face an increased demand for added services involving students from the ghettos who require special educational remedial work. Other people, such as those who need hospital tests and psychiatric services, may require attention from charitable institutions on a custom-tailored instead of a programmed basis. Technological advances can significantly improve the quality of the services to individuals, but the advances do not necessarily lead to what economists call "economies of scale"—meaning a lowering of unit costs as the volume of output increases. In fact, in the field of medicine it may work the other way around. Improvements in the quality of services rendered because of technological advances may increase costs per unit and at the same time reduce the number of patients yearly attended to by each hospital employee.

None of this says that there is no ground for hoping and urging that increases in the "productivity" of our charitable organizations can and should help offset the increased costs they have incurred for the reasons just detailed. It means simply that the task is more difficult for these organizations than it is for manufacturing enterprises. A rough approximation showed not only that the "unit costs"[2] of charitable services rose sharply between 1962 and 1968 but that the extent of the increase markedly exceeded the rise in the consumer price index and even the rise in salaries for the personnel of charitable organizations.

2. Appendix III elaborates on these findings. By "unit cost" we mean the cost of providing one unit of charitable service; for example, a hospital patient-day. Clearly it is impossible to make precise comparisons of these costs since the quality of these charitable units changes over time.

What about the future? With that question in mind, the commission asked Chicago philanthropic organizations to think about their 1975 prospects and to choose, from three descriptive statements, the one that corresponded most closely to their prognosis. The statements and the percentage of affirmative answers each received were as follows:

To be sure, costs are rising and charitable needs are growing, but I'm also confident that outside revenues and contributions will also go up fast enough to meet our needs   17 percent

I'm quite concerned about rising costs and increasing charitable needs. I'm not at all sure that outside funds will be adequate to meet these needs, and some cutbacks will probably be necessary to make ends meet   26 percent

I believe that by 1975 our organization will be facing a real budget crisis unless some major new sources of funds are developed   57 percent

The trend shown in our study of Chicago charitable institutions is by no means unique. The evidence is overwhelming from many sources that the operating costs of nearly every kind of nonprofit organization throughout the country have risen and will continue to rise in coming years faster than prices or even the gross national product will rise. Some of the specially commissioned studies which promise to be of great value are not yet made public. But a few made available during the last two or three years buttress the conclusion repeatedly and persuasively.[3]

3. American Hospital Association, "Financial Requirements of Health Care Institutions and Services," *Hospitals Magazine, Journal of the American Hospital Association,* 1 January and 16 April 1970. William Baumol and William Bowen, *Performing Arts: The Economic Dilemma* (New York: Twentieth Century Fund, 1966). Howard R. Bowen, *The Finance of Higher Education* (Carnegie Commission on Higher Education, 1968). (One quotation from this pamphlet: "Every educational administrator who attempts to project institutional costs for five or ten years ends up with the gloomy conclusion that they are bound to rise, even if he assumes no price inflation and no qualitative improvement. Faculty salaries have been rising by 5 or 7 per cent a year and are expected to continue to rise, though possibly at a slower rate, for as far as the eye can see.") William G. Bowen, *The Economics of the Major Private Universities* (Carnegie Commission on Higher Education, 1968); *The Economics and Financing of Higher Education in the United States, a Compendium of Papers Submitted to the Joint Economic Committee, Congress of the United States* (Washington, D.C.: Government Printing Office, 1969). Gideon Chagy, ed., *Business in the Arts '70* (New York: Paul S. Eriksson, Inc., 1970), especially the essay "Economic Crisis in the Arts" by C. Douglas Dillon. Cresap, McCormick, and Paget (management consultants), three studies for clients (a Negro college, a prestige women's college, and a major national museum) showing anticipated cost increases exceeding 90 percent in the next ten years, without any change of program. W. McNeil Lowry,

The judgment of our own commission that on a *national* basis the real and justifiable costs of charitable organizations can be expected to rise significantly faster than the GNP was also reinforced by our survey of national leaders who have firsthand knowledge of the financial prospects for charitable organizations in their own professional areas.[4] We asked a sample of these leaders the following question: "Over the next five to ten years, what would you expect to be the trend in financial needs of the charitable organizations in the particular field or area of society in which you feel most knowledgeable about philanthropy?" While the results varied somewhat by field of interest, a very substantial majority in each foresaw rapidly increasing financial needs. The percentage of response to the four possible answers to the question is as follows:

Financial needs will go up rapidly over this period, significantly more rapidly than the GNP, for example   72 percent

Financial needs will go up but at a relatively modest rate— about like the GNP   26 percent

Financial needs will stay the same as they are now   1 percent

Financial needs will go down over this period   1 percent

Thus, philanthropy is now caught in the cross-tensions between an existing set of old demands and an emergent set of new demands. On the one side are the claims of sustaining the traditional and priceless objects of support in universities, medical research institutions, hospitals, religious institutions, museums, symphony orchestras, and the like. All these are part of things which already exist, have the sanction of society, and their support on a continuing, sustained basis speaks its own importance. On the other side are the claims posed by an assortment of

---

The Economic Crisis in the Arts: The Need for a National Policy (Ford Foundation Annual Report for 1968). Robert J. Myers, statement to U.S. Senate Committee on Costs of Medicaid and Medicare by chief actuary, U.S. Social Security Administration, *New York Times*, 27 February 1970 (predicting 70 percent increase in hospital costs in next five years). Michael W. Robbins, ed., *America's Museums: The Belmont Report* (a Report to the Federal Council on Arts and Humanities by a Special Committee of the American Association of Museums, 1968). Helen M. Thompson, for American Symphony Orchestra League, *Summary of Financial Data of U.S. Symphony Orchestras* (prepared for Conference of Presidents and Managers of Symphony Orchestras, 1969). McKinsey and Company (management consultants), Memorandum on Symphony Costs for the Presidents of the Boston, Chicago, Cleveland, New York and Philadelphia Symphony Orchestras, 1969 (indicated need to double 1967–68 nonoperating income in order to meet 1971–72 costs).

4. This national study of distinguished citizens is reviewed in appendixes I and II.

new projects or new institutions which lie on the beckoning frontier of social change. The common justification for all the new-style projects is that they will help promote an accelerated and orderly transition from that which *is* to that which *ought* to be.

The cross-tensions threaten philanthropic donors with schizophrenia. In trying to meet the needs of both with the limited amount of total funds available, philanthropy can deliberately forsake one in favor of the other, or be split down the middle in trying to satisfy both. Neither prospect is a happy one. Each has its own distinctive dangers. Philanthropy can break out of the trap only if it secures for itself a significant increase in funds that will significantly increase its options.

To sum up: Our assessment of the present and future needs of charitable organizations in America leads the commission to believe that the American public and those who formulate public policies must now face two harsh facts: first, that the needs of America's vitally important charitable organizations are rising rapidly; and second, without important new sources of funds amounting to many billions of dollars our society will feel the full force of what can be called *the charitable crisis of the 1970s.*

4

Tax Incentives
and
Philanthropy

The logic of the preceding analysis forced the commission to consider the public policies which could conceivably deal with the growing budget crisis among charitable organizations. Many options were weighed, but the main ones were reduced to the following three:

First: Permit a significant number of charitable organizations to decline or to die on the vine by deliberately failing to provide them with major new funds through either private or governmental sources.

Second: Decide that the problems now dealt with by charitable organizations are in fact public problems, and that the work of the organizations should be supported largely or entirely with tax dollars, while incentives for private philanthropy should be reduced.

Third: Stimulate an increased flow of private resources to philanthropy by offering higher government inducements to contributors and in ways which would underscore the importance of private philanthropy in our overarching social arrangements.

The commission, for its part, rejected the first option, and for this reason: if charitable organizations are sharply reduced in numbers in consequence of a deliberate policy of attrition, the effect on a society already torn could be an irrevocable breach in the whole of our social fabric.

The commission also rejected the second, and for reasons which require a restatement of what has already been said. Briefly, if the government were the main source of support for private charitable organizations, the process for choosing organizations to receive direct government payments for services rendered would be invaded by a number of negative forces. It would become enmeshed in the less attractive aspects of partisan politics, and from there it would be subjected to greater government control, with a consequent drop in private financial support for these organizations, their still greater reliance on direct government support, the loss of their independence, and hence a loss of their freedom to make special kinds of contributions to our society.

The commission endorsed the third policy—namely, the one whereby one government would stimulate an increased flow of private resources to philanthropy. A policy of this kind could be congruous with the proposition that the federal government, on its own, should and must play a major role in the solution of social problems. It would also formally recognize that private philanthropy has a crucial role to play, independent of but complementary to that of the government, in dealing with the complex problems that haunt our society.

At this point in its analysis, the commission considered the kinds of government inducement that might stimulate an increased flow of private resources to philanthropy.

One such inducement could conceivably be arranged outside the existing tax system. The government, for example, would directly match part of the amount which private individuals contributed to philanthropic organizations but would not earmark the uses to which the organizations put the portion of the funds received from it. There are, however, objections to this arrangement. First—and this repeats what is by now a leitmotif—the process for choosing organizations qualified to receive government funds on a matching basis with private contributions could lead to political complications or to a loss of elasticity in the programs of the organizations. Second, it could be a waste of effort to create a separate structure outside the tax system for matching government grants with individual grants when the existing tax system already provides a suitable means to accomplish the main objective of stimulating private giving.

The commission favors the use of incentives for charitable giving within the existing tax system. At the same time, it is aware of the general objections to the use of tax incentives in lieu of direct government payments. Tax incentives tend to be hidden. Their effectiveness is often difficult to measure. They do not show up in government budgets. There is often great uncertainty about who gets the benefits. A tax rate structure can also have undesirable side effects; for example, in the course of encouraging charitable giving, it has made it possible for the taxpayer to make money for himself. And again, there is usually a low degree of not very discriminating government control over the way the incentives are administered.

In addition to these general drawbacks, the commission candidly recognized that there are drawbacks to tax incentives which apply specifically to private philanthropy. Precisely because these incentives put private philanthropy in a tax context, tax administrators understandably look at the matter through their own knothole. They tend to focus attention on the collection of tax revenues without giving due attention to the philanthropic benefits of tax incentives—even though the government itself, in the absence of private giving, would undoubtedly have to support with its tax revenues many of the activities dependent on charity. Also, it is generally acknowledged that the Internal Revenue Service and the Treasury does not assign an adequate staff to philanthropic activities, though it should be quickly added that the power to change the case for the better does not lie with the Treasury Department itself. It lies in a public policy decision by the Executive, the Congress, and the general public that philanthropic activities are allies of the national interest, backed by an entry in the national budget with respect to the employment of the added personnel needed for a balanced coverage of charitable giving.

Also, as became apparent during the hearing held by the commission at which a number of eminent tax experts drawn from the universities, the government, and private enterprise offered testimony, there is an obvious dearth of current information about philanthropy itself, or specifically, about who does the giving and for what purpose. These experts observed that the very facts they most frequently cited were dated 1962—the year in which the Treasury Department issued one of the last reasonably complete statistical studies it has made of certain key issues in philanthropy. The same lack of information about the size and scope of the foundations fosters gross misconceptions about their activities. The misconceptions go unchallenged, and, as was noted in the case of the 1969 tax reform year, result in decisions harmful to philanthropy.

Meanwhile, the tax administrators' almost exclusive concern with the collection of revenues leads to a preoccupation with tax issues divorced from their consequences for philanthropy. The 1969 tax reform experience is instructive. The House-passed version of the bill contained tax reforms which had been carefully calibrated to achieve certain effects on tax revenues. No such estimates had been made on the specific effects of these same provisions on philanthropic giving. Only later did it become clear that the effects on private giving would have been seriously inhibiting. The tax technician has an understandable and even praiseworthy interest in achieving equitable tax effects. But there are policy questions to be asked and answered. Is the effect to encourage or discourage charitable giving? Is it worthwhile to pay some price in uniformity of tax treatment if doing so stimulates private charitable giving, or should no such price be paid? These questions are too important to be answered by a technical staff alone. They call for a top policy voice that can guide the technical staff and thus help put government philanthropic decisions in the broader context where they belong.

Indeed, if philanthropy had strong, committed, rational, and informed representation at a high policy level—a level concerned not merely with the collection of tax revenues but with the social consequences of philanthropy—the way would be cleared for a major next step: the designing of a system of tax incentives that could stimulate the flow of more private resources into philanthropy. The step itself, admittedly, would not easily be made. It would have to consider the general drawbacks noted in connection with tax incentives. It would also have to achieve simultaneously a number of objectives that are not wholly compatible with each other: for example, that private resources be drawn into truly charitable channels; that the dollars given up by the government in taxes be highly efficient in eliciting private funds for charitable purposes; that the distribution of the inducements among taxpayers not offend any strong community sense of fairness.

The difficulty of reconciling all these objectives is complicated straight away by one fact. It is that today, as in the past, philanthropy depends heavily on the generosity of the well-to-do. The commission, faced by a paucity of data on charitable giving, was unable to get a precise estimate of the extent to which total charitable giving is concentrated among the wealthy.[1] Yet experience says that it is the large gift which raises the sights of a philanthropic enterprise, sets the pace for fund raising, and enables new philanthropic organizations to take root. This is not likely to change in the foreseeable future. Moreover, because the wealthy have surplus resources beyond those used to maintain a desired standard of

1. See appendix V, "Philanthropy and the Economy," by Mary Hamilton, which includes data on some relationships between reported income and charitable giving. In 1966, the last year for which these data were available, it was interesting to see that for those with annual incomes of all the way from $5,000 to $100,000, charitable contributions were at about 3 per cent of income. Above $100,000, the percentage contributed goes up substantially.

living, any increase in tax incentives (measured in terms of tax dollars forgone by the government) is almost sure to draw a greater response from the wealthy than from people of modest means.

This reality in turn underlies a two-part question. Are tax incentives really necessary to encourage adequate levels of charitable giving? Would not wealthy contributors in particular give almost as much as they do without the spur of tax incentives?

As in so many other philanthropic matters, there is little readily available evidence that bears directly on this important question. The commission, however, gathered indirect evidence showing the effects tax incentives have on the charitable giving of the wealthy and large donor. Some eighty-five donors who had made large charitable contributions over the years were asked to indicate their reaction to the following statement: "For the moment, let us assume there *were no tax benefits at all* for charitable giving—in other words, let us assume you had to make all your charitable contributions out of your after-tax income. What effect would this have on your charitable contributions?"[2]

Only 4 percent indicated that it would have no effect on their giving. The remaining 96 percent replied that it would *reduce* their giving, and the median reduction was 75 percent.

Due allowances must be made here for the possibility of a self-serving declaration. Yet it is interesting to note how *few* large donors felt that the absence of tax incentives would have but little effect on the amount of their giving.

TABLE 1.
ESTIMATED REDUCTION OF DONATIONS WITHOUT TAX INCENTIVES

Percentage of Reduction	Percentage of Donors
0	4
1– 19	0
20– 39	7
40– 59	27
60– 79	33
80–100	29

Indeed, the importance of tax incentives to at least the large donors is suggested by the pervasive involvement of tax counsel in their charitable giving.

In another approach to the possible effects of tax incentives, the com-

2. See appendix I for description of this survey.

mission studied the *form* of the charitable gifts of wealthy donors. The tax law now provides additional incentives for making gifts in the form of appreciated property instead of cash. The consequent effects are suggested in the findings of our surveys, which show (1) that approximately 70 percent of direct gifts of large donors is in the form of appreciated property; (2) that gifts of appreciated property account for nearly three-fourths of gifts to foundations.

If, therefore, the concern were only with the relative ease of mobilizing more private support for philanthropy, there is little doubt that the incentive should be designed primarily to capture the attention of the rich. However, it is not desirable to design a system whose operational effect would be to give the wealthy disproportionate benefits from the new tax stimulant. A dollar given to private philanthropy is not, from the giver's perspective, the equivalent of a dollar paid in taxes. The major difference is that, within limits, the philanthropic donor can determine and direct how and by whom his dollar is spent for public purposes.[3] The taxpayer has no comparable control over the dollar he pays in taxes. And it is largely because of this difference that the donor is in a position to obtain a greater and more direct personal satisfaction from his dollar contributed to charity than he can get from his dollar taken in taxes.

With all the foregoing considerations in mind, the commission recognizes the need for a tax incentive system that will not only induce the relatively well-to-do to make substantial increases in the level of their support to philanthropy but will also have a stimulating effect on people of lesser means—while taking care that government revenues will not be unnecessarily impaired.

The optimum solution will not be easy to achieve. We emphasize the need for careful exploration of many possible ways that can make it significantly more attractive for people who are not wealthy materially to increase their contributions to philanthropy.

It is probable that most of the mechanisms for stimulating philanthropy through taxation have already been noted by commentators. Very little is known, however, about the impact or cost of particular measures applied one by one or in combination. If a prudent decision is to be made about the combination that can achieve the desired effect, there must first be a marriage between the wealth of data now available

3. For example, there is a marked difference between the purposes to which the wealthy allocate their contributions, and the pattern of allocations among Americans as a whole. In contrast to the general pattern, the wealthy give substantially more to higher education, cultural institutions, and hospitals. They give substantially less for religious purposes.

only to the government and the judgment of a wide spectrum of outside experts in the realms of taxation and philanthropy.

It remains to be said that the commission's support for increased tax incentives to philanthropic giving should not be construed as a blanket endorsement of the incentive system as it now exists. We recognize that the existing system is vulnerable to criticism in points of detail. We also recognize and strongly affirm that much work remains to be done at both a conceptual and an administrative level before a new tax incentive approach attains its full potential. All we say here is that tax incentives are the "growing root" that needs to be cultivated, and that, with due recognition of the difficulties entailed, the formulation of new and better tax incentives for charitable giving should be accorded a high priority.

Part 2
Foundations

5

Foundations:
Their Characteristics
and Work

The power of speech was given to man alone as an authentic gift straight from heaven, and, for this reason perhaps, a holy insecurity went along with the gift. That insecurity is clearly evidenced whenever the word "foundations" is used. It means many different things to different people who use the word in different contexts. The commission has tried to define foundations in ways that consistently describe a common set of realities.

Basic Characteristics of Foundations. A foundation serves as an intermediate entity between a donor and the recipients of his philanthropic giving. As the commission uses the term, a foundation is primarily a *grant-making* organization supported by contributions from an individual, a company, or a small group of persons. We distinguish foundations from organizations which are broadly supported by the general public. Our definition excludes so-called "feeder" organizations which support only a single charity, as well as "operating" foundations which devote most of their funds to the direct conduct of charitable activities. A foundation, within our use of the term, may be organized in the form of either a trust or a nonprofit corporation; it may have an endowment or distribute contributions for charitable purposes as they are received. Its grants may be limited to a specialized purpose or cover the whole range of permissible charitable purposes.

In a further refinement of its definition, the commission decided that two basic characteristics distinguish foundations from other charitable organizations: first, they receive their contributions from a single person or a relatively small group, and second, their major function is *giving (grant making) rather than doing.* We decided that the existence of an endowment, which has been used in some definitions of foundations, was not essential for our purposes. As long as the sources of contributions are relatively narrow, we did not think the presence or absence of an endowment made a major functional difference.

It is worth noting here that our definition of foundation differs from that in the Tax Reform Act of 1969. The act for the first time introduces the term "private foundations." The definition thus excludes other charitable organizations from this category. Schools, churches, and hospitals are explicitly excluded. For other organizations, the primary test for exclusion corresponds to the first characteristic of foundations we have mentioned: a charitable organization is not considered a "private foundation" under the new law if it is broadly supported. "Broadly supported," as defined in the law, means that the organization normally receives more than one-third of its support—exclusive of capital gains—from the public in relatively small amounts and less than one-third as income from investments.

The new law does not, however, make use of the second trait we have mentioned: the fact that an organization is "operating" rather than "grant-making" is not a basis for exclusion from "private foundation" status.[1]

In one sense the activities of foundations are like those of an individual donor: a foundation, like an individual, chooses among competing requests for charitable funds. Unlike most individuals, however, a foundation can often commit funds over a prolonged period and may therefore have a marked effect on the activities of the recipients of its funds. Recipients are accustomed to negotiating with foundations about the use to which grants will be put, while individual donors are generally expected to provide funds with few strings attached. As an institution, a foundation is more likely than an individual to develop an organized method of making its charitable contributions. It may employ a staff or seek the assistance of consultants to develop expertise in particular specialties.

In addition to being an intermediate entity—a middleman for philanthropic giving—there are two other major attributes which distinguish the foundation from other institutions.

First, it has funds which are not committed to its own ongoing ac-

1. For a few limited purposes under the new law, a distinction is made between "private operating foundations" and "private non-operating foundations." Grant-making foundations, as we use the term, would be "private non-operating foundations," but because of the mechanics of the legal definition some other organizations will also fall in that category.

tivities. Practically every other organization in our society, whether a government agency, a corporation, a church, or a university, is likely to have its future activities dictated in part by the momentum of its continuing programs. Budget pressures from existing programs generally make it very difficult to find funds for different kinds of programs. But foundations have substantial amounts of uncommitted money, which their trustees can spend next year for purposes quite different from those pursued now. This gives foundations a degree of flexibility unmatched by any other institution in our society and imposes correspondingly heavy responsibilities on them. The ability of foundations to undertake new tasks—besides giving sustained support to continuing programs of great importance—is of great potential significance to society in an era of rapidly accelerating change.

Second, a foundation is not required to raise funds either because it is endowed or because future contributions may be expected to come from the same donors as did previous funds. This in turn means that a foundation does not have to worry about the impact of its activities on contributions. It is therefore free from an element of external control to which most other institutions are subject. Government agencies must satisfy congressional authorization and appropriations committees as well as the Budget Bureau. Business corporations must satisfy both their customers and their investors. Universities must satisfy a variety of existing and potential sources of funds, scholars, and beneficiaries of scholarship. A foundation, however, may stick to a single field of concentration, or it may totally alter its areas of interest on its own initiative. It may determine the extent to which it may wish to prescribe or supervise the activities of a grantee, without reference to the effect of this involvement on its relationship with potential contributors. It is relatively free to sponsor experimentation, since it has the resources and the independence to afford failure and the opportunity to learn from it. It is thus one of the few institutions in our society that can take the long view, can take the time to explore solutions to our most intractable problems.

The Legal Framework for Foundations. As entities formally separate from the individuals who contribute to them, foundations have special legal privileges. They also have special legal obligations. Because they are exclusively charitable organizations, they are subject to forms of public scrutiny—including disclosure of their grants and financial operations—which would be considered an intrusion upon an individual donor's privacy.

Foundations, like most other legal entities, are created under state law as trusts or as not-for-profit corporations. As states grant foundations the right to exist in perpetuity and as charitable entities, foundations enjoy an exemption from state taxes of various types. In turn, they are subject to state regulation of their activities. In practice, however, few states have developed active programs to regulate foundations.[2] Federal law has been far more important for foundations. Under the tax code, an organization operated exclusively for charitable purposes qualifies for exemption from income taxation. Charitable purposes are very broadly defined in the tax law to include "religious, charitable, scientific, testing for public safety, literary or educational purposes and the prevention of cruelty to children or animals." The tax exemption applies both to income from endowments and to income obtained from charitable activities. However, the tax exemption does not apply to income from the active conduct of a business unrelated to the foundation's charitable purposes.

Perhaps even more important than the tax exemption on foundation income is the tax deduction available to contributions to foundations. Contributions to the organization (up to specified percentages of adjusted gross income) are deductible by individuals and corporations for income tax purposes, and bequests are deductible for estate tax purposes.

Prior to the Tax Reform Act of 1969, foundations were subject to the same basic limitations on their activities as other charitable organizations. For example, they could not be used for personal profit; they could not participate in partisan politics; and they could not attempt to influence legislation except as an insubstantial part of their activities. In addition, foundations and some other charitable organizations were prohibited from engaging in financial transactions with donors and other related parties ("self-dealing") except on an "arm's length" basis. They were also prohibited from unreasonably accumulating income or from using their income in ways that did not benefit charity. Violation of these prohibitions could result in loss of tax exemption. In practice, the harshness of this sanction and the difficulty of administering the legal restrictions meant that regulation was seldom invoked.

The Tax Reform Act of 1969 for the first time separates "private foundations" from other charitable organizations. These "private

2. The state of New York is one of the best examples of an exception to this general statement.

foundations," which are defined to cover some other organizations besides grant-making foundations, are subject to a new and far more comprehensive set of legal restrictions. Monetary sanctions for violations of these restrictions are imposed on the foundation itself, on responsible foundation officials, and on individuals involved in prohibited transactions.

The new law is quite complicated, and the wording is frequently ambiguous. Thus the complete impact of the new law cannot be assessed until the Treasury Department issues regulations covering it and until it has been in effect for several years. We can, however, indicate the basic legal framework in which foundations will operate in the future. (Chapters 17 through 19 contain definite legislative and regulatory recommendations.)

First, with regard to programs, foundations continue to be permitted a broader flexibility in their grant making than an individual is in his tax-deductible charitable giving, but they are subject to several special restrictions:

1. Foundations are prohibited from making any expenditure to attempt to influence legislation either by attempting to affect public opinion or by contacting individuals involved in the legislative process. There are two limited exceptions to these prohibitions: (i) making available the results of "non-partisan analysis, study, or research," and (ii) rendering technical assistance to a governmental body at its request.

2. Foundations are prohibited from spending funds to attempt to influence the outcome of a specific election. Voter education and voter registration activities are permitted only under very limiting conditions.

3. Foundation grants to individuals must be awarded on an objective and nondiscriminatory basis, for specified purposes, and under procedures approved by the Internal Revenue Service.

4. Foundation payments to government officials are prohibited (with minor exceptions, such as providing reimbursement for expenses incurred in charitable work).

5. Foundations are required to monitor the activities of some grantee organizations to see that the funds are spent for permissible purposes.

Subject to these specific restrictions, foundations may make grants to charitable organizations (including other foundations), to individuals, to foreign organizations, or to organizations not themselves charitable, provided that the spending is exclusively for charitable purposes. In addition to grant-making programs, foundations can, as a legal matter, engage in the direct conduct of charitable activities.

Under the new law, foundations are for the first time required to make a minimum annual payout for charitable purposes. They are required to expend an amount each year equal either to their net income (excluding long-term capital gains) or to a percentage of the market value of their assets (initially established at 6 percent for new foundations with a transition period for existing foundations), whichever is the higher amount.[3] Under the prior law there was no payout requirement but only a loose rule against unreasonable accumulation of income.

In addition to the basic requirement that they not be operated to benefit private parties, foundations are subject to specific restrictions on their financial and investment activities:

1. Foundations are absolutely prohibited from engaging in any transactions with persons related to them ("self-dealing"). Under the prior law such transactions were not prohibited but were mainly subject to an "arm's length" or "reasonableness" standard, which was difficult to administer and subject to abuse.

2. Foundation speculation and other questionable investment activities are prohibited.

3. Foundation ownership of a controlling interest in a business comes under substantial new restrictions in the new law. The rules are complex but apply generally to stock holdings in excess of 20 percent. Holdings existing in 1969 are subject to special transition rules. The percentage limitation applies to stock held either by the foundation alone or in combination with persons related to it.[4]

3. For existing foundations the 6 percent minimum payout is to be phased in over a transitional period: 4½ percent in 1972, 5 percent in 1973, 5½ percent in 1974, and 6 percent in 1975 and thereafter.

4. For foundations with corporate control holdings on 26 May 1969, less stringent divestiture requirements are applied. In general, they are subject to a 50 percent limit (in conjunction with the holdings of those related to the foundation). Those whose holdings were above that level on 26 May 1969 are given a period of time ranging from ten years for those with from 50 percent to 75 percent to twenty years for those with over 95 percent to reach the 50 percent limit for combined holdings. They then have an additional period of fifteen years to reduce the foundation's own holdings to 25 percent (or 35 percent if related persons own less than 2 percent).

No foundations may purchase corporate control stocks. Those which receive such stock under a will executed before, or a trust instrument irrevocable on 26 May 1969 are subject to the rules for existing stockholders. In other cases of gift or bequest, the foundation has five years to dispose of the stock it acquires.

The general limit on foundation stock ownership in a corporation is, along with those persons related to the foundation, 20 percent of the voting stock of the corporation. If a third party has effective control of the corporation, then the limit is raised to 35 percent. In addition, if the foundation owns less than 2 percent of the stock of a corporation, then the attribution rules for related persons do not apply.

Foundations have been required for some years to file information tax returns (Form 990-A's) to the Internal Revenue Service. These returns have been available for public inspection. Under the new law, foundations are required to file an expanded version of this return. In addition, they are required to file annual reports containing additional information and to have these reports available for public inspection at their offices.

The new law places grant-making foundations at a relative disadvantage to other charitable organizations as recipients of tax-deductible contributions. A donor to a foundation can deduct only 50 percent of the appreciation in value of stock and certain other property which he contributes to a foundation and which is not distributed by the foundation in one year. If the same property is given to a "broadly supported" or operating charity, then the full amount of the appreciation is deductible. Because a high percentage of large donations consist of appreciated stock, the less favorable treatment accorded to foundations is likely to have a serious impact on new contributions to foundations. The new law also places foundations at a disadvantage with respect to the ceiling on deductible contributions by individuals. The ceiling on deductions for foundation endowments remains at 20 percent of the individual's annual income. The ceilings on other charitable contributions have generally been raised to 50 percent of income with a right to carry over excess contributions.

Finally, unlike other charitable organizations, foundations are required to pay a special federal "excise tax" at an annual rate of 4 percent of their net investment income. We shall say more about this tax later.

The net result of all this is to make the foundations under the new tax law no better than "second class" charitable organizations.

Reasons for Establishing Foundations. The reasons why donors have established foundations instead of giving directly to operating charities are highly varied. In most cases, there has undoubtedly been a mixture of "pure" philanthropic motives and personal motives, including tax advantages. In combination, these motives have resulted in a proliferation of foundations. In the last thirty years, the number of foundations increased one hundredfold.

Probably the strongest attraction of a foundation is that it enables a donor to obtain a tax deduction for a charitable contribution while still retaining a limited but substantial control over the assets contributed to the foundation. In this respect, a contribution to a foundation differs markedly from contributions to most other philanthropic organizations, where, at the time the contribution is made, the property passes out of the donor's control.

The donor's control over assets contributed to a foundation has two main features. First, the donor who controls his foundation maintains flexibility in choosing how and when to devote the foundation's assets to charitable purposes. By contributing stock or other property to his foundation he has merely committed himself to devote the income to charity. The property can be maintained intact (subject to the payout requirements of the new law). The decision to contribute money to the foundation, rather than giving directly to a university or other charitable organization, leaves open the donor's future options both as to purpose and as to ultimate recipient.

The second feature of control relates to the nonphilanthropic decisions which the donor is in a position to make with respect to property he has contributed to a foundation under his control. This point is of particular importance when the property consists of stock in a closely held corporation. The ability to maintain control of the corporation by voting the stock held by the foundation has been an important reason for contributing to a foundation rather than to another type of charitable institution. The new tax law severely restricts the use of foundations as a means of controlling corporations. Under the prior law the donor also had considerable flexibility to make personal use of assets contributed to the foundation. For example, the donor could obtain loans from the foundation subject only to an "arm's length" or "reasonableness" standard. The enactment of statutory prohibitions against "self-dealing" transactions between a foundation and its donors should prevent such personal use of foundation assets in the future.

Foundations are also a useful means of "evening out" gifts. A company or an individual may put more money into a foundation in a good earnings year, less in a poor, and still maintain a relatively constant level of support of charitable organizations. Alternatively, the foundation can accumulate several years' contributions (subject, of course, to the requirement that it make a minimum payout to charity) and make a large grant at a later date.

Many donors desire to continue to support the recipients of their charitable giving after their death, and most achieve this goal through direct bequests to these charities. Some individuals, however, may not want to give their entire contribution either at one time or for one purpose. Far from reflecting the "dead hand of the past," their motive in establishing a foundation as a conduit for their bequests may stem from a realization that needs may change and that a foundation provides flexibility in patterns of giving in response to these changes.

Another attractive feature of a foundation involves a point already touched on—namely, that a foundation is a legally separate entity from the donor. For this reason it is permitted to make certain types of grants that would not be tax-deductible if made by an individual or corporate donor directly to a recipient. It is anomalous, and some would say a legislative accident, that merely by creating a foundation an individual can expand the permissible scope of his tax-deductible charitable giving. This fact alone appears to justify increased government surveillance of foundation grants.

An individual with a foundation may, with tax-deductible dollars, hire a professional staff to systematize and develop expertise in giving, whereas an individual may not claim deductions for such expenses.

A foundation also provides a convenient conduit for making special kinds of charitable contributions. For example, a donor who wishes to use property rather than cash for his charitable contributions is likely to find it more convenient to transfer the property to the foundation and then let the foundation sell the property and make donations to his various philanthropic interests. This is generally simpler than transferring property piecemeal to many recipients.

A foundation may also provide some degree of insulation from direct appeals for contributions. Executives of business corporations can avoid having to respond to personal solicitations by referring requests to the company foundation.

Finally, personal considerations are often of the greatest importance as reasons for the creation of a foundation. A foundation bearing the family name gives a donor a degree of status and distinction during his lifetime and creates an opportunity for perpetuating his name and charitable interests after his death.

The Types and Distribution of Foundations. One clear sign of the lack of public understanding of foundations is the widespread belief that there is a monolithic sameness to them, when, in fact, few types of organizations are as varied as they are in every respect. Foundations vary in size from those with no endowment and only a few thousand dollars in annual grants, to the Ford Foundation with approximately $3 billion in assets and annual grants of roughly $200 million. They may have received contributions from an individual, a single company, or a number of unrelated persons. Contributions may have been received on only one occasion, such as by bequest or on a regular annual basis. The foundation may be independent of the donor, or completely controlled by him, or in some intermediate state of independence.

A foundation may have a specialized charitable purpose or make grants for many different types of charitable purposes. Its grant making may be confined to one locality or may be worldwide. It may employ a large professional staff with substantial discretionary authority, or no staff at all, all grant-making decisions being made by the donor. It may make grants that are innovative or controversial or it may make only grants to well-established public charities. Foundations can play a very active role in their fields of interest. Some, in fact, carry on sizable "operating programs." Others limit themselves to check writing with little or no follow-up on what happens to the money.

Assets and Geographic Concentration. Earlier in these pages, data compiled by the Foundation Center in New York was cited which indicate that in 1968 there were approximately 22,000 foundations in the United States with assets estimated at $20.5 billion (see chapter 1 at note 1). Their annual grants of $1.6 billion were approximately 9 percent of the $17.6 billion total of voluntary giving in 1969. The Foundation Center estimates that foundation assets and grants, in the period 1964–67, were compounding at a rate of 11.4 percent and 16 percent a year, respectively. The Center's statistics on the number of foundations differ from those compiled by others. Such differences are inevitable because, as has been observed, there is not yet any agreement on the definition of a foundation. In 1968 the Internal Revenue Service published a list containing 30,262 foundations.[5] Representative Wright Patman has contended that there are 45,000 foundations.[6]

No one has even attempted to estimate the number of organizations which will be classified as "private foundations" under the definition in the 1969 Tax Reform Act. The statistical problem will be exacerbated by the new definition contained in the Tax Reform Act which includes non-grant-making organizations in the "private foundation" category but excludes community foundations.[7]

5. We understand this was the first major attempt of the IRS to do this, and it is not yet entirely satisfied with the definitions and inclusions.
6. Patman's estimate would appear to include many exempt organizations not normally considered "foundations." This underlines the need to define what is meant by a "foundation."
7. We consider the designation of foundations as "private" distinctly unfortunate.

The commission has found that the assets reported by many foundations on their Form 990-A returns to the Internal Revenue Service are carried at cost or some other basis rather than market value. A leading example is the Irvine Foundation, which until 1969 carried its assets at approximately $6 million. In 1969 it filed a Form 990-A which reflected assets in excess of $100 million, and there have been estimates that the market value of that foundation's property is considerably higher. It is highly probably that the Foundation Center's $20.5 billion figure for the total asset value of foundations is low.

Using the Internal Revenue Service list of foundations, we have prepared a breakdown of the number of foundations in each region of the country and compared these results with population distribution. Foundations are found in every state in the Union, although a disproportionately large number are located in New York (see chart 3).

This geographic concentration would be greatly magnified if asset value were used as a standard of comparison. The situation probably reflects a time lag between the creation of large fortunes and the transfer of accumulated funds to foundations. As new centers of wealth arise throughout the country it is reasonable to expect that new foundations will become more dispersed, though some major foundations have migrated eastward from their place of origin.

The commission surveyed a sample of grant-making foundations in order to determine where their grants go, the form of contributions to foundations, and methods of operation. Questions were framed to elicit basic data about foundations which had not previously been available.

Many foundations responded, and our information came largely through personal interviews with representatives of 201 foundations, including seventeen of the twenty-six largest. We divided foundations into five categories by asset size: over $100 million; $10–100 million; $1–10 million; $200,000–1 million, and under $200,000. We treated company foundations and community foundations separately.

An understanding of the concentration of assets is crucial to an understanding of the foundation structure in America. Thus, the twenty-six largest foundations hold over $10 billion in assets—at least one-third of total foundation assets—and account for over $475 million in

---

By the same token, neither is it accurate to refer to them as "public," for while their purposes are public, their operation is private. This commission would prefer a designation such as "philanthropic foundation" to remind everyone, including the foundations, of their essential purpose.

CHART 3
FOUNDATIONS VERSUS POPULATION BY REGION

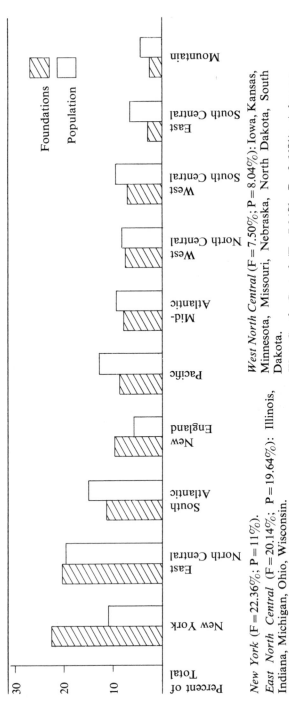

New York (F = 22.36%; P = 11%).

East North Central (F = 20.14%; P = 19.64%): Illinois, Indiana, Michigan, Ohio, Wisconsin.

South Atlantic (F = 11.14%; P = 14.99%): Delaware, District of Columbia, Florida, Georgia, Maryland, North Carolina, South Carolina, Virginia, West Virginia.

New England (F = 9.87%; P = 5.71%): Connecticut, Maine, Massachusetts, New Hampshire, Rhode Island, Vermont.

Pacific (F = 8.88%; P = 12.95%): Alaska, California, Hawaii, Oregon, Washington.

Middle Atlantic (F = 7.84%; P = 9.38%): New Jersey,

West North Central (F = 7.50%; P = 8.04%): Iowa, Kansas, Minnesota, Missouri, Nebraska, North Dakota, South Dakota.

West South Central (F = 7.04%; P = 9.66%): Arkansas, Louisiana, Oklahoma, Texas.

East South Central (F = 2.89%; P = 6.50%): Alabama, Kentucky, Mississippi, Tennessee.

Mountain (F = 2.34%; P = 4.02%): Arizona, Colorado, Idaho, Montana, Nevada, New Mexico, Utah, Wyoming.

F = Percentage of total foundations

grants per year or slightly less than one-third of the annual grants. Of this total, the Ford Foundation is by far the largest, and, wherever necessary in our survey, we have its permission to show its figures separately. The hundred largest foundations account for roughly half of the total annual grants of all foundations.

It has been charged that foundation assets account for a very large and growing proportion of the nation's financial wealth. When Charles Schultze of Brookings Institution calculated the ratio of foundation holdings to total holdings of stocks, bonds, and mortgages, he found the foundations hold a *very small* and *declining proportion* of that wealth. In 1968, using two different methods of computation, he showed the ratio of foundation holdings to be between 1.29 and 1.39 percent of the nation's total holdings. In 1958, these ratios were somewhat larger, or between 1.47 and 1.57 percent.

Two types of foundations merit a special word:

1. *Community Foundations.* The Cleveland Foundation, the Permanent Charities Fund of Boston, and the Chicago Community Trust are examples of this type, and they differ from other foundations in several important respects. Their endowment assets represent the pooling of gifts and bequests from a number of donors within the community, and their trustees are usually widely representative of the community. Their grants are almost entirely within one metropolitan area. There are at least 214 community foundations with assets estimated by some sources at $665 million. Because many of these community foundations receive widespread support, they may legally be classified as "publicly supported charities" rather than as "private foundations" and may therefore be unaffected by federal tax law affecting foundations.[8] Although the "publicly supported" community foundations do not meet the definition of a foundation used by this commission, they are primarily grant-making organizations, and therefore we have included them in our survey. Not all of our recommendations, however, necessarily apply to them.

Community foundations are of great importance in the foundation field. Family foundations without professional staffs frequently draw upon the expertise of a community foundation either for advice on particular grants or to coordinate their grant-making activities with those of other foundations. Assets of a small or medium-sized founda-

---

8. The rules for deduction of contributions for federal income tax purposes, as amended by the Tax Reform Act, specifically treat community foundations in the same way as broadly supported charities rather than as private foundations.

tion are frequently transferred to a community foundation after the death of the donor. Various methods are used to maintain the identity of the individual donors.

2. *Company Foundations.* These are usually closely tied to the corporation which created them, with company officers serving as trustees. Company foundations are a convenient method for a company to even out its annual corporate giving by contributing more to the foundation in good years and less in poor years. Some company foundations are so-called conduits—that is, annual grants are roughly equal to the annual contributions received from the corporation. These conduit foundations have little or no endowment. There are, however, a number of company foundations which have substantial endowments and which operate in much the same way as foundations established by individuals.

Survey Findings—Geographic Focus of Foundation Activities.[9] Because of the heavy concentration of assets and grants in relatively few foundations, we have shown the findings of our survey both in terms of numbers of foundations and in terms of dollars of grants or assets. Large foundations operate in quite different ways from small ones, and to show our data only in terms of numbers of foundations would give disproportionate emphasis to small foundations. For example, if we

TABLE 2.
GEOGRAPHICAL FOCUS OF FOUNDATION ACTIVITIES

	Percentage of Foundations	Percentage of Foundation Assets, End of 1968	Percentage of Foundation Grants, 1968
Regional	65	36	32
Cities, counties or metropolitan areas	47	24	23
State	9	4	3
Multistate region	9	8	6
National (but not international)	19	21	38
International only	6	2	3
National and international	10	42	27
	100	100	100

9. For detailed data on the geographical focus of the activities of foundations of different asset size and type, see appendix IV, table A.30.

look at the geographic scope of foundation activities in terms of *dollars of grants*, we conclude that over two-thirds of foundation activity is represented by foundations that operate on a national and international scale. Had we looked at this only in terms of *numbers of foundations*, we would have concluded that foundation activity was predominately regional, because two-thirds of all foundations focus their efforts on specific metropolitan areas, a particular state, or a multistate region.

A side glance at foundations in Europe shows a marked contrast to the American picture. In European countries generally, the status of a foundation depends heavily upon the ministerial or parliamentary decree that the donor is able to get for the creation of his trust. In practice this is difficult to get, or a foundation is compromised in its work because of the great difficulty in getting a tax exemption. The one exception is in Great Britain, where all charitable organizations, including the foundations, have remained exempt from payment of income taxes even under a Labour government. In Britain, as in the United States, the creation and operation of a foundation is a relatively simple legal procedure requiring only the formality of incorporation; hence, there are a great number of them, though most are relatively modest in size. Elsewhere in Europe, however, foundations are both few in number and small in size, with minimal tax exemptions or none at all.

Aside from the general opposition of most European governments to the creation of foundations, and tax-exempt foundations at that, there have been two other inhibiting factors to their development. One is the shrinkage of the large fortunes in Europe under the combined effects of war, taxation, and inflation. The other is that large industrial corporations are likely to have committees of workers sitting with management, and these labor representatives are zealous about seeing that company workers, instead of society at large, are the main beneficiaries of any generous impulses.

6

Financial
Abuses of
Foundations

In the 1960s the number of foundations in America grew at a rate estimated by some observers to be as high as two thousand a year. To critics suspicious of this growth, the foundations seemed to be a device whereby donors not only could avoid paying taxes but could enjoy numerous additional advantages not otherwise within their reach. When these suspicions seemed to be confirmed by public disclosures of spectacular and particular instances of abuse, the revelations had the effect of making the line between the guilty and the innocent as indistinct as a line drawn in water. In consequence, extensive new regulations of foundations were enacted as part of the Tax Reform Act of 1969.

A major source of increased public awareness of financial abuse involving foundations was the investigation of foundations begun by Representative Wright Patman in 1961 and still continuing. Patman has thus far issued seven voluminous reports consisting of many studies of the financial activities of individual foundations along with a vast amount of statistical material. He has also conducted two sets of full-dress public hearings, the second of which, held in 1967, centered on one particular organization with a spread-eagle title: Americans Building Constitutionally or, in abbreviation, ABC. The organization undertook for a fee to guide its constituent members in organizing foundations—but in suspect ways.

Patman's reports have been attacked on the ground that they were inaccurate in fact, and exaggerated in the general conclusions and recommendations he drew from the examples selected. Nonetheless, it would be wrong to conclude straight off that where there is smoke, there is only a smoke machine. Under the spur of Patman's early revelations, the Treasury Department undertook its own study of private

54

foundations. In a report issued in 1965, the department concluded that foundations "can constitute a powerful instrument for the evolution, growth, and improvement in the shape and direction of charity," but it also found abuses in the use of the foundation instrument. Among a number of regulatory recommendations contained in that report, several formed the basis for provisions which were incorporated in the Tax Reform Act of 1969.

The main financial abuses charged against foundations spring, in essence, from too clever an exploitation of their advantages. The advantages themselves have already been detailed in these pages, and so it is not necessary to dwell on them again. What needs to be said here is that a donor's ability to control a foundation is the precondition that makes financial abuses potentially possible. Indeed, the common elements in the various types of financial abuse all involve benefits accruing to a private person—generally a substantial donor to the foundation—but at the expense either of charity or of government revenues. When impropriety has involved contributions to the foundation, the decisive factor has been the ability of the donor to accept his own contributions on behalf of the foundation—or, to be more precise, to *impose* them on the foundation. When the impropriety involved the foundation's investments, administrative procedures, or grants, the decisive factor was again the control exercised by the benefited party over the foundation's actions.

On the side of *contributions to foundations*, one kind of abuse can occur in connection with a deduction from taxes of contributions to any charitable organization, either by overvaluing the amount contributed or by making an outright false claim of a contribution. Property which is contributed, for example, may be overvalued by the donor to increase the amount of his deduction. This is particularly likely to occur with property for which there is no readily ascertainable market price. Some types of contributions, such as gifts of the use of property, may be so grossly overvalued that the only practical remedy is the one adopted in the Tax Reform Act of 1969—namely, to disallow any deduction for such gifts.

These two kinds of abuse—overvaluing contributions or falsely claiming deductions for gifts never made—are likely to occur more frequently in the case of foundations than in that of other charitable organizations. The reason is, in part, the nature of the contributions they receive. As our survey data on foundations indicated, the major share of the contributions made to them has been in the form of appreciated property, and a substantial share is in the form of stock in a closely held corporation. These are the kinds of gifts that are most likely to be overvalued, especially for income tax purposes.

Foundations have also been given unproductive property which conferred no benefit upon charity but gave the donor a current tax deduction for full—and sometimes inflated—market value. In its 1965 report on foundations, the Treasury Department cited some awesome examples of such gifts. In one instance, a taxpayer claimed a tax deduction of $39,500 for the gift of family jewelry to her husband's foundation. The jewelry was kept for years in a safe deposit box rented by the foundation and presumably was available for loan to the woman who gave it. In another instance, a company donated vacant land adjacent to its plant. The foundation held the land for eleven years, during which period it produced no income for charity. In that interval, however, the company had a double advantage: a tax deduction and what amounted to a free option to purchase the land when it was needed for expansion.

Deals of this kind are possible through charitable organizations other than foundations. The former, however, generally have little interest in receiving unproductive property which cannot be sold. A foundation, for its part, may accept a gift only because the donor controlling the foundation wants to take a tax deduction. The foundation may also continue to hold the unproductive property for no more compelling reasons than the donor's own desire that it should.[1] Nor is this all. The donor's control of "his" foundation may aid him in overvaluing his contributions to charity. One abuse of this kind—the back-dating of contributions—was identified in a survey of accountants which Arthur Andersen and Company conducted for the commission. The worth of a share of stock today, for example, might be only half of its value six months ago; by back-dating the contribution, the donor takes a larger deduction.

On the side of *investments or use of foundation assets*, there is the kind of abuse where contributions resulting in a personal benefit to the donor entail further financial transactions between the foundation and the donor or a related party. An example of this kind cited by the Treasury in its 1965 report involved a contribution which was immediately loaned by the foundation to a business controlled by the donor. The donor, in effect, received an immediate tax deduction for funds

1. Assuming it has other resources to meet its annual payout requirement.

invested in his business—a form of pledge to devote the sum to charity at some future date. No taxpayer without a foundation could have obtained a deduction for a pledge to charity, though his pledge may legally have been just as collectible as the loan.

It has already been noted that prior to the Tax Reform Act of 1969, the tax law permitted transactions between a donor or those related to him and his foundation if they were at "reasonable" or "arm's length" terms. However, because a stringent sanction was applied in a case of violation—namely, a loss of tax exemption—courts tended to interpret the "arm's length" standard liberally, permitting a variety of doubtful transactions to occur. Administration was also difficult since the Internal Revenue Service had to scrutinize transactions in detail to ascertain if they met the "arm's length" standard.

Even when a financial transaction between a donor and "his" foundation appeared reasonable on the face of things, the terms could still give concealed advantages to the donor. In borrowing from his foundation, for example, a donor would not have to give the same detailed statement a bank would have required. He could be sure of a favorable response to his request and an extension of maturity dates if necessary. Again, a foundation could receive an apparently reasonable interest rate on its loan to the donor, but the loan could be made when the money market was too tight for him readily to find another source of funds. A foundation could pay a fair price when it bought property from a donor, but it might have made the purchase either because the donor needed cash and could not easily find another buyer or in order to permit the donor to retain effective control over the property.

Further, though the foundation could pay a fair rental on property leased from the donor, the latter would have the advantage of a docile lessee when he needed advance leases to secure financing for the acquisition of the property or for construction purposes. The donor's knowledge that he could use the foundation's assets for his personal benefit could affect the decision he made as a foundation official concerning the productive investment of its assets or the amount to be distributed to charity. His knowledge that its assets could be used as a source of capital could cause the donor to see to it that the foundation retained its assets in a form in which they could quickly be converted into cash rather than making either the best investments possible or making distributions to charity.

The commission recognized the self-evident potential for abuses in the foregoing kinds of transactions. But how *often* and how *serious* have these abuses actually been? The question, which goes to the heart of any reformist proposal, was difficult for the commission to answer because it had no subpoena or auditing power to get at the hard facts. Thus, the commission had to use various indirect approaches.

One of these was based on the law prior to the Tax Reform Act of 1969, which permitted self-dealing transactions between the donor and his foundation if they were at arm's length or met a standard of reasonableness. Foundations, however, were required to report such transactions to the Internal Revenue Service on their Form 990-A annual information return, regardless of whether or not the foundation believed the transaction was fair or at arm's length. Hence, transactions reported indicate the level of potential rather than actual abuse from self-dealing transactions. (Of course, some foundations may not have reported transactions at all.) When the commission tabulated the incidence of reported self-dealing transactions in a sample of nearly five hundred foundation Form 990-A's, the results showed what the following count makes clear—that the vast majority did not report any self-dealing transactions:

	Percentage of Foundations *Reporting Transaction*
Borrowing income or corpus	1.5
Receiving compensation for services	2.5
Using services or assets	0.5
Purchasing securities or other property	3.5
Selling services or property	5.5
Receiving income or corpus in any other transaction	1.1

Meanwhile, since it was generally assumed that self-dealing abuses were more frequent among small foundations than among larger ones and because less was known about small foundations, the commission had Arthur Andersen and Company survey accountants anonymously for their impressions of such self-dealing abuses by small foundations. The nature of the proposition put them and the manner of their response was as follows:

"There are loose financial self-dealings between small foundations and the donor or friends which work to the advantage of donor or friends."

Very infrequent	70%
Not common	21%
Fairly common	7%
Very common	2%
	100% (N = 212)

(Nine respondents expressed no opinion.)

The accountants were also asked about the record-keeping practices of small foundations and the extent to which any loose practices among them might make it difficult to determine whether self-dealing and other abuses occurred. The proposition elicited the following responses:

"There is loose record-keeping by small foundations which makes it difficult to know whether personal advantage is being taken by the donor or his friends."

Very infrequent	69%
Not common	24%
Fairly common	5%
Very common	2%
	100% (N=211)

(Ten respondents expressed no opinion.)

The replies here suggest two things: while self-dealing abuses are not frequent among the small foundations, they do occur and may be difficult to discover.

Investment transactions for the benefit of private parties have not always involved direct transactions with the donor. As a source of ready capital, foundations have been used for speculative investments, either to aid the donor in profiting from his personal speculation or simply as a convenient device to enable him to indulge in such activities without the risk of personal financial loss. Representative Wright Patman and the Treasury Department in its 1965 report cited several examples of the range of investment activities that have been carried on under the tax-free auspices of a foundation.

The Tax Reform Act of 1969 now imposes an absolute prohibition on self-dealing transactions, including indirect transactions (to manipulate stock prices, for example) to benefit those related to the foundation. Other types of speculation are also prohibited when investments jeopardize the foundation's charitable purposes. The new act also tightens restrictions on the use of borrowed funds by tax-exempt organizations, a device which had been used to benefit private parties in the so-called "Clay Brown" transactions.

On the side of *foundation administration*, instances have been uncovered of foundation funds' being used to provide personal amenities for the donor, his family, or others associated with the foundation, under the guise of administrative costs. In some cases, administrative expenses have had no charitable purpose. In others, expenses for legitimate purposes have been excessive.

In the anonymous survey of accountants conducted by Arthur

Andersen and Company, the accountants were asked whether, in their judgment, small foundations had high administrative costs. Though there had been a few widely publicized examples of this condition, the accountants apparently did not believe the condition was widespread. The nature of their response to the proposition put to them was as follows:

"There are high operating expenses relative to the assets or the income of the small foundations."

Very infrequent	72%
Not common	23%
Fairly common	3%
Very common	2%
	100% (N = 209)

(Twelve respondents expressed no opinion.)

One detail should here be added. The Tax Reform Act of 1969 prohibits the payment of excessive compensation to donors, trustees, officers, and those related to them. It also limits the inclusion of administrative expenses to reasonable amounts for purposes of calculating the required distributions to charity. It does not, however, include a direct prohibition of excessive administrative expenses.

On the side of *foundation grants*, there have been some instances where a foundation was used to funnel funds from a donor so that he could claim a charitable deduction although the ultimate recipient was not a "charitable purpose." Since the foundation itself was a charitable organization, the contribution to it was deductible. But the foundation's use of the contribution in ways which benefited the donor went underground and was difficult to trace.

Company foundations occasionally have made grants which could more legitimately be considered business expenses. Thus, they might support research in a field in which the company is interested, with an informal or formal arrangement under which the company gets access to the results before its competitors or the general public. In another form, company foundations might make grants to charitable organizations which are its customers, thus in effect giving them a price rebate.

Since a foundation has flexibility in making charitable grants with tax-deductible dollars, it can make grants to individuals and to foreign organizations as well as to nonprofit organizations and even profit-making businesses as long as the grant is for charitable purposes. One result is the establishment of foundations primarily to serve as conduits for funds to charities outside the United States or to individuals.

These activities are not necessarily improper. But abuse of this privilege has occurred. An example of this kind of abuse—now clearly prohibited by the new tax law—may be something like the following. A foundation makes a "scholarship" grant to a donor's child or the child of a friend of the donor, sometimes as part of a mutual assistance pact where the friend's foundation makes a similar grant to the first donor's child. In such instances, the donor receives a charitable contribution deduction for amounts given the foundation, though the amounts were used indirectly to benefit the donor or others in ways which would not be deductible if done directly.

Some 8 percent of the accountants surveyed for the commission indicated that, in their judgment, individual grants not based entirely on merit were "fairly common" or "very common" among small foundations. Here is the nature of the proposition put to them and the manner of their response:

"Grants by the foundations to *individuals* are based not so much on merit, but on friendship or kinship with those in charge."

Very infrequent	70%
Not common	22%
Fairly common	7%
Very common	1%
	100% (N = 197)

(Twenty-four respondents expressed no opinion.)

The Tax Reform Act of 1969 prohibits many of these grant-making abuses—through self-dealing provision, restrictions on individual grants, and a catch-all requirement that all foundation expenditures be in furtherance of its charitable purposes.

A national audience hearing of the real or potential abuses of privilege by foundations is in the position of an audience looking at a newsreel. Things suddenly flash into view, and just as suddenly flash out of view—all in snippets, all without context. A sensational instance where an actual abuse is uncovered is followed by an instance where an alleged abuse which had nothing to do with the foundation's special privileges but where the foundation was simply a convenient vehicle for a legitimate transaction. Yet the two were merged into a composite impression that foundations are tax dodges rather than valuable charitable enterprises. Moreover, that impression owed much of its currency to the fact that the foundations were subject to few restrictions and minimal scrutiny. A determination of the frequency with which the alleged abuses have occurred—or, to put it directly, a determination of the large truths about the whole of the matter—required a thorough audit of the foundations by the Internal Revenue Service. Yet the extent of IRS auditing was, unfortunately, very small, as was brought home to the commission when each of the foundations we surveyed was asked the following question: "To the best of your knowledge, has the foundation been audited in the past ten years by state officials or the federal Internal Revenue Service?"

If our sample is an adequate indication of the general picture, only 36 percent of all foundations have been audited during that period. Only 9 percent have been audited by state officials and 30 percent by the IRS, while a few foundations have been audited by both. At the time of our survey, the Ford Foundation was undergoing only the second audit since it was established in 1936. IRS auditing of foundation grants abroad is virtually nonexistent, largely, we believe, because of inadequate budgets.

Every abuse, by definition, is bad. Yet it needs to be repeated that the air of the illicit that has settled on foundations generally is at least partly due to the fact that so little has been known about the actual frequency of abuses charged against them. In place of the careful inquiries we need, we have had guesses made airborne by the winds of suspicion. In place of the stable body of hard facts we need, we have had a mental process whereby a person looking at the foundation picture finds only what he is looking for. Worst of all, instead of isolating the spectacular case of an abuse so that it can be carefully examined to determine whether it is unique or part of a pervasive pattern, we have set it loose to undercut public confidence in all foundations and even charity as a whole—and this at a time when charitable organizations desperately need added support.

It is the firm conviction of this commission that it is irresponsible, shortsighted, and unfair to permit all foundations to suffer from the broadest anecdotes of individual cases of abuse of privilege without using available tools of auditing and public reporting to get at a balanced judgment. If there are significant levels of abuse, both their nature and their level should be identified and made the subject of a public report. Conversely, if there are no significant levels of abuse, this too should publicly be made clear.

It is urgently necessary to stop all abuses. It is just as urgently necessary to cleanse from the foundations any taint of abuse which unjustly adheres to them.

7

Politics and
Public Concern
over Foundations

In the 1960s, suspicions which led to attacks on foundations went beyond the charges that financial abuse and tax avoidance outweighed philanthropic motives as a reason for the mushroom growth of small foundations. Attacks were also made on foundation ideology, foundation power, and foundation involvement in politics.

Ideologically motivated attacks on foundations are not by themselves something new under the sun. They resulted in major investigations of foundations years before the Patman inquiries, which have concentrated on financial abuses. The noteworthy feature of such attacks is that in the course of a half century there has been a full swing of the pendulum in the ideology of the complaint. Thus, whereas foundations were once denounced as "tools of capitalism," they have lately come to be denounced as the promoters of "creeping socialism."

In the twentieth century, the first sustained attack on the foundation occurred in 1910–12, when the Rockefeller Foundation sought a federal charter to administer its initial gift of $50 million in Standard Oil of New Jersey stock. An influential group of social workers (whose ranks included Jane Addams) led by Dr. Edward T. Devine, denounced the proposal as a "new form of the dead hand" and insisted that the income be taxed and that the government have a voice in choosing trustees. The cry of "tainted money" was raised in Congress, and after three years of fruitless effort, the Rockefeller interests abandoned the contest and turned to the New York legislature, where, within the brief space of a week, a state charter was unanimously voted.

Coinciding with the hubbub of this controversy, in 1912 a Presidential Commission on Industrial Relations was appointed pursuant

63

to an act of Congress. Its chairman was Frank P. Walsh, and its assignment was an investigation of the "general conditions of labor in the United States." The immediate events behind the investigation were the violent strikes in the Colorado coal fields; among companies affected was one in which Rockefeller interests were believed to own controlling stock. Having noted that the Rockefeller Foundation had sponsored a general study of labor conditions under the direction of William L. Mackenzie King, later the Liberal prime minister of Canada, the Walsh Commission extended its inquiries during 1913–15 into "the concentration of wealth and influence."

When the Walsh Commission eventually submitted its report, a majority of its members agreed that "the domination by men in whose hands the final control of a large part of American industry rests is not limited to their employees but is being rapidly extended to control of the educational and social service of the nation." The report argued that since foundation funds were heavily invested in the shares of corporations, the policies of the latter must inevitably be tailored to conform to the wishes of the foundations. This fear of the power of big business and great wealth, resulting in charges of "creeping capitalism," rose to heights of near-hysteria during the Progressive era. The alarm declined rapidly after 1915; the Rockefeller Foundation itself had dropped its labor inquiry and devoted a large fraction of its 1915 expenditures to Belgian relief. Congress, for its part, gave little attention to the Walsh report.

The activities of the General Education Board, one of four foundations created by John D. Rockefeller, Sr., also came under attack in this era of trust busting. The public had been alarmed by disclosures concerning industrial combinations. Along with its efforts to enhance education in the South, the General Education Board had worked with the Department of Agriculture to operate demonstration farms which spread knowledge of improved methods. A number of congressmen charged that this joint arrangement was a "dark plot" by which the board not only was "undermining the fabric of government" but by its aid to teachers was attempting to "warp public opinion throughout the country." Other congressmen, however, were persuaded by their constituents of the value of the board's work, and demands for a full-scale investigation were dropped. As part of this quiet climax, when a Senate resolution required executive department heads to report the extent of involvement of government employees with Rockefeller or Carnegie philanthropies, the inquiry turned up a total of one zoologist who had served as an adviser to a Rockefeller commission.

By the 1950s foundations were no longer feared as agents of "creeping capitalism" but, on the contrary, as promoters of left-wing political causes. An article in the *American Legion Magazine* entitled "Let's Look at Our Foundations" concluded that these organizations constituted a danger to society because they were financing "outright communists, fellow travelers, socialists, do-gooders, one-worlders, wild-eyed Utopians and well-meaning dupes." The concern was sufficiently strong to impel Congress in 1952 to authorize an investigation proposed and headed by Representative Edward E. Cox of Georgia, whose charges had inspired the Legion article.

Discussing the complex motives which influence the words and actions of those involved in such situations, Harold M. Keele, who was counsel for the Cox committee, has attributed the responsibility for the 1952 investigation to three separate groups, with a common purpose but different motives.

There was one group which, for convenience, may be termed the "Bricker Amendment" group. This group felt that the foundations had lent very considerable support to the United Nations and to those organizations which, in the opinion of the Brickerites, threatened to undercut our Constitution by treaties.

There was a second group motivated largely, if not entirely, by political considerations. This second group was very interested in Taft's nomination for president. The members of this second group believed that General Eisenhower offered the greatest threat to Taft's nomination and they also believed that Eisenhower would draw much of his support from what may be termed "the Eastern crowd," among whom was John Foster Dulles and other prominent persons who were either trustees or officers of foundations, including Paul Hoffman, president of the Ford Foundation. This second group believed (1) that if they could establish that Columbia University was a hotbed of Reds, a sufficient amount of carmine would rub off on its then President, General Eisenhower, to render him unavailable as a candidate, and (2) that by showing, as they believed, that Communists had infiltrated and received the blessings of the foundations they could neutralize the influence of certain key men behind Eisenhower because of their connections with foundations.

The third group working for the 1952 investigation was composed of a very small but hard-hitting number of individuals and organizations which indulged a very real distrust and hatred of foundations generally, and was particularly distrustful of the newly created Ford Foundation and of those in control of it, especially Paul Hoffman and Robert Maynard Hutchins. This extreme right wing group, composed both of Republicans and Democrats, had within it many of the "professional Red-baiters" to use their self-applied term, as well as a hard core of sincere, patriotic and well meaning conservatives who constituted the "fundamentalists" of politics.[1]

The atmosphere had been electrified by the perjury conviction of Alger Hiss, president of the Carnegie Endowment for International Peace, in a case involving communist espionage. In this climate, the Cox committee inquired into the possible infiltration of communists into foundations. As a companion inquiry, it sought evidence of financial aid to communist causes, and it broadened its study to look at possible abuses of tax exemption and the place of foundations in American life. Confining its investigation to a small segment of large foundations, the committee laid to rest the expectation that it would be merely a Red-hunt; some forty witnesses made a generally favorable case for the foundations.

The report of the committee was unanimous. It hailed the importance of foundations in American life and noted that "their most significant function had been the supplying of venture capital for advancing the frontiers of knowledge." It called attention to the great service foundations had rendered in medicine, public health, education, and natural science. It noted with approval their significant support in the sometimes controversial field of the social sciences. The committee concluded that the foundations had not used their resources to undermine the capitalist system and that on balance their record was good in forestalling efforts of communists to infiltrate their organizations. Out of 35,731 grants which were examined, only 63 were pronounced "questionable."

The next encounter for the foundations was an investigation headed by Representative B. Carroll Reece of Tennessee in 1954. Reece had been a member of the Cox committee, but attended only one of its eighteen sessions. The bent of his thinking was indicated in his speech on the floor of the Congress when he proposed a new investigation of the foundations:

Some of these institutions support efforts to overthrow our government and to undermine our American way of life. . . . Here lies the story of how communism and socialism are financed in the United States. . . . There is evidence to show that there is a diabolical conspiracy back of all this. . . . Organizations which are primarily committed to a given ideology have received large grants from big foundations over many years.

1. "Foundations under Investigation: A Review and Evaluation of Cox, Reece, and Patman," an address given to New York University's Ninth Biennial Conference on Charitable Foundations, May 1969.

The evidence to which Reece referred had been submitted to the Cox committee and rejected on the ground that the research was sketchy and inaccurate, that there was insufficient time to pursue the leads presented, and that the "international conspiracy" charges were beyond the authorized limits of the Cox inquiry. The method of the Reece committee evoked strong criticism. Studies presented by members of the staff constituted the principal evidence. Of nine nonstaff witnesses who testified, only one was a representative of foundations, although foundations were later afforded an opportunity to file written statements, and thirteen did so. The hearings were marked by stormy exchanges between committee members and between members and staff, and eventually they became so turbulent that they were recessed and never reconvened.

The majority report of the Reece committee was gentler than its proceedings. It accused foundations of controlling research in the social sciences "in the interest of the political left" and directed toward collectivism. Among the recommendations were a federal law to unseat trustees who made grants to "subversive organizations"; expansion of the Internal Revenue Service to keep closer watch on foundations; a prohibition of the use of foundation funds for political or propaganda purposes, and a reduction of foundation expenses by cutting staff and the dissolution of "intermediary" organizations.

The minority report attacked the majority for an "unseemly effort to reach a predetermined conclusion."

One of the major conclusions of the majority report was that foundations exercise power far out of proportion to their respective funds. The report further found that this power was greatly magnified by an interlock, or concert of action, of which—as the report conceded—foundations might not be aware. The committee assembled evidence of a tendency of foundations to channel their support to those individuals and organizations which support the liberal view, which the majority report evidently equated with radicalism. No legislation, however, resulted from the committee's work.

In the course of recent expressions of concern about foundation power and programs, Senator Albert Gore has called foundations "free-floating, non-owned, non-public accumulations of economic assets" which form part of a "silent revolution in property devolution" —separating ownership from control of our national wealth. Representative Patman has asserted that "the multimillion dollar foundations

have replaced the trusts which were broken up during the Theodore
Roosevelt administration."[2]

There is doubtless a vague uneasiness at the sheer size of foundation
assets, corresponding to the fear of big government, big business, and
big labor. The largest foundation, Ford, with $3 billion in assets, is in
fact relatively small compared to the largest of America's industrial
Leviathans like General Motors. Yet in the eyes of some people it nonetheless appears to be a fearsome aggregation of capital with a potential
for economic domination of our society. There is also an egalitarian or
populist sentiment which invests virtue in small things and evil in large
ones, and especially in large fortunes, holding that these owe their existence to the denial either of just wages to workingmen or of fair value
to consumers.

On top of everything else, there is a conspiracy theory which holds
that foundations are part of an "Eastern liberal establishment" united
in a desire to "move the country to the left." This view is fleshed out by
stressing foundation-financed projects that seem to advance the concept of community responsibility for programs to solve new or aggravated social problems, or by pointing to exchanges of key administrative
personnel between government and large foundations. The association
of executives and the similarities in directorates between large foundations and powerful business and financial institutions is cited to add the
patina of credibility to the conspiracy theory.

It is also worth noting that, in a meeting of extremes, the same facts
serve equally as ammunition for the political left. Critics from the left
also say that the executives and the directorates of foundations on the
one side, and powerful business and financial institutions on the other,
tend to resemble each other like figures duplicated in a hall of mirrors.
Thus, say the critics, the same group of men become defenders of class
institutions, "conscious not merely of parochial economic interest but
of the necessity of preserving a total social system, international in
scope, on which their whole wealth, power and prestige depends."

Social action programs sponsored by foundations have also led to
criticism. The role of the Ford Foundation in the New York City
school decentralization controversy was easily misconstrued and widely
resented. Experimental programs in slum areas, including grants to
"street gangs" in Chicago, have angered some local officials. These
programs have also disturbed some politicians because of their potential

2. The study made by Charles Schultze of the Brookings Institution, refuting the
implications of this charge, has been cited in chapter 5.

for changing the political balance of power, particularly by mobilizing the electoral strength of black communities. And programs for minority groups have aroused some whites.

Foundations have also seemed to some to be heavily involved in politics and not charity. Instances cited were a Ford-supported voter-registration drive in Cleveland, Ford travel-study grants to aides of the late Senator Robert F. Kennedy, and grants by the Richmond Foundation, controlled by a candidate for Congress, to charitable organizations in the district where he was running. Some in political life, moreover, believe that foundations constitute pools of capital available for research or other assistance to candidates or issues that they oppose, but not to themselves.

In another direction, a critic of the foundations like Wright Patman struck an exposed political nerve when he assailed the foundations on the ground that they were giving millions for projects outside the United States—in India, Mexico, and other foreign countries—but practically nothing in Utah and Wyoming. Patman also contended that these foreign grants were an important contributing factor to the deficit in the country's balance of international payments. More will be said about this charge later. It is in point here merely to ask a question. What if this line of criticism were to be taken to its limits? It would follow that the United States government itself should go isolationist and that American corporations should be greatly restrained in creating manu-facturing plants abroad, since our foreign commitments and the over-seas investments of our industrial enterprises can also contribute to the nation's balance of payments problems in a given year—without doing anything immediately visible for Utah and Wyoming.

Other specific complaints have been leveled at the foundations. They range from the conflict-of-interest controversies dramatized by the role of the Wolfson Foundation in a long-term agreement for sizable annual payments to Justice Fortas of the Supreme Court, to the sensational disclosure that some foundations were used as channels whereby the Central Intelligence Agency supported a variety of overseas activities, to the use of foundations to help finance extremist groups on both the left and the right.

In the 1969 Tax Reform setting, there can be little question that a substantial part of the hostility to foundations sprang directly from members of the Congress. A considerable number of them became con-vinced that foundations had become partisan political instruments. A passionate element to this charge was added by individual members of the Congress who seized upon isolated projects of a few foundations and read into them an electioneering intent aimed at encouraging the defeat of incumbent legislators in the areas where the projects were carried out.

To sum up: Foundations have encountered criticisms from virtually the entire political spectrum. They have been an easy and convenient target for politicians who, in order to prove their zeal as guardians of the Republic, need a "threat" or a "conspiracy" to "expose." They have been an all the more convenient and easy target because of a general oversight on the part of the public that the Capitoline geese did not cackle only at the approach of a real enemy to Rome. They sometimes also cackled at random.

There is an ironic element in all of this which cannot be overstated. It is that despite the fears voiced about the imperial power of the foundations to control everything in sight, the foundations are ill prepared to defend themselves when under attack. Unlike operating charities, they have no ready-made constituencies—no alumni as with colleges and universities, no parishioners as with churches, no out-patients as with medical installations, no audiences as with symphony orchestras, no viewers as with museums, and no parents as with the Boy Scouts and Girl Scouts.

Their constituency is in a sense an abstraction called "the public interest." In serving it, the foundations must necessarily reject the claims of many more applicants for grants than they can satisfy. The rejected applicants form an army of people who naturally doubt the foundation's judgments and are ready to lend their voices to the chorus of critics, while the successful applicants tend to be content with their own position—that is to say, they till their own garden without taking time off to openly defend the foundations which were of benefit to them.

As a general rule, the foundations have felt no need to justify themselves to the public. In ways recalling the habit of the ermine, which would rather die than soil itself, the foundations have tended to adhere to a conventional wisdom that seems to say that they should not become publicly visible in the forum for forensics. Thus, only a handful of foundations make public reports, and even these are generally not directed to a wide audience. The smaller foundations have presumably felt that in a free society they were as free to give their money away as they were to acquire it—without public explanation so long as they observed the legal requirements of their tax exemption. The result is that large segments of the public are only superficially aware, if at all, of the accomplishments of foundations. To the casual observer, impressed by the magnitude of the attack on foundations, their silence may take on the appearance of a tacit admission of guilt. Even the most extreme attacks gain some adherents when there is no voice on the other side.

Foundations, to repeat, have tended to overestimate their immunity from public criticism and from accountability to the public. Their financial independence has given them a level of freedom not available to other organizations, permitting them to operate and even experiment in sensitive fields. But that freedom is not absolute; if existing foundations do not need to raise additional funds, they still need protection from restrictive or crippling governmental regulation. The main source of this protection—perhaps the only source—is an informed public that comprehends the need to maintain an atmosphere in which foundations can function effectively for the betterment of society. Like most institutions, foundations have to rely upon continued public acceptance for their lives. They are not exempt from a political law noted by Abraham Lincoln when he said that with public opinion behind you, everything is possible; without it, nothing is. Some of the allegations about foundations—as to both financial and program abuse—are valid. They are rooted in concrete instances of abuse and errors of judgment by some foundations. But the charges hurled at foundations in the late 1960s also included willful distortions, uninformed or prejudiced statements, and gross exaggerations. We shall return to this matter.

8

Foundation Funds: Sources, Investment Performance, and Amount of Payout

One of our key findings about the sources and forms of contributions to foundations have been touched on already in our discussion of tax incentives (chapter 4). We noted that gifts of appreciated property have been extremely important in the creation of foundation endowments. Indeed, nearly three-fourths of all foundation contributions have been in the form of appreciated intangible property—principally corporate stocks.[1] Our data also showed the following:

1. The most important type of appreciated intangible property has been stock in a company in which the donor and his family owned a substantial interest (20 percent or more). Such stock has accounted for 44 percent of all contributions to foundations and 70 percent of the contributions to foundations with over $100 million in assets.[2]

2. While ownership of a "controlling" interest in a corporation (20 percent or more) by a foundation has been, and continues to be, relatively infrequent, it is found primarily among large foundations. Our survey data indicate that only 7 percent of all foundations have ever owned a "control" block of stock. But two-fifths of those foundations with over $10 million in assets have owned such a block. At the time of our survey, our data suggest that only 4 percent of foundations still owned a "control" block. But 27 percent of those with over $10 million in endowment held control stock, and, in all, foundations with a controlling interest in a company held nearly three-tenths of all foundation assets.[3]

3. The preponderance of foundation assets—perhaps as much as

1. See appendix IV, tables A.31, A.32, and A.33 for detailed statistics.
2. Ibid.
3. See appendix IV, table A.34.

three-fourths—is accounted for by contributions from a living donor (or a corporation), for which income tax incentives were probably available. Testamentary gifts—that is, those from an estate—accounted for less than one-fourth of all foundation assets.[4]

4. Over half of all foundations expect future contributions. Most of these expect lifetime gifts rather than bequests. Forty percent of them expect cash only, 27 percent property, and 33 percent both forms of contributions. And 11 percent expect to receive stock in a company controlled by the donor or his family. Smaller foundations more often expect future contributions than large ones.[5]

How have foundations managed their assets? The commission had two main reasons for considering this question. One was the legitimate interest society itself has in knowing how much the assets of the foundations produce for charity. The second goes back to what was said earlier about the financial crisis philanthropy as a whole faces in the 1970s: the commission, conscious of that impending crisis, wanted to know if the foundations were managing their own investments in ways that could produce the greatest possible investment return for the greatest possible payout to charity.

There was nothing exceptional about the yardstick the commission used in measuring the investment performance of the foundations. It was the one almost universally used by mutual funds, profit sharing funds, pension funds, and other endowment funds. All these are judged and judge themselves by the *total rate of return* on their assets—interest, dividends, realized and unrealized capital gains. In the case of the commission's survey of the foundations our estimates of the total return on their assets are necessarily imperfect,[6] since different foundations valued their assets differently. We therefore show below the median return on assets for each class of foundations, and an estimated median for

4. Ibid., table A.35.

5. Ibid., tables A.36, A.37.

6. Where possible, we utilized a number of sources of data. First we referred to our questionnaires on the market value of assets at the beginning and end of 1968. In some instances, however, market value was not available, and we had to depend on book value, as shown on the 990-A forms filed by the foundations. (This was more often true for small foundations in our sample than for larger ones.) In an attempt to verify our data, we calculated similar figures for a larger sample of foundations (roughly 800) using 990-A forms for all of those for which we had no questionnaire. The median figures did not differ significantly for any class of foundations. We could not, of course, adjust either type of data to reflect the timing of receipts or expenditures.

all foundations. Use of the median helps offset any disproportionate effects—upward or downward—of those foundations which did not report assets at market value. We should also say that for the largest foundations the data on market value were more readily and accurately ascertained.

TABLE 3.
TOTAL RETURN ON FOUNDATION ASSETS AS A PERCENTAGE OF ASSETS, 1968[a]

	Median Total Return on Assets (percent)
Foundations with assets	
under $200,000	4.7
$200,000–$1 million	6.7
$1 million–$10 million	6.0
$10 million–$100 million	7.7
over $100 million	8.5
Company foundations	5.8
Community foundations[b]	5.2
Weighted figure for all foundations	5.6

a. "Return on Assets" is based on net income plus increase in value of assets held by the foundation at the beginning of 1968.

b. The median return on assets may give an inaccurate picture for these foundations because some hold assets subject to an income interest which is not reflected in their valuation.

We are informed that, in 1968, average total return was 15.3 percent for so-called common stock mutual funds, and 14.9 percent for balanced funds. While it might be said that one year is not an adequate period for evaluating investment return (the marked decline in 1969 total return compared to 1968, for example), it seems significant that, *in every category, foundation investment performance is substantially lower than the balanced funds performance of nearly 15 percent in 1968.*

What has been a reasonable total return for investment portfolios over a longer period? As might be expected, funds that have concentrated on equity stock have done better than balanced funds, with a substantial percentage of bonds and other debt instruments. Between 1959 and 1968 the total return, as presented in a recently published study conducted under Ford Foundation auspices entitled "Managing Educational Endowments," is as follows:

	1959–68 Annual Average
Twenty-one balanced funds	9.2 percent
Ten large general growth funds	14.6 percent

When the commission discussed the subject of foundation investments with a number of investment experts, the latter were in general agreement that returns on foundation assets were significantly lower than on other types of professionally managed funds. Further, an echo of this consensus sounded in an article in the *Institutional Investor* of November 1968 entitled "Foundations: The Quiet $20 Billion." The article asked whether there was "a place yet untouched by the revolution on money management," a place "where the winds of performance are not felt." It answered that "such a place does exist," and it is called "foundation land," where a tax-exempt twenty billion dollars, "one of the biggest pools of capital in capitalism" is "still run the way money used to be. The way it used to be, that is, for Widows and Orphans, before currency began to depreciate." In foundation land, "the managers do not often buy their stocks, because they already have them—they were given them many years ago, and now they sit, quietly watching."

To clinch the last point, the article referred to a Securities Exchange Commission study of the stock turnover rate for foundations showing that the rate was in the range of only 1–2 percent—which is extraordinarily low by a factor of 10 or more compared to a variety of other funds. Investment experts have different explanations for this low turnover rate. One is that a significant portion of a foundation investment portfolio is often control stock in a company, and it has not been thought desirable to trade these securities. A second is that the managers of the foundations have not given a high priority to the effective management of funds. A third is that in some cases the legal instrument setting up the foundation bars the sale of the securities donated to the foundation (though the commission's own data suggests that this is true for only a small percentage of the foundation). Finally, it is observed that some managers of foundations feel restricted in their investment activity by their concept of the "prudent man rule" as they believe it affects foundations.

The commission itself makes no claims that it has exhaustively reviewed the investment performance of foundations. Yet all the signs it has seen tend to say the same thing: that the investment performance of foundations is below par, and perhaps significantly so. This is not something that can be lightly dismissed. The public, whether it is aware of the fact or not, has a stake of its own in the matter, and for the following reasons: Since each percentage point of added total return on foundation investments would yield between two and three hundred million dollars of additional funds for charity, the costs to society of a lackluster management of these investments could be on the order of hundreds of millions of dollars annually. To gain what is now being lost would not by itself forestall the impending financial crisis in philanthropy. Yet to gain what is being lost is not a small thing in itself.

Payouts to Charity. There is an obvious link between what has just been said and this further point: better foundation investment performance makes more funds available to be paid out each year for charitable purposes. From the commission's survey of foundations for 1968, the payout figures expressed as a percentage of beginning-of-the-year assets (computed at market value, where available) were computed.

These payout figures are overstated for two reasons. First, some foundations report their assets on the basis of cost rather than market value. Since the former is generally lower than the latter, the percentage of the dollar payout in proportion to the value of the assets is made to appear higher than it actually is. Second, the payout figures include substantial amounts which are given to the foundation and paid out in the same year. The inclusion of these "pass through" funds in the return to charity from foundations inflates the proportion of the payout on actual endowments. This is especially true of smaller foundations, since a larger proportion are "pass through" or conduit foundations.

Yet even when the figures are accepted as given, our data show that a substantial proportion of foundations pay out a very small percentage of their asset values. In 1968 specifically, 47 percent of all foundations paid out less than 6 percent of asset values. Ten percent paid out less than 1 percent; 17 percent paid out less than 2 percent; 22 percent paid out less than 3 percent; and 27 percent paid out less than 4 percent.

TABLE 4.
MEDIAN PAYOUT AS A PERCENTAGE OF FOUNDATION ASSETS, 1968

	Median Payout (percent)
Foundations with assets	
under $200,000	8.0
$200,000–$1 million	5.9
$1–10 million	5.9
$10–100 million	5.2
$100 million and over	4.4
Community foundations	5.8
Company foundations (significant number of conduit foundations)	19.3
All foundations	6.6

The foundations in question clearly are not providing an adequate payout to society in return for the immediate tax deductions society has given their donors.

9

How Foundations
Have Spent
Their Money

In its examination of the purposes for which the foundations actually spend their money, the commission's lead-off question was: Is it really true, as some people assert, that the foundations grant a large percentage of their funds to individuals engaged in politically oriented activities?

The commission asked foundations to classify their 1968 grant expenditures by type of recipient and purpose of grants. The returns show that 94 percent of all grant dollars made in 1968 went to qualified charitable organizations, that is, organizations to which an individual donor could himself make a deductible contribution. A breakdown of that 94 percent shows that 72 percent went to "public charities—churches, schools and colleges, hospitals, and publicly supported charitable organizations; the remaining 22 percent went to other qualified charitable organizations. Only 6 percent of all foundation grants went to recipients to which individual contributions are not deductible; 3 percent went directly to individuals; and about 4 percent went to noncharitable organizations. The latter included tax-exempt nonprofit organizations such as social welfare groups, civic leagues, labor unions and trade associations, foreign organizations, and profit-making businesses—generally as an investment in or a grant to a fledgling ghetto enterprise.[1] Table 5 shows the general distribution picture.

The extent of the grants to individuals was a very sensitive subject at the time of the commission's study, largely because of the controversy over the travel and study grants the Ford Foundation had made to

1. The figures cited are based on the aggregate grants of large and small foundations combined. When the grants of the smaller foundations are viewed on a plane of their own, what they show is that the smaller foundations give a greater percentage of their grants than do the large ones to charitable organizations. The comparisons are set forth in appendix IV, table A.41.

TABLE 5.
DISTRIBUTION OF 1968 FOUNDATION GRANTS BY TYPE OF RECIPIENT

| | Percentage of Grants | |
	Including Ford	Excluding Ford
Qualified charitable organizations		
"Public charities"	72	72
Other charitable organizations	22	23
Noncharitable tax-exempt or nonprofit organizations	†	†
Foreign organizations (and profit making organizations)	3	1
Individuals	3	3
†Less than 0.5 percent.		

former members of the late Robert F. Kennedy's staff. The commission's survey helped bring the parameters of the matter into clearer focus. It showed that, of all foundations, viewed numerically rather than by the aggregate amount of their grants, 12 percent made grants only to individuals and not to charitable organizations; these particular foundations were generally small, and their grants represented only 2 percent of the total grant expenditures for all foundations. Only 17 percent of all foundations had ever made grants directly to individuals.

Of the 3 percent of total foundation grants which went to individuals in 1968, the uses made were these: scholarships and fellowships—62 percent; research—23 percent; support for creative endeavors—7 percent; direct aid to the needy—7 percent; awards and prizes—1 percent; travel and study—1 percent.

In a shift of perspective, when we asked foundations to classify all their 1968 grant expenditures by *purpose*, the results undercut the charge that foundations spend a substantial part of their funds on political and social activist purposes. Table 6 shows that the principal beneficiaries of the funds allotted were: education—31 percent; health and medicine—21 percent; general welfare—14 percent; cultural institutions—11 percent; religion—4 percent; community services—4 percent. These represent aggregate figures of all grants for all foundations. When the smaller foundations are examined by themselves, the pattern of their expenditures for philanthropy corresponds closely to the pattern of an individual donor. They allocate a higher proportion of their grants than do the large foundations to purposes such as health and medicine, religious institutions, and the Community Chest.

TABLE 6.
PURPOSE OF FOUNDATION GRANTS, 1968

	Grants Including Ford (percent)	Grants Excluding Ford (percent)
Education: educational research, elementary, secondary, higher, and adult education programs (except manpower or vocational training)	31	31
Health and medicine: medical research, treatment, and education, including hospitals, clinics, public health education, and services such as birth control clinics, etc.	21	22
General welfare: support of Community Chest, United Fund, Welfare Council, and similar general welfare agencies	14	15
Community action and services: organizing or supporting designated groups (including, for example, youth groups such as "gangs"), neighborhoods or regions, planning for community improvement, and provision of community facilities not elsewhere classified	4	4
Community, racial, or ethnic relations: improvement of intergroup understanding and relations	3	3
Religion: support of a church, synagogue, or other religious organization primarily for religious instruction, practice, or other predominantly religious purpose	4	5
Science and technology: all nonmedical research and development in the physical and natural sciences and technological applications of scientific knowledge	2	2
Social sciences: all social science research and publication not elsewhere classified	2	1

TABLE 6.—Continued
PURPOSE OF FOUNDATION GRANTS, 1968

	Grants Including Ford (percent)	Grants Excluding Ford (percent)
Conservation and recreation: provision of recreation facilities and programs, parks, conservation of natural resources, wildlife preservation	1	1
Manpower and vocational training: research on manpower problems, vocational and job training and related programs	1	1
Housing: design, construction, or provision of housing and improvement of housing conditions or access to housing for designated groups	1	†
Cultural institutions: libraries, art galleries, museums, symphonies, theater, educational television	11	11
Arts and humanities: support of artistic endeavors—writing, fine arts, music and research and publication in the humanities	2	1
Individual and family services: provision of food, clothing, and other necessities and services (except medical or educational services) for the needy	1	1
Political-process-related activities: voter registration, voter education, schools for political candidates, etc.	†	†
Other	3	3
	100	100

†Less than 0.5 percent.

Earlier in these pages, notice was taken of a charge by Representative Wright Patman and others that substantial amounts of foundation grants have gone overseas. No data were cited to support the charge— or, for that matter, to refute it. The commission's data show that only

9 percent of all foundation grant dollars were for programs having an international objective, and most of the recipients were individuals and grantee organizations in the United States. Further, our review of these grants suggests that a substantial part of them was probably spent in the United States and not abroad. Numerically, more of the smaller foundations—such as those which support Israel—than the larger foundations granted dollars with an international objective. The larger foundations, however, spent more in aggregate dollar amounts. We also found that 75 percent of all foundations, making 63 percent of 1968 grant expenditures, supported only domestic programs and projects in 1968.[2]

TABLE 7.
PERCENTAGE OF 1968 GRANT EXPENDITURES FOR DOMESTIC AND
INTERNATIONAL PROGRAMS AND PROJECTS

	Domestic Programs and Projects (percent)	International Programs and Projects (percent)
Foundations with assets		
under $200,000	73	27
$200,000–$1 million	100	†
$1 million–$10 million	98	2
$10 million–$100 million	98	2
over $100 million	77	23
Excluding Ford	86	14
Ford alone	70	30
Company foundations	99	1
Community foundations	100	0
Weighted average, all foundations	91	9
†Less than 0.5 percent.		

A further analysis of foundation grants for international activities in the years 1967–68 was made by the commission from data at the Foundation Center in New York. The Foundation Center's published reports includes only significant grants, and, for this reason, its findings understate the total of actual grants. But the figures on hand showed that in the two-year period 1967–68, foundations support for international activities came to $221 million. Of this amount, almost three-fourths is accounted for by Ford Foundation grants, and 82 percent by seventeen of the twenty-five largest foundations including Ford.

2. See appendix IV, table A.44.

The largest share of the 1967–68 grants went to programs involving neutral or uncommitted nations of Asia and Africa and Latin American countries. The preponderance of grants were made to established educational institutions, largely in the United States. Little went to individuals or institutions which were dependent on American foundation grants for their support. Very few direct grants to foreign governments were made. Over four-fifths of the grants for international activities went for education, technical assistance, international studies, and health and medicine; the remainder went to programs bearing on cultural relations, peace and international cooperation, exchange of persons, and relief and refugee problems.

The ability of foundations to tackle controversial subjects and to finance social action projects is one of the frequent justifications for their existence, although attitudes toward controversy vary among foundation people. Controversy, however, does not rest easily alongside other qualities which characterize what many foundations may desire for themselves, whether or not they are openly talked about. The other qualities are perhaps prudence, civility, and discretion. Indeed, some foundations have been so "discreet" that, on the few occasions when they forged ahead with "controversial" social action projects and encountered strong opposition, it was widely believed that some had not meant to be controversial. One is reminded of Macaulay's description of an English statesman who had so great a reputation for sagacity and cunning that, each time he acted, people spent sleepless nights probing the secret and complex motives behind what were in fact his very simple blunders.

In our attempt to come a little closer to the realities of the matter, we asked the foundations three related questions bearing on their activities in the three years 1966–68 inclusive:

1. Had they made any grants for certain specified types of projects which some people might consider controversial or undesirable.[3]

2. Had they made any grants or gifts to projects which *they* considered to be controversial or particularly unpopular?

3. Had they made any grants or gifts which *they* considered to be innovative, experimental, or out of the ordinary?

As to the first question, we were particularly interested in the extent

3. The list of specific categories to which answers were requested (see table 8) is not to be construed as a judgment on our part about the merits of a particular grant or particular type of project.

to which foundations were active supporters of a project much commented upon in the press—namely, the registration of voters. The responses, when analyzed, indicated that foundation involvement in this realm amounted only to a "hail and farewell." Even the Ford Foundation, a leader in the matter, had spent a total of only $440,000 for grants for voter registration between 1966 and 1968. In that same three-year period, the total of foundation grants for all purposes considered undesirable or sensitive by some people outside of the foundations was also very small. The amounts, measured against the grand total of foundation grants, ranged from less than 0.05 percent for purposes such as sex education and grants to government employees, to 1.5 percent for purposes such as community organizing (see table 8).

TABLE 8.
PERCENTAGE OF FOUNDATION GRANTS, 1966–68, FOR SPECIFIED PURPOSES
    CONSIDERED CONTROVERSIAL BY SOME*

Specified Purposes	Foundation Grants (percent)
Voter registration and voter education	0.1
Studies of subjects directly related to public policy issues and for dissemination of such studies to the general public by publication or discussion	0.3
Community or neighborhood organizing of an ethnic, ghetto, or impoverished group	1.5
Grants to individuals employed by government or persons acting as assistants to government employees or related persons	†
Birth control	0.9
Sex education	†
Urban youth groups (including gangs)	1.3
Student organizations	0.8

*We also asked about grants for schools for potential political candidates and grants connected with a specific election. No foundation surveyed reported any expenditures for these purposes.
†Less than 0.05 per cent.

On the second question asked—whether the foundations considered any of their grants and gifts between 1966 and 1968 to be controversial or particularly unpopular—the responses indicated first that only 1 percent of all foundations viewed any of their grants as controversial; second, that the grants involved amounted to only 0.1 percent of the total grants made between 1966 and 1968 and, as such, were almost totally centered in the large foundations. Table 9 gives details on the ways foundations, classified by size, answered the question: "Have any of the projects supported by your foundation's grants or gifts in the past three years been considered controversial or particularly unpopular?"

TABLE 9.
PERCENTAGE OF GRANTS CONSIDERED CONTROVERSIAL, 1966–68

	Foundations Answering "Yes" (percent)	Grants (percent)
Foundations with assets		
under $200,000	...	...
$200,000–$1 million	...	...
$1–10 million	16	1
$10–100 million	5	†
over $100 million	38	3
Company foundations	...	...
Community foundations	16	1
Total, all foundations	1	0.1

†Less than 0.5 percent.

With respect to the third question—"Has the foundation made any grants or gifts in the past three years which you consider innovative, experimental, or out of the ordinary?"—only 13 percent answered in the affirmative, while the grants involved represented only 3 percent of the total grants made between 1966 and 1968. The pattern of the response again says something about the way the inner life of foundations—or more precisely, the inner life they claim for themselves—can be a function of their size. The large foundations, few in number but far more important from the standpoint of expenditures, are much more likely to claim that they engage in innovative activities compared with any such claims by the more numerous smaller foundations. Table 10 shows how the foundations answered the question.

TABLE 10.
PERCENTAGE OF GRANTS CONSIDERED BY FOUNDATIONS TO BE INNOVATIVE, 1966–68

	Foundations Answering Yes (percent)	Grants (percent)
Foundations with Assets		
under $200,000	7	2
$200,000–$1 million	20	3
$1–10 million	31	8
$10–100 million	53	7
over $100 million	81	37
Company foundations	23	2
Community foundations	63	13
Total, all foundations	13	3

With respect to all that has been said up to this point on the grant patterns of foundations, the commission has reached two conclusions.

First, the grants made by a great number of foundations appear to be simply extensions of the individual donor's giving patterns. Many make a large number of relatively small contributions (often of $100 or less) to well-established charities, just as many individuals do. Other foundations—whether because they have no staff assistance or because their trustees devote relatively little time to foundation affairs—also fail to achieve their institutional capability. Their descriptions of their grant-making process and the patterns of their grants suggest that many give primarily in response to requests they receive "over the transom" or in person. They support charitable causes only if they are informed about them, and their sources of information may be limited.

Second, both the critics and the panegyrists of foundation grant programs appear to have greatly overstated their claims. The facts do not bear out the charges that much of what foundations support is not charity at all but rather political and social activism, and that most foundation grants go to individuals, foreign organizations, and noncharitable groups. Conversely, those who would have us believe that the typical foundation program is venturesome, innovative, and at the "cutting edge" of social change are making their personal and romantic hopes the source of the glorifying touches they add to the facts of the foundation picture.

It will be shown later in this report that when foundations are viewed in an historical perspective, *some* of them acting in *some* fields have been a source of key initiatives of great benefit to Americans and even to mankind generally. In some cases, moreover, the qualitative importance of a single significant initiative can outweigh the quantitative importance of a thousand routine acts. The word *some*, however, does not mean all, or even a majority. A majority of foundations spend most of their funds on conventional projects and in conventional ways that are similar to the traditional patterns of individual giving.

To take note of this simple truth is not to indict the foundations but to correct the extreme charges leveled against foundations and the extreme claims made on their behalf. Traditional patterns of individual giving have, after all, a merit of their own. Moreover, it is indispensable that existing institutions in our society—such as colleges and universities, hospitals and clinics, symphony orchestras, opera companies, and museums—be supported not merely in spurts, but on a sustained basis. Their life depends on sustained support.

10

Management of Foundation Grants

We noted earlier that a foundation, as an intermediary between donors and grantees, can hire an expert staff to define and administer its grant programs in ways which will enable it to make distinctive contributions to American life. It is true, of course, that a committed donor might devote much of his own time and effort to that end. Yet our review suggests that this kind of donor is relatively rare. Further, our survey of foundations shows that only one-fifth of all foundations have any paid staff at all, including secretaries. Only 5 percent have any full-time paid staff.

As would be expected, there are sharp differences in this respect between small and large foundations. All foundations in our survey with assets over $100 million had a staff, but only one-sixth of those with assets of less than $1 million did.[1] Even foundations with staffs generally have a small number of employees, while full-time professional personnel for all foundations probably do not exceed a few thousand. These figures comment in their own way on the rather widespread belief that foundations have high administrative overheads. The hint that the belief is unfounded is confirmed by our additional figures which show that the median administrative overhead for all foundations in 1968 was only 2.9 percent of grant expenditures.[2]

In addition to staff, it would seem reasonable to suppose that founda-

1. See appendix IV, table A.38.
2. The point needs to be made that "administrative" expenses in some foundations are not easy to separate out and are reported in a way that includes the costs of carrying out specific charitable projects. Thus, in a foundation that both makes grants and operates charitable programs, the "administrative" expenses, in our terms, may be overstated.

tion board members would be an important force in determining the foundations' grant program. Our data suggest, however, that in many cases the board is little more than a source of platitudes and beatitudes. On the basis of how foundations themselves have characterized the functions of their respective boards, we estimate that in nearly two-fifths of the foundations, board members play so small a role in foundation grant-making as to border on the invisible. A donor or another single individual dominates many of these foundations. Table 11 indicates the way the foundations themselves have reported the role of their boards.

TABLE 11.
ROLE OF BOARD MEMBERS IN GRANT MAKING

	Foundations (percent)	1968 Grants (percent)
Hardly any role at all	30	26
Formal approval of recommendations; reversal of recommendations extremely rare	9	7
Review of recommendations on most applications within program area of foundations	5	19
Approval or rejection of all applications within program area	12	9
Approval or rejection of all applications	44	26
Other	1	14
	101	101

It might be assumed that board members could perform one distinctive function. They could recommend new program areas or types of recipients for the foundation to support. Our survey, however, suggests that in nearly half the foundations this never or only rarely occurs (see table 12).

TABLE 12.
FREQUENCY WITH WHICH BOARD MEMBERS SUGGEST
NEW PROGRAM AREAS OR TYPES OF RECIPIENTS

	Foundations (percent)	1968 Grants (percent)
Often	19	10
Sometimes	33	68
Rarely	21	17
Never	28	5
	100	100

Our survey suggests something further. Though the trustees of a foundation are legally responsible for what it does, they often fail to devote time to foundation business. Indeed, the boards of 9 percent of the foundations never meet; the boards of another 33 percent meet once a year or less, while 15 percent meet for one hour or less a year. It should be added, however, that these figures primarily represent the small foundations. A few of the largest foundations have quarterly or monthly meetings of a day or more in length, with an agenda that probes deeply both into programs and purposes, which are faithfully attended by some of America's best-known and most thoughtful citizens (see table 13).[3]

TABLE 13.
FREQUENCY OF FOUNDATION BOARD MEETINGS BY DURATION OF
AVERAGE MEETING, ALL FOUNDATIONS (IN PERCENTAGE)

Frequency of Meetings	No meetings	One hour or less	1–2 hours	2–6 hours	6 hours or more	Total
Never	9	...	...	...	...	9
Annual or less often	...	15	13	5	1	33
Quarterly or semi-annually	...	13	22	8	†	43
Monthly	...	2	3	2	0	6
Whenever necessary	...	8	†	1	†	9
Total	9	37	37	15	2	100

†Less than 0.5 percent.

The commission used the focusing lens of information in *Who's Who in America* and other sources to look at both the geographic spread and the human profile of the trustees of twenty-five of the twenty-six largest foundations. We found that only four of these foundations have boards whose members might be considered broadly representative of the nation's various geographic regions. The remainder tend to represent only single regions with the New England–Middle Atlantic regions in the clear lead. Moreover, half of the trustees of the twenty-five largest foundations attended Ivy League colleges, and roughly two-thirds have business, banking, or legal backgrounds. Of the foundation trustees for whom information was available, none had a background in organized labor. There were very few Catholics, Jews, or Negroes, or, for that matter, women or young trustees. An overwhelm-

3. For additional data on foundation board meetings, see appendix IV, tables A.39, A.40.

ing majority of the trustees of the large foundations are white, Anglo-Saxon, and Protestant.

These facts do not in themselves imply that the large foundations are somehow guilty of an ineffable sin. Such a construction would do a gross injustice to the distinguished Americans who are presently serving as board members for the large foundations. The implication of our study is simply this: these boards clearly lack the kind of diversity that could further enlarge their perceptions about the raw surge of American life—a diversity, moreover, that could help establish a firmer public footing beneath the foundations at a time when they are involved in activities of great public sensitivity.[4]

"The laws," said Edmund Burke, "reach but a very little. Constitute the government however you will, infinitely the greater part of it will depend on the uprightness and wisdom of the chief ministers of state." The same truth applies all the more forcefully to the great foundations because, compared with the government, foundations have far fewer formal decision-making processes, far fewer checks and balances. These kinds of discretionary powers are better used when a diversity of men give direction to their use only after they have asked the kinds of questions a democratic people should ask about matters in the public domain. Has anything become clear to us since we were last together? What are we looking at now? How do we know what we think we know about it? What, if anything, should we do about it?

In addition to the way foundations choose grantees to receive funds, the commission inquired into the way foundations monitor and evaluate the grantee's actual use of the funds. The commission recognized that the nature of the grant and of the recipient determines the extent of the need to follow up the grant. No single policy can cover, or would be appropriate to, all cases from the standard grant to the radical one. A grant to an endowment fund of a university or an unrestricted grant to a church or to a united welfare fund—representing the majority of all grants—does not require the same follow-up as a grant to a newly-formed agency for a specific activity such as a community organization. If foundations rigidly supervised the work of all grantees, the character of foundations would clearly be changed in an unwholesome direction, in terms both of increased administrative overhead and costs and of the degree of foundation intrusion into the affairs of recipient institutions.

---

4. The composition of the boards of these largest foundations differs very widely of course from that of the vast majority of other foundations, whose trustees are typically donors, kin, and donor-linked.

Nevertheless, the commission's data on present policies among foundations underlines a need facing many foundations themselves to reassess their own follow-up procedures.[5] Some of our findings, however, should be mentioned here.

For one thing, 41 percent of all foundations—the figure is weighted for the entire foundation field—never take any steps to monitor their grantees or follow up their grants. Not surprisingly, this negative fact was truer of the small foundations, which accounted for only 25 percent of 1968 grant expenditures, than of the larger foundations with their full complement of professional staffs. For another thing, over half of the foundations never make field visits or use any other device for periodic personal checks on grantee activities; 72 percent never require periodic reports as a requirement for payment of installments of the grants; 91 percent never require independent auditing of the grantee's expenditures. Table 14 shows how things generally stand in this matter.

TABLE 14.
MONITORING OR FOLLOW-UP OF GRANTEES

	Foundations (percent)	1968 Grants (percent)
Never taking monitoring steps	41	25
Sometimes, but not always, taking monitoring steps	45	27
Always taking monitoring steps	15	48
	101	100

Aside from the fact that the standard grant, say to the endowment fund of a university, does not require a close follow-up, the commission realized that there are many kinds of innovative social programs which, by their very nature, seem to defy an evaluation even by the most sophisticated and talked-about cost-benefit analytical techniques. In many cases, for example, it is far from easy to decide what is meant by "successful" and how long an interval of time is needed before one can be sure that a given approach to a program is the right one to take. There is also the sensitive problem of knowing how to use an evaluation after

5. See appendix IV, tables A.45, A.46, and A.47 for full data bearing on this point. The commission also explored on an individual basis a few of the celebrated cases of foundation "political" grants. It was not a reassuring picture.

it is made, especially when it is highly critical of an individual grantee. Finally, this evaluation and follow-up process can be a costly one. Yet to acknowledge all these difficulties does not efface the commission's strong impression that most foundations apparently find the process of conceiving or making grants more satisfying and more worthy of their time and resources than evaluating the success or failure of these grants, what was learned by means of them, and the extent to which the results were disseminated to interested publics.

11

Foundation Achievements:
An Overview

When Thales, the Greek astronomer, fell into a well while stargazing, he was laughed at for staring at the heavens to the neglect of what was at his own feet. Yet the history of science has a different reaction to this man. It says that the critical spirit he brought to the study of the heavens—his work to emancipate human perceptions from the prison of myths and his struggle to produce reasoned explanations of natural phenomena—was a major first step in the development of Western science. It says that there is, in fact, a direct connection between this stargazing man and the landing of American astronauts on the moon.

In the case of foundations, as with Thales, no episode on a single day, neither a success nor a failure of the moment, is a fair basis for judging the quality of their work. Only when the passing years reveal what the days hide is it possible to see how a foundation set in motion a train of progressive developments which might never have occurred at all, or at least might have been long delayed, were it not for the fact that the foundations took the first step. It is, therefore, from a historical perspective that the achievements of the foundations must be viewed and judged.

The emergence of the modern American foundation dates from the post-Civil War period, coincident with the birth and growth of great American fortunes. Education seemed to have been the main beneficiary of the new-style institution for philanthropy. One example was the $2 million George Peabody Education Fund, established in 1867 for the promotion and encouragement of education in the South, and another was the $1 million John F. Slater Fund, founded in 1882 for the education of freed men. Even so, the foundation concept remained in a rudimentary form—as did the general concept of American philanthropy—until two protean figures appeared on the American scene.

The two were Andrew Carnegie and John D. Rockefeller. As religious-minded men, both were convinced that their surplus wealth was a "sacred trust" to be used for the benefit of the community—and in the distinctive American way of helping people to help themselves. The best means to help the community, said Mr. Carnegie, "is to place within reach the ladders upon which the aspiring can rise." Mr. Rockefeller, as if in a continuation of the sentence, said: "If people can be educated to help themselves, we strike at the roots of many evils of the world." The foundations created by each of these men administered philanthropy on a broader and more sophisticated basis than ever before.

Other major foundations, often bearing the names of their donors, came to birth in twentieth-century America. It is possible here only to indicate a few of them. The Milbank Memorial Fund, created in 1905, specialized in studies of nutrition and, more recently, in population control. The Russell Sage Foundation, noted for its work in the development and application of the social sciences, dates from 1907. The Phelps-Stokes Fund established in 1911 and the Rosenwald Fund established in 1917 made Negro education their special interest. The Juilliard Music Foundation was created in 1920. The Laura Spelman Rockefeller Memorial—a great force in modernizing American social science—was created in 1922, and the Duke Endowment with its emphasis on regional development came in 1924. Then came the Spelman Fund in 1928, a spin-off from the Laura Spelman Rockefeller Memorial and, like it, a major force in American social science: the development of the science of public administration in America is its great monument.

There was also the creation in 1929 of the John Simon Guggenheim Memorial Foundation, which has given opportunities for travel and creative work to thousands of American scholars and artists. The W. K. Kellogg Foundation too was created in 1929, for broad purposes. Two years later, the Richard King Mellon Foundation was formed. It remains to be added that, despite the belief that progressively higher income taxes would so inhibit the development of large fortunes as to impede the growth of foundations and philanthropy, nine of the thirteen largest foundations have been funded mainly since World War II. These include Ford, Lilly, Sloan, Pew, and Rockefeller Brothers.

A list of sonorous names, of course, does not by itself prove that the activities covered by the names are of exceptional merit. The commission decided to look at the fields in which foundations do their work by means of a sampling by experts who might be expected to discern the significance of any foundation contributions. Accordingly, the commission asked three of its members who have expert knowledge in separate fields affected by philanthropic financing to prepare an analysis bearing on what, if anything, foundations have done to stimulate worthwhile advances in their own areas of interest. Medicine and health were reviewed by Dr. Philip R. Lee, chancellor of the University of California San Francisco Medical Center. Science was reviewed by Franklin A. Long, vice-president for research and development at Cornell University. Martin Friedman, director of the Walker Art Center, Minneapolis, reviewed the arts. The commission also asked experts in education and population studies to review foundation contributions to those fields.

Medicine. Long before the federal government became a sponsor for various programs related to medicine and medical care, the foundations were a major force in this field, and they have to their credit a long list of brilliant successes. Medical education, for example, is the point of departure for everything else in medicine. And if American medical education is now unsurpassed anywhere in the world, it owes its excellence to Abraham Flexner's Rockefeller Foundation financed study of what American medical education was like, what it *should* be like, and what it would take to make it what it ought to be. The study, and a follow-through on it with foundation support, marked a turning point in the way America's future doctors were trained.

There was a matching piece to this in the field of public health. New knowledge about the prevention or treatment of diseases could go forward in research laboratories. But the knowledge gained was no better than a good dream unless it could be extended beyond the laboratory into the broad domain of public health. The means for doing that, however, were hobbled by the shortage of trained professional personnel— until the Rockefeller Foundation entered the picture. It made an initial grant to Johns Hopkins University to establish a School of Hygiene and Public Health. The founding of this one school, under the direction of Dr. William Welch, had a revolutionary effect in moving public health education from the plane of primitive guesswork and folklore to a foundation in science. It provided the model for imitation by other schools of hygiene and public health. Though shortages persist to this day in the supply of professionally trained public health workers, without the innovative work of the Rockefeller Foundation in this field there is no calculating how many millions of Americans would have been afflicted by diseases they were spared.

Foundations have also pioneered in the support of modern experiments in medical care. The record of success ranges from the eradication of hookworm, a debilitating infection that plagued the South, to the development of insulin by a team of scientists at the University of Toronto who were working on the control of diabetes, to the early assistance rendered to Dr. Jonas Salk's polio vaccine research that has since helped bring polio under control.

In other forms, foundation funds helped launch the two largest experiments in improved medical care, the Health Insurance Plan of Greater New York and the Kaiser Health Plan. A key development in rural group practice, the Hunterdon Medical Center in rural New Jersey, was initiated with Commonwealth Fund support. The Macy Foundation supported two experiments in group practice, one at Montefiore Hospital and a less successful venture at New York University Medical Center. It also supported a searching study of medical care by the New York Academy of Medicine.

An experiment uniting medical education with medical care which was to have a significant impact on American medicine resulted from a unique combination of the Mayo Foundation and the Mayo Clinic. The foundation provided support for research and education while the clinic staff provided services and financial support for the foundation. Thousands of physicians trained at the Mayo Clinic have established small, medium, and large-sized groups throughout the Midwest and western United States.

Nor is this all. Foundations have been active in the hospital field, although on a smaller scale than government and usually for specific purposes. The Commonwealth Fund has provided assistance for rural hospitals; the W. K. Kellogg Foundation has made grants for the construction of nursing schools operated by hospitals, and in 1956 the Ford Foundation made grant funds available to all hospitals in the country for special purposes that were not part of their regular operating budgets. This was part of a $560 million grant to privately supported colleges, medical schools, and hospitals.

On another front of medicine, and again before the federal government entered the medical picture, foundation support was forthcoming for basic research in medicine. The initiative here came from the Rockefeller Foundation in the early 1930s, when it determined to support basic sciences concerned with the "constitution, structure and function of living organisms and their component parts." In the twenty-five years that followed, the foundation invested approximately $100 million in fundamental research work, with vast consequences for medicine, medical care, and medical education alike. Today, for example, the fields of molecular biology and genetics are among the most exciting and creative in the life sciences largely because of the sustained support the Rockefeller Foundation provided for research and research workers in this area. Other foundations have played no less a central role in developing the field of psychiatry.

It does not detract from what the foundations have done in the field of medicine to note that the federal government, by its extensive support for medical research in the past thirty years, has made a massive contribution to public health. These foundation-backed studies gave powerful evidence of what scientists could do when they were adequately financed for an attack on the afflictions of the human body and mind, and helped muster public support for the government's assumption of a great role of its own in the common effort.

Nor was the government of the United States the only body thus aroused. In the medical field, the foundations fly the international flag of human patriotism. The Rockefeller Sanitary Commission is a case in point. Its fight against hookworm, which began in the southern part of the United States, was extended by the International Health Board to include work on a world scale in malaria control and yellow fever. These and other international health efforts by the Rockefeller Foundation have been vastly expanded since World War II by the World Health Organization, the Pan-American Health Organization, and some one hundred countries, many aided by grants and technical assistance from the United States.

Many of the old basic problems such as malnutrition and malaria still remain to be overcome on a global scale. Yet two sets of new problems now face public health authorities. The first is the population explosion, due in part to the successful conquests of many of the infectious diseases of yesterday—a population explosion that presents the world with more hungry mouths to feed. The foundations were among the first to tackle the equation between people and food. Thus, they supported the kind of agricultural research that could help increase the food supply in areas of the world where daily hunger was the rule. They also supported research in the control of human fertility and reproduction.

The second set of new problems consists of some of the ailments of an affluent, urban, and industrialized society like America. The ailments include the health hazards associated with cigarette smoking, pollution of the air and water, the increasing volume of partially treated municipal wastes indiscriminately dumped into America's rivers and lakes, the millions injured and thousands killed annually by traffic accidents, the rising problems of mental illness, alcoholism, drug abuse, and the like. With respect to all these matters, which bear heavily on the conditions of American life, different foundations are again out in front searching for remedies that can be underwritten later by the government.

The Broad Realm of Scientific Research. American science in the past fifty years has changed from a position of almost complete intellectual subservience to the science of Western Europe to one of demonstrable world preeminence. To be sure, many other factors outside the foundations have contributed to it. One was the establishment, more than a hundred years ago, of land grant colleges, with their specific obligation to support the fields of agriculture and the mechanical arts. These gave American institutions of higher learning a devotion to applied science which remains strong to this day, as does the support from American industry for scientific research and development. Another contributing factor to American preeminence was the haven the United States gave to many scientists and skilled technicians who fled from a Europe dominated by the Nazis and Fascists. Above all, there has been the increase in federal support for science from negligible amounts in 1945 to the current scale whereby more than half the nation's efforts in basic scientific research is paid for by federal agencies.

Yet there are important gaps in government support for science, and foundations alert to national needs have been at the forefront of efforts to fill them. While the government, for example, has financed basic research and graduate education in science, its support did not extend to undergraduate education. The Sloan Foundation, recognizing this fact, gave substantial grants several years ago to some dozen leading American colleges to be used in undergraduate education in the natural sciences. The grants were of great importance to the colleges and permitted them to upgrade their scientific facilities and staff. They were of almost equal importance in dramatizing the need for more attention to undergraduate programs at all levels.

Developments in new areas of scientific teaching and research have also found foundations taking important initiatives not forthcoming from government. A good example is the grant the Sloan Foundation made to Cornell University in 1963 to develop a new department in computer science. By that year, the importance of computers to universities was well recognized, but it was not yet clear that the field of computer science would also be an intellectual area for study. In fact, only one or two significant teaching programs existed in the country at that time. Support from Sloan permitted Cornell to move rapidly and effectively into this field to create within only a few years a high-caliber department to meet a rapidly growing need.

Private foundations, meanwhile, have played an essential role in supporting the kind of teaching and research that cuts across different disciplines. Interdisciplinary activities are always somewhat awkward for universities to handle because they lack congruence with the normal departmental structure. They are just as awkward to the federal government because of the government's tendency to tie its support to the programs of agencies oriented to particular missions. Foundations often provide the saving grace of their help. The "area" programs to develop interdisciplinary regional studies and the related Centers for International Studies—both extensively supported by the Ford Foundation—are good examples of the kind of assistance they render.

Federal funds for new buildings for scientific teaching and research have been in short supply and even when available have provided only partial support. In particular, there have been almost no funds for buildings for undergraduate education. Even for graduate training and research, federal building support is normally limited to a maximum of 50 percent of the total cost. The problem has not escaped the attention of foundations such as the Olin Foundation. It has provided substantial help to a number of institutions of higher learning which have been in urgent need of new physical quarters for students.

Most federal agencies are uneasy about giving grants for the support of individual American scientists, particularly for travel abroad, and federal funds for this purpose have generally been skimpy. Conversely, it is difficult for federal agencies to support foreign scientists who visit or want to visit the United States to consult with their co-workers in a field. Foundations, however, have been available to support this two-way traffic of research-oriented minds, just as they have come to the support of able young men and women in the natural sciences who are at the start of their careers.

Population Studies.[1] The field of population studies provides a strik-

1. The commission is indebted to Frank W. Notestein and Bernard Berelson, who provided much of the raw material from which this brief summary was written.

ing example of the way in which foundation pioneering can demonstrate the need for an activity so unmistakably that public funds take over its support. In 1968, government agencies became the major source of money for population studies, but foundations previously furnished the major support. On the commission's questionnaire, Ford's International Division cited its grants of $23 million to the Population Council between 1954 and 1969 as among its most significant. (The scale of Ford's total giving in this area, however, is on the order of $100 million.)

Shortly after World War II, the increasingly rapid growth in world population resulting from triumphs in public health measures was noted with widespread alarm. Those who were suddenly concerned about the population explosion found that foresight, working through a foundation, had already created a fund of scholarly information on the political and social implications of population growth. The Scripps Foundation for Research in Population Control had been established in 1922; its director, Warren S. Thompson, became the first of a new breed of demographer. In 1928, the Milbank Memorial Fund began to support research in population problems that included studies of the efficacy and acceptability of methods of contraception—at the time a "dangerous" subject. The first grant to a university for population studies—$250,000 to Princeton—was made by the Milbank Fund in 1936. With the resulting establishment of the Office of Population Research, the field of study had achieved full academic respectability.

Among those keenly interested in the problem of the world's food supply was John D. Rockefeller III, who became the prime mover in the formation in 1952 of the Population Council, which he financed initially with gifts of about $250,000 a year. Its mission was to develop the scientific knowledge and the personnel to deal effectively with the population explosion. Others took note of the same problem and made large grants to expand the council's work. Among its many projects was investigation of the efficacy of the plastic intra-uterine device. Forty research projects over three years in medical schools, clinics, and hospitals, at a cost of $2 million, established the ring as a safe, effective, and acceptable contraceptive. The method has since been widely adopted in underdeveloped countries with acute problems of overpopulation.

At the outset, foundations taken as a whole moved into the population field cautiously. Some foundation staffs and trustees were reluctant to make substantial population grants since they perceived risks of heavy religious opposition in countries with pivotal foundation public health programs. Later, so rapidly was the importance of population studies recognized, that support was widely generated for their continual expansion. No government funds went into the early work of demography—in contrast to the situation in Europe, where, especially in France and Sweden, public money was devoted to research on the subject. Yet it was the United States that was able to provide the trained experts to meet the cry for help that came from backward countries whose teeming millions faced the threat of mass starvation.

Now, of course, federal, state and local governments are moving into the field on a large scale. An analysis of the total financing of activities in the area reveals that, while in 1968 American foundations invested about $25 million in population studies, government contributions were $145 million—$55 million for research and $90 million for family planning services. The whole story remains an illustrious one in the catalog of imaginative, innovative work by foundations at a critical time.

Ford's entrance into this field in the early 1950s is sometimes mentioned as an example of a foundation's willingness to enter controversial areas. A better example, however, is the Rockefeller Foundation's support of the Kinsey sex studies. The Rockefeller Foundation gave more than $1 million to the Committee for Research on Problems of Sex—part of the National Research Council—for twenty-five years starting in the 1930s. The committee, in turn, gave $400,000 to support the studies of Dr. Alfred C. Kinsey and others at Indiana University. This, according to the Rockefeller Foundation's book *Toward the Well-Being of Mankind*, was "one of the most controversial series of grants in the Foundation's history."

Other Dimensions of Education. Among the experienced observers to whom this commission turned for informed comment on the work of foundations was Robert C. Weaver, a Harvard-trained economist, president of Bernard M. Baruch College, and former Secretary—the first—of the United States Department of Housing and Urban Development. He was for many years a member of the awards committee of the Fulbright fellowships. He was a consultant to the Rosenwald Fund, which was concerned primarily with Negro students. He was the first director of the Opportunity Fellowship Program of the John Hay Whitney Foundation and is an official of the National Scholarship Service for Negro Students. Opportunity Fellowships have gone to members of disadvantaged groups, to Negroes and Americans of Mexican and Puerto Rican background, persons displaced by Nazis,

American Indians, Japanese and Chinese Americans. The NSSFNS concerns itself primarily with undergraduates in integrated schools.

Weaver reports that at the time the Rosenwald Fund was established there was a dearth of fellowships, particularly at the graduate school level. There were a few fellowship programs—Guggenheim being probably the outstanding exception—which were devoted to the performing arts as well as to scholarship and creative work. The Rosenwald fellowship program greatly accelerated the number and the quality of Negroes who went into these fields. When the Rosenwald Fund was dissolved, a proposal was made to the John Hay Whitney Foundation that a similar program, but with wider coverage, be established. This is still operative under the name of the Opportunity Fellowship Program. The alumni of that program are quite outstanding. Robert Weaver told the commission:

The issue now before us is what, in perhaps the specific field of fellowships, might be done today by a foundation in a new milieu. There are many new sources of support for graduate students in private colleges and institutions where scholarships and fellowships are much larger and much more prevalent today than they once were. In addition, a larger number are earmarked for minority groups, Negroes in particular. Similarly, the black artist or the black writer, the black playwright, the black composer today, even the black performing artist today, certainly in the theater, in opera, and symphony has a much greater opportunity both for training and for employment than existed even a decade ago. Since these various sources of support are so much greater today than they were even a decade ago, does philanthropy have a role to play as a source of fellowships?

The answer is yes for two reasons. First, the needs are much greater today than they have ever been, and the opportunities of employment are much greater. It is of the utmost importance that these opportunities should become actualities rather than remain as theoretical possibilities. Secondly, there are several new areas of research and of training which offer unique opportunities coupled with unique preparatory requirements. A failure to pursue these actively and effectively will dim a bright prospect.

With the tremendous expansion of public support for higher education, foundation support for education now becomes increasingly what in some degree it has always been: a type of financial support for experimental innovations. There will always be areas in education that cry for new and bold solutions. Foundations do not have the assets to compete with publicly supported programs. They can, however, act more quickly and be more innovative —with fewer constraints—than is true of public institutions. Unless foundations play the latter role they will become the very small tail on a kite of safe activities already established and more generously financed by public sources. If the foundations retreat and simply accept the fact that they will last longer if they are safer, it seems to me they have really foreclosed their reason for being.

Some of the grants in education listed by the major foundations are so basic in character that they can be seen in perspective only against the whole background of American education. Have foundations made an overinvestment in higher education at the expense of the elementary and secondary grades? Have they, by the promise of funds, diverted universities from more important goals? Could tax-supported agencies have done the same things? To whom did the benefits flow from foundation-supported educational programs?

All of these questions and many more may well be answered by a high-level commission now surveying the field of higher education under the sponsorship of the Carnegie Foundation for the Advancement of Teaching (most of whose funds come from the Carnegie Corporation of New York). The Carnegie Commission on Higher Education, led by Clark Kerr, former president of the University of California, has embarked on the task of forecasting the financial and other needs of the country's colleges and universities in the decades that lead into the twenty-first century.

Many foundations have tried to meet the special needs of education through scholarship programs. A prime example is the National Merit Scholarship Corporation, set up by the Ford Foundation in 1955, which administers a national program of scholarships to academically gifted high school students. The foundation has given the corporation, or pledged, $38,500,000 to administer the program through 1973. Ford also supported the Woodrow Wilson National Fellowship Foundation, which gave fellowships to doctoral students—$55,600,000 for the period 1957–70. Ford says, "This was the first major effort to meet the estimated future need for college teachers by systematically recruiting qualified college seniors for doctoral study."

The Kansas City Association of Trusts and Foundations provided almost a half-million dollars between 1962 and 1968 for a scholarship program for marginal students in the "central city." The 450 young people sent to college under the program established a better survival rate (83 percent) than college students generally. "In addition to the obvious importance," the association wrote, "a second and unexpected benefit occurred. A number of the graduates thus far (some 10 percent) have elected to go into teaching and have accepted jobs in the inner city schools whence they came as students."

Many programs of grants directly to colleges have also been devised. Ford's enormous programs are most notable, but much innovation has occurred in smaller programs. A company-sponsored foundation, Esso

Education Foundation, began a program in 1955 of grants ranging
from $2,000 to $5,000 to undergraduate colleges. In 1964, the program
was changed to a presidential contingency program: grants ranging
from $2,500 to $7,500 are given to the president of the college for use on
unbudgeted items.

Smith, Kline, and French Foundation, sponsored by the phar-
maceutical company, has taken a special interest in medical education.
Since 1953 it has given over a million dollars in relatively small grants
for a somewhat novel program: money is granted for unrestricted use
to newly appointed medical educators—deans and department chairmen—in the belief that those newly in office have the most ideas and
motivation but the fewest funds. The foundation has also helped a
program at the University of Pennsylvania to carry young medical
researchers through the "lean post-doctoral years."

The Arts. Norman Cousins, editor of the *Saturday Review*, has observed that "an artist is not of a separate species capable of living indefinitely on art and adulation." For every story of a famous artist who
continued to work creatively despite hunger, sickness, and misery, there
are countless instances of those who stopped working when they stopped
eating. "A good artist," Cousins added, "is a prism for refracting
beauty; he is to be supported not because it is good to keep people from
being hungry—that is the function of charity or government—but
because the human community cannot live fully or joyously unless its
sense of beauty is exercised and proclaimed." The painter, sculptor,
and composer are likely to create their best works of art from periods
of sustained study and experiment, which in turn require sustained
financial support.

Not all foundations have been alive to this truth, and only recently
has there been sustained support of the arts and artists in any significant
way. Yet here is a beckoning frontier for foundation activity. The need
is all the greater precisely because America in the 1960s seemed at last
to have "discovered" the arts and to provide a remarkably large
audience for the offering of individual artists in the different media.

Dance, long the most indigent of the arts in America, enjoyed an
unexpected renaissance in the 1960s, and there are now between 110 to
200 professional and amateur dance companies. American museums
and art centers also proliferated in the 1960s to an amazing extent so
that there are now over 620 art museums, while American painters and
sculptors have become the new "form givers" of international art.

American architecture during the 1960s revealed itself as astonishingly innovative, visually and technically. There are now 1,450 orchestras and somewhere between 600 and 700 opera companies. The American theatre generally, so long a captive of Broadway tastes and its hard economics of production, has begun to decentralize.

Against this burgeoning, seemingly ideal, situation of a "cultural renaissance," we must weigh the factor of support. Opera, theater, and dance performances require substantial, consistent subsidy if the curtain is even to go up; $12, $15 and now $25 Broadway ticket prices are out of the reach of the average non-expense-account buyer, though the prices realistically express high production overhead. The regional theaters' performances, and most concerts and dance programs, would be empty at these rates; subsidy becomes the determining attendance factor. Meanwhile, American museums are in fact subsidizing their audiences. They offer many educational services, such as school tours, exhibitions and low-cost publications, but are often unable to cover operating expenses. The costs of presenting important traveling shows, publishing catalogs and buying and maintaining distinguished works of art for permanent collections are not being adequately met by most of our museums.

The realities of the matter need to be put sharply and directly. There is a growing economic crisis in the arts in spite of, or perhaps because of, the demands of a vast new audience. Our population has an increasingly higher educational level. It has a longer life expectancy. It has more time and motivation to use its cultural resources. But even as the audience grows for these reasons, American artists and arts institutions are in the same financial quicksands they were in before government and foundation aid became even modestly available. Performing arts companies and museums are pressed to offer expanded programs. This calls for the development of highly professional staffs. Yet in view of the economic uncertainty in this area, the best qualified candidates are reluctant to pursue careers as administrative heads of museums, theaters, or symphony orchestras, and arts specialists find more security and less ulcerating conditions in universities.

Many young actors and musicians give up their artistic ambitions to pursue other careers rather than perform for low wages. It is paradoxical yet true that the artist's survival, even in our age of affluence, is incredibly risky. His productive work is regarded as inseparable from culture and affluence, yet he is too often part of a neglected, unsupported subculture. The exceptions are the relatively few painters, sculptors, writers, actors, and musicians who have won recognition and a measure of financial security, but the overwhelming majority must teach or work at other jobs in order to practice their art. The vast American resource of fertile individual talent can be aborted unless the valuable people involved have access to some security. Nor are our established cultural institutions beyond the reach of peril. Income from endowments, long the main source of funds for nonprofit institutions such as museums, is no longer enough to meet rapidly rising operating expenses.

While America has had an honorable history in the evolution of major cultural institutions such as museums, symphony orchestras, and opera companies, support for this work has become associated with economic and cultural elitism. Private patrons of the arts have often been enlightened and imaginative, but just as often the arts, under that kind of sponsorship, have become an exclusive province of the wealthy. Though these established patrons are now unable to provide sufficient support, it is still the individual—not the foundation, corporation, or government—who shoulders the greatest load in supporting the performing and visual arts in the United States. According to 1966–67 estimates, individual giving to the arts accounts for about 68 percent of total contributions; foundations, 12 percent; corporations, 8 percent; and local, state, and federal governments, 12 percent.

Although federal funds have been available to the arts for decades through a variety of agencies—the Smithsonian Institution, the Library of Congress, the Office of Education, the State Department, and so forth—the first direct interest of the federal government found its legislative expression in 1965 with the establishment of the National Endowment for the Arts. The National Endowment, during its brief history, has done important work. Through it, matching funds are provided to state arts councils, which, in turn, attract private and foundation assistance to maintain arts programs in metropolitan and rural regions. National Endowment grants include a 1967 housing project for artists (in collaboration with the J. M. Kaplan Fund), which provided low-cost living quarters and studio space for qualified artists in New York City. The endowment has supported an annual American Literary Anthology and the establishment of the American Film Institute. Programs and grants of the endowment have been varied, imaginative, and extremely effective.

Thus far in the arts, there is no consistent pattern where private philanthropy initiates pilot projects that are then picked up by the government. Indeed, in some instances it is the other way around. Examples include the Federal Laboratory Theatre Project, the American Film Institute, and state touring programs and, in New York, the State Arts Council touring attractions which are now funded principally by local sources with some additional assistance from the state; initially, the state provided 100 percent of the funds. State support for the arts is new; it is also experimental and highly diversified, though very limited. Some foundations have devoted part of their budgets to arts sponsorship. (The Solomon R. Guggenheim Foundation, the Rockefeller Foundation, and two Mellon foundations—the Avalon and Old Dominion—were active in this area even before the 1960s.)

Our commission's study of foundations shows that about 2 percent of the total foundation grants go to "arts and humanities," and even this small amount tends to be concentrated in the larger foundations. A notable exception to the general rule is the Ford Foundation, which in 1957 established its program in the arts, far outstripping any single private, government, or other foundation source. Since then, the Ford Foundation has granted $182.5 million in the creative and performing arts. Its biggest year was 1966, when $85 million in matching grants was given to American symphony orchestras. Even so, a McKinsey and Company study of several of our major symphony orchestras makes their painful financial situation distressingly clear. Last year the Ford Foundation's total new appropriation to the arts was $13.5 million for such projects as museum collection catalogs, resident theater, symphony development, and Negro theater.

Another exception is the Rockefeller Foundation, which has been interested in university-based arts programs that result in closer relationships between departments of art, music, and theater and professional artists and groups. Rockefeller's policies on giving include an entire division called "Cultural Development." A recent quarter showed a $400,000 grant to the Public Theater for new plays in New York and a $388,000 grant to the University of Minnesota Drama Program to help young playwrights.

The John Simon Guggenheim Memorial Foundation, for its part, has made important grants to writers, composers, artists, and other creative individuals. This is one of the most respected individual grant programs in the arts, and the foundation's award making has been exemplary. The list of those who have received Guggenheim grants is virtually an index of this country's creativity. In another direction, the T. B. Walker Foundation of Minneapolis has been since 1927 almost the sole support of the Walker Art Center, a contemporary art museum whose membership and activities are entirely public. The Juilliard Musical Foundation supports a single institution, the Juilliard Music School. While this situation is repeated throughout the United States in the support of regional museums, musical and theatrical organizations, the giant foundations that do little or nothing in the arts clearly outnumber those that give substantial support. A list of a hundred of the largest foundations shows that about seventy-five give less than 5 percent to the arts, and many give nothing at all.

Foundations can help identify, through their research and programs, areas of need in the arts. But the need for arts support is of such magnitude that it cannot be met adequately by foundations, individual donors, and corporate donors. Only through a committed program of government support for the arts can the potentialities of serving an enormous public be fully realized—but until such support is forthcoming as a generally recognized need in our national life, foundation support remains essential to the survival of the arts in America.

Preservation of Historical Sites and Parks. A federally chartered organization whose existence has been almost completely dependent on private philanthropy is the National Trust for Historic Preservation, which saves historic sites and notable architecture from decay and destruction. Since the national park sites are well known, it is widely believed that the field is dominated by government agencies. In fact, it has been almost exclusively private until recent years.

Although the preservation movement began with government action when the New York legislature, in 1850, acquired the farmhouse at Newburgh that had served George Washington as headquarters, this for many years remained an isolated example of government concern for historic shrines. Mount Vernon was saved and restored, and is still maintained, by a private organization of women. (A foundation created by another woman, Mrs. Frances P. Bolton, former Congresswoman from Ohio, saved the view from Mount Vernon when it was threatened in recent years.) Thomas Jefferson's home, Monticello, was preserved by another private group. Private endeavor was the pattern, a pattern that reached its apogee in 1927 when John D. Rockefeller, Jr. began the restoration of Virginia's colonial capital at Williamsburg. Colonial Williamsburg not only began on an unprecedented scale of private spending, but continues so: despite its heavy endowment and hordes of visitors, it still receives an annual Rockefeller subsidy approaching $2 million.

Restoration is one thing. Preservation is another, and the case for it is clear cut. A nation, like an individual, can be a victim of amnesia. It can lose the memories of what it was, and thereby lose the sense of what it is or wants to be. We need the signs of where we came from and how we got to where we are, the thoughts we had along the way and what we did to express the thoughts in action.

These ideas were implicit in the 1935 decision of Congress when it passed the Historic Sites Act and declared it to be a national policy to preserve historic sites of national significance. However, private endeavor remained of such importance in carrying out this policy that Congress chartered the National Trust for Historic Preservation in 1949. It was not given public funds but received congressional blessing to accept donations and do what it could to stimulate interest in preserving historic sites.

In its answers to the commission's questionnaire, the Avalon Foundation and the Old Dominion Foundation (now merged to form the Andrew W. Mellon Foundation) each listed contributions of $1,250,000 to the National Trust first among its most significant grants. The chairman of the National Trust, Gordon Gray, corroborated this assessment. He wrote in a personal communication that the trust now has assets of more than $10 million in addition to ten properties, an expenditure budget of $1,265,305 in 1969, and 20,000 individual and 1,200 organization members. "Thus, the Trust has come a long way from the one property (Woodlawn), the 100-member organizations, the 500 individual members, and the annual budget of approximately $90,000, which the Trust had when the Avalon and Old Dominion Foundations first came to the help of the Trust."

Private philanthropy, including that of Paul Mellon and Ailsa Mellon Bruce, has also bought historic property for the National Park Service. John D. Rockefeller, Jr. bought a significant property in Yorktown, Virginia—the Moore House—when the Colonial National Historical Park was being planned, and held it until the Park Service could reimburse him. This particular function—by prompt action helping government agencies to circumvent real estate speculation—is seen more clearly in the preservation of natural areas.

The role of private philanthropy as an ally of the federal government in this field was discussed for the commission by Conrad L. Wirth, former director of the National Park Service. He pointed out that, until the creation of the Cape Cod National Seashore, none of the big National Park Service areas had been purchased with federal money; all came from the public domain or from gifts. Among single benefactors, John D. Rockefeller, Jr., was preeminent, his gifts stretching from Acadia in Maine to the Great Smoky Mountains and the Grand Tetons.

Old Dominion and Avalon cited, in their answers to the Foundation Center questionnaire, their help in creating Cape Hatteras National Seashore. Each gave $400,000 in 1952 to help the state of North Carolina buy the property; in 1966, each gave an additional $100,000 for the extension called the Cape Lookout National Seashore. Old Dominion and Avalon also cited their gifts totalling about $700,000 to the Matching and Loan Fund of the Nature Conservancy. The fund has been used to buy natural areas for preservation. The Nature Conservancy has the simple goal of guaranteeing that the country holds on to at least one sample of each of its characteristic landscapes. It has been successful as a land-acquiring organization which gets property and then turns it over to another agency, such as a state park system, for preservation.

In 1968, the Ford Foundation made public the details of an arrangement with the Nature Conservancy designed to enlarge that organization's activities by strengthening its credit. The foundation guarantees the Conservancy a $6 million line of credit so that it can borrow money to buy land in at least twenty-seven states. The Conservancy can buy strategic parcels when they become available and hold them until a public agency can reimburse it; this is expected to be an effective measure against speculators and the delays of legislative appropriations.

Accomplishments of Smaller Foundations. A few of the smaller foundations have shown a diversity and a lively imagination which, particularly when coupled with the ability to act quickly, has enabled them to perform important services. The small foundations, as the instruments of a single individual's enthusiasms and interest, may thus often discover useful projects that others neglect.

The Spaeth Foundation has sponsored traveling exhibitions of religious art; many company and individual foundations have purchased works of art for presentation to museums. The Ittleson Foundation, the Grant Foundation, the Josiah Macy Junior Foundation, and the Samuel Z. Levine Foundation for International Child Health have all contributed importantly to work in international health, particularly in the training of leadership personnel.

The Elas U. Pardee Fund of Midland, Michigan, has financed a number of individual research projects in medicine which have produced radioactive drugs now in wide use. An advantage of the small foundation is its capacity for quick action when it perceives a need. It was a small foundation, for example, that reacted immediately to the riots in New York in the summer of 1963 by bringing together ministers in slum areas to organize an employment program for idle youths. Small sums often prove to be the seeds of growing developments. For example, in 1963 the Chicago Community Trust made an initial grant to enable the Welfare Council to establish an Open Lands Project. This had the object of helping to organize efforts to preserve for public-recreation purposes some of the fast-disappearing open land around Chicago. The Chicago Community Trust has made a series of grants that seek to bring about increased placement of blacks on the boards and committees of a variety of civic, social, and cultural organizations, with the purpose of providing leadership training and interracial and intercultural experience. When the Circuit Court of Cook County (Chicago) appointed a citizens' committee to investigate conditions in its juvenile court division, it was soon apparent that an investigative staff was essential for a satisfactory result. The Woods Charitable Fund, the Wieboldt Foundation, and the Chicago Community Trust joined in providing funds to finance a report that brought significant improvements in the treatment of juveniles in the court's custody.

In the mid-thirties and for the following two decades, the largest single cause of blindness in children was an ailment known as retrolental fibroplasia. Most of the victims were premature babies, and a puzzling aspect was that the condition was most frequently found in infants who were receiving the best medical care. When oxygen therapy was improved, with more efficient incubators, the hospitals with the best equipment seemed to have the largest number of cases of retrolental fibroplasia. Starting in 1954, the Chicago Community Trust financed research by Dr. Arlington C. Krause of the University of Chicago Medical School which, in conjunction with research elsewhere, established that too much oxygen was the major culprit. There has since been a dramatic decrease in the incidence of this disease.

12

Other Views of Foundation Achievements

In the course of its appraisal of foundation achievements, the commission offered foundations a chance to speak for themselves. With the help of the Foundation Center in New York, we asked a selected group of foundations to list several grants which they considered to be especially significant. They were to do this first for the period from the foundation's creation to recent times, and then for the past five years. They were also asked to list a few grants which they considered disappointing or unproductive.

Replies came from about twenty foundations, including the largest and most prestigious and various smaller ones. What we wanted to know specifically was whether there are cases that could stand as modern counterparts of the "classic" foundation accomplishments such as the Flexner report on medical schools and the campaign against hookworm. The answers were also examined for instances that would support claims made on behalf of foundations—that foundations have pioneering spirit, flexibility, willingness to enter controversial areas.

A "classic" modern case was quickly apparent. Two foundations cited grants in an area that may have more profound meaning to the nation today than the eradication of hookworm or the upgrading of medical schools had a generation ago. The area is national educational television.

The claims of the Ford Foundation and the Carnegie Corporation in the area of national, noncommercial television are large but simple. The Ford Foundation's claim is that it kept noncommercial television alive so that America has the option of creating a distinctive alternative to commercial television. The Carnegie Corporation's claim is that it supported the study that suggested a mechanism by which the second service could be established—the mechanism that did in fact become the Corporation for Public Broadcasting, which Congress created in 1967 following the Carnegie study.

According to the Ford Foundation's Public Broadcasting division, Ford has put a total of about $180 million into public television in the past seventeen years. The amount seems staggering until it is measured in the scale of national television spending. The commercial networks spend money nearly two hundred times faster—a rate of about $2 billion a year. The costs of national television created one boundary to public television; the American belief that the federal government should not control or influence channels of public information created another. In between were few agencies with resources of any size. Noncommercial television can be cited, therefore, in support of the contention that in some areas foundations can work more effectively than any other institution.

From the beginning of the television age in the 1940s, there were thoughts of a second, noncommercial service. The idea of reserving air space for such a service was presented to the Federal Communications Commission in 1944, but nothing came of the proposal. However, in 1948 the FCC declared a moratorium on assignment of new channels while technical studies were conducted. The freeze lasted until 1952, and during this time the forces interested in educational television formed a Joint Council on Educational Television, which repeated to the FCC the proposal that channels be reserved for noncommercial television. In this same period the Ford Foundation expanded to multibillion-dollar size. Education was to be one of its major interests; the foundation was attracted almost immediately to educational television as a way to surmount the postwar teacher shortage. Before the FCC's freeze ended, the foundation made an ambitious effort to exploit commercial television for culture. From 1951 until 1957, the foundation supported *Omnibus*, which ran for an hour and a half on Sunday afternoons. Although *Omnibus* thus far remains an isolated experiment for commercial television, the foundation is still proud of it. On the Foundation Center's questionnaire, Ford's Public Broadcasting division cited the grants totaling $11,400,000 in support of *Omnibus* as among its most significant.

When the FCC's freeze ended in 1952, the basis for noncommercial television was established by the Commission: 242 channels were reserved for noncommercial educational television stations. Ford's money began to flow into noncommercial television through three conduits: the foundation itself and two independent agencies that had been created by the foundation—the Fund for the Advancement of Education and the Fund for Adult Education.

The Fund for the Advancement of Education supported the organization of the Educational Television and Radio Center. The name was soon changed to the less cumbersome National Educational Television (NET). It was an exchange service—one that would find and distribute programs for local stations—and direction was primarily in the hands of educators rather than broadcasters. The shortcomings of this system were apparent to the foundations by 1959. NET's headquarters were moved to New York so that the system would be at the center of national communications. The concept of a fourth network that would offer the public an option to the three commercial networks was beginning to grow.

The year 1962 was crucial. About $30 million in federal funds flowed into noncommercial television. The money, authorized under the Educational Facilities Act, went for construction costs and station equipment. In the same year, the Ford Foundation decided to continue support of noncommercial television as a major activity. NET was reorganized. The balance of power shifted from educators to broadcasters, and Ford raised its support from $1 million a year to $6 million. The money was to finance production of five hours of programs a week, with emphasis on quality.

McGeorge Bundy, after he became president of the Ford Foundation, proposed to the FCC that the system of communication satellites established over the continents be used for the benefit of public television. The satellites enable television signals to be transmitted without the need of long land-lines, thus saving the networks many millions of dollars each year which could be used to support noncommercial programming. The FCC took the proposal under advisement. About a year later, a commission financed by a $500,000 grant from the Carnegie Corporation made its report, holding that "a well-financed and well-directed educational television system, substantially larger and far more pervasive and effective than that which now exists in the United States, must be brought into being if the full needs of the American public are to be served." It recommended specifically that Congress charter a non-profit Corporation for Public Broadcasting to direct the effort. By 7 November 1967, the major recommendations of the Carnegie commission had been translated into law.

The Carnegie commission estimated that the system it envisaged would cost $270 million a year (noncommercial television now spends about $70 million a year). Ford's rule of thumb is that a public educational TV system will be considered healthy and competitive when it has an annual budget of $300 million. This problem of financing remains to be solved. In the meantime, the joint funding of *Sesame Street*—conceived initially by the Carnegie Corporation—as the first major experiment to help prepare children, particularly ghetto children, for public schooling could be one of public television's most important and exciting successes.

Some provocative answers were elicited by the last section of the Foundation Center's questionnaire, which asked about grants considered to be disappointing or unproductive. Some of the answers appeared to be candid, some appeared trivial, and some foundations ignored the question.

Of the failures listed, most involve human failure on the part of the recipient: "We had a good idea and we acted in good faith, but the person who got the money misspent it." The next biggest categories were: the program was not properly assessed before funding; the program was simply not productive; the program was successful enough but it failed to attract continued support when the foundation funds ran out. The answers give no reassurance that the foundations truly look on their failures as being as significant as their successes. Instead, the suspicion is raised that they would bury their mistakes just as quickly as any other human agency.

Are failures simply written off? Foundations have the risk capital and the freedom to make mistakes; the parallels with the researcher who carefully lists the materials that do *not* make good filaments for light bulbs, and with the oil explorer who maps the location of dry holes, are obvious. Very few foundations show much willingness to chat with the public at all; even fewer to talk about any of their "bad experiences." The foundation world can hardly be blamed for being as success-oriented as the rest of America, though it is ironic that foundations which have initiated so many evaluative projects of other institutions and their programs seem reticent either to evaluate or to talk candidly about their own programs.

As part of this commission's study of the role of foundations, we asked our sample of Chicago charitable organizations what their experience with foundations had been.

Their overall verdict is a distinctly favorable one.[1] Most charitable organizations confirmed the foundations' flexibility and willingness to support new projects. In doing so, these same charitable organizations expressed their concerns about government funding; namely, rigidity of categories, enormous quantity of paperwork, and the whims of the annual appropriation process.

We also explored the criticism that foundations try to impose their own thoughts and policies, their own "fads" on grantees. There was three-to-one agreement that foundations are not likely to do this. Although the charitable organizations we questioned are understandably protective of the hand that feeds them, there is considerable ambivalence about the innovative role of foundations. They appreciate the fact that they can get support for new ideas from foundations that they sometimes could not get from the government. On the other hand, they express the somewhat wistful desire for more "bread and butter" support as well from foundations.

At the same time, the commission encountered a point of view about the relative interest that foundations display in the conception of new projects as compared to later follow-through and implementation of projects. The thought is worth sharing: "The problem I see with foundations—and I could almost make a generalization—is that this old bugaboo 'innovation' is a strangler. And I think that this is one of the most serious problems that affect the nonprofit sector today. Foundations should think very carefully about responsibility for innovation and later support—not just beget the baby."

1. This study is reviewed in appendix 3 in greater detail. Also, the commission surveyed 885 distinguished citizens with experience in various fields of charitable work. Their verdict too is distinctly favorable.

13

The Commission's Assessment of Foundations

It can be agreed that foundations have contributed to our society in past decades. But this does not answer the questions that are rightly asked about the future. With the future in mind, do the benefits to society of such tax-favored institutions outweigh the risks of abuse? Do foundations have advantages over other means for promoting the general welfare?

In weighing these questions, the commission did not find it possible to make a "cost-benefit" analysis whereby an estimate of the loss of tax revenue could be measured against the social benefits produced by foundations. Take the "clear" and "simple" case of the discovery of a polio vaccine. How do we measure the "benefit," its value to society? What value do we place on the foundation grant that made the discovery possible? What would have happened in the absence of foundation support? Would the discovery have been delayed? How long? What is the earlier discovery of a polio vaccine worth to society? Would the results have been similar if funds went directly from donor to recipient or if the project had been funded by government? Would someone else have supported the project?

The problem of evaluation here is further aggravated by the fact that foundations are grant-making institutions. How can one accurately apportion the credit (or blame) for a foundation-financed program between the money that made it possible and the recipient who did the work? Did the foundation provide some of the ideas or suggest an approach, or did it merely disburse funds? Clearly, no balance sheet can be drawn with the gains and losses neatly totaled.

There are two levels at which we can attempt to assess foundations as an institution. One is quantitative. The other is qualitative.

At the quantitative level, we can ask: Does this institution increase the total level of private funds that are made available for charitable purposes? This commission believes deeply in a strong system of dual public and private funding. At a time when the needs of charitable organizations have increased to the point at which their financial situation may fairly be described as a crisis, we think it is of no small value if an institution does nothing more than add significantly to the private-sector side of this dual system.

We have studied the sources of the twenty to thirty billions of dollars of foundation assets that are now pledged to charity. We have considered the financial and the psychological advantages of foundations, including the donor's obtaining a tax deduction for a charitable contribution while still retaining some control over the assets contributed to the foundation. Thus, particularly in the case of some large fortunes represented by significant ownership of companies, we reach the conclusion that billions of dollars now pledged to charity through foundations would not have been devoted to charity if a foundation could not have been used as the means.

It is not enough, however, to say that foundations have attracted new funds to charity. Nor is it enough to say that most foundation funds go for what are nearly universally considered beneficial purposes, and that the abuses which have occurred are not sufficiently widespread to warrant serious curtailment of foundation activities. Every institution should search for things that it alone can do well or that others cannot do at all. Every institution should define its areas of "comparative advantage," to use the economists' term—apply its highest capabilities and live up to its unique potential.

It seems to us that foundations are uniquely positioned to make a large and distinctive contribution to the general welfare of a society in a world of change. On the one side, they can promote the cause of order by their sustained support for unglamorous but indispensable charitable activities that act as stabilizers in daily life. On the other side, in contrast to virtually all other institutions, they have pools of funds that are not committed to sustaining ongoing, normal activities. This leaves them free to respond quickly and significantly to new, unmet needs. It also leaves them free to take the longer view, to sense the revolutions of the future, to understand earlier the causes of tomorrow's problems. In human society, as in the practice of medicine, it is far better to get at a problem when the diagnosis is hard and the cure is not costly.

Furthermore, because foundations have an independence that is also unique among institutions, they can test new or different approaches to problems in order to determine whether they justify broad support. Embryonic ideas urgently need such supportive institutions in an environment where the unfamiliar often meets with general hostility. Foundations can thus help develop the talent and knowledge demanded in a world of bewildering and increasingly complex change. Foundations, in a word, can be one of our preeminent institutions of reform.

In sum, foundations must be judged against their own potential. There are few more compelling stories in the twentieth century than that of some foundations in upgrading both the quality and the prospects of human life throughout the world. The examples of a new world rice, polio and yellow fever vaccine, public television, unrivaled achievements in higher education, and others would perhaps by themselves more than justify our society's investment. Yet we must also ask what this foundation contribution might have been if more than a special few had come closer to fulfilling their unique potential. The record of distinctive foundation contributions is the record of a comparative handful.

While the public rhetoric of foundations stresses continuing bold, venturesome leaps into the future, a more complete picture would include a rather pervasive passivity, and a sluggishness that marks not only their financial investments and payout to charity but also the quality of grant making of most American foundations.

The commission strongly affirms the work of many of the traditional purposes to which foundations devote their funds. Yet many more of them must face up to a high priority task. They must fulfill their unique potential for the public good in a world of change. They must earn and build the public's trust and confidence if they are to tackle our society's unmet needs.

Part 3
Recommendations

14

Angle of Vision

"If we could first know where we are, and whither we are trending, we could better judge what to do and how to do it." In the spirit of these words of Abraham Lincoln, voiced in his "House Divided" speech, the commission has tried to know where American philanthropy now stands and where it is trending.

The three great ends we have in view are clear.

First: We want to stimulate an increase in funds available and actively devoted to philanthropy. We have presented evidence showing that charitable needs will continue to rise rapidly in the 1970s, and we have stated the reasons why private philanthropy should be encouraged to help meet these needs.

Second: We want to make sure that foundation funds are devoted to legitimate charitable purposes, and not diverted either to private gain or to activities that are not truly charitable.

Third: We want not only to increase but to diversify and improve philanthropic efforts in the private sector in such a way that more charitable organizations and foundations can make unique contributions to the general welfare. If foundations are to be way-showing institutions of social modernization and orderly change, they can be that only if they build for themselves a far broader base of public understanding and enthusiastic loyalty.

These aims, to repeat, are clear. There are, however, different schools of thought about the best means to attain them. Some would rely on voluntary self-regulation by the foundations themselves. Others would rely heavily if not entirely on legislative solutions and government supervision and regulation. The commission rejects an "all of one thing or all of another" sort of approach. We favor a "mixed economy" approach, combining government supervision in some matters with private self-direction in others.

We have been guided in our recommendations by the following principles:

1. We do not favor voluntary self-control in the specific financial realms in which foundations can abuse tax-exempt privileges either by using their resources for private gain or for purposes that are not charitable. In these areas, the temptations to abuse are too great—and the detection of possible offenders is too difficult—to make voluntary self-control a reliable deterrent to wrongful conduct. The Treasury report of 1965 which spotlighted some of the different types of financial abuse by foundations did not lead to any significant movement for self-reform among foundations. It is now too late to wait for such a movement to develop.

The commission therefore, strongly favors government supervision of the foundations in those financial areas in which the creators of foundations can take advantage of their fellow citizens and can corrupt the integrity of the tax system.

2. We believe that full and early disclosure and public reporting of foundation activities not only serves the public right to know but can serve as one of the most powerful ways of attaining fuller accountability to the public. "Sunlight," as Justice Brandeis said, "can be the most powerful disinfectant." Government regulation can provide only a partial answer; the foundations themselves must realize that an informed and understanding public is essential.

3. We believe that the society's critical needs for tax-supported projects require that the billions of dollars of existing foundation funds which reflect significant tax deductions already granted must make their full contribution to society. Again, government regulation is a necessary but not a sufficient answer. The foundations must recognize their deep responsibility to invest these precious assets productively.

Granted this, we believe that it is also essential to increase the flow of new funds into foundations. The birth of new foundations is needed to deal with growing problems and—equally important—to provide added diversity and fresh insights. Variety is one of the surest ways of dealing with the twin concerns of foundation passivity and power.

4. We recognize that government regulation of foundation grant programs can become punitive and a form of indirect control over all aspects of foundation life. Since the freedom of decision the foundations have had in the nature of the grants they make is one of the great sources

of their utility, the commission looks first to the foundations themselves to make a distinctive and responsible use of their freedom. This implies that foundation trustees and managers must become deeply involved in the work of their respective foundation—to help devise meaningful programs and to help make sure that funds are competently and conscientiously applied to the ends for which they were granted. The commission, in a word, urgently recommends that the foundations cleanse and invigorate themselves from within in programmatic matters.

From these general considerations, the commission has a number of specific recommendations to make, beginning with those addressed to foundations and continuing with those addressed to government.

15

Recommendations to Foundations

I. A BETTER DEFINITION OF THE FOUNDATION'S MISSION

The commission received suggestions that it define the highest priority areas of our society that should command foundation support. It was meant by this that we should formulate a hierarchy of programs—civil rights, the fight against pollution, education, and the like—all weighted in the order of their importance as subjects to which the foundations should address their own efforts. The suggestion was rejected, and for a reason aside from the fact that the commission did not conceive itself to be God's Vice-regent on Earth. It was rejected on the ground that the whole idea of a private sector for philanthropy rests on the interest the public has in private freedom and individual choice. In the case of the foundations, they would probably do better work if they defined their own missions by carefully considering what they can do better than any other institution.

Inevitably, in considering the potential missions of foundations, one cannot ignore the burgeoning and often dominant role of the government in the traditional areas of philanthropy. Those who speak fearfully of the "enormous" size and power of foundations should be reminded that all foundation grants total about three-quarters of 1 percent of the federal budget, and even in education, where the largest single amount of foundation grants go, they account for less than 1 percent of total expenditures.

Further, if foundation efforts are not qualitatively different from government programs, then we believe foundations will have lost one of the most powerful reasons for their existence. If foundations and individuals do not vigorously support heterodoxy, who will? If private-sector philanthropy will not support worthwhile activities that are neither self-supporting in the market place nor have sufficient political support for public funding, who will?

We believe that foundations can in fact do a number of things differently and better than government agencies.

1. *Experimentation.* It is much easier for a foundation to sponsor certain kinds of controversial experiments than it is for a government agency. The political framework in which government programs are conceived and executed makes it extremely difficult to tolerate failures. It also makes it very difficult to operate on a small scale. Political administrations are often not around long enough to wait the five or more years it may take to know whether a given approach works. This introduces a twofold handicap. An experimental program which looks as though it may produce negative results may well be killed too early. A program which looks promising may well be given broad application prematurely. The political pressure from hundreds of congressional districts to get in early accelerates this unfortunate tendency.

Many knowledgeable observers suggest, for example, that one of the major problems with such antipoverty programs as Community Action has been that experimental approaches were proliferated too widely too early, with inadequate evaluation of results.

Foundations are, in the main, freer than government to experiment. It is generally possible for a foundation to sponsor a project in one community without being exposed to irresistable pressure to duplicate the experiment in every other community. Similarly, the flexibility of a foundation as a grant-making institution makes it possible to write off an unsuccessful experiment without the dangers this would involve in a government program.

We remind foundations that studies, however helpful in defining problems, are not a substitute for experimentation and action in solving them. We also remind foundations there are very few, if any, other institutions in our society better able to support innovation in the social sector.

2. *Work in Sensitive or Controversial Areas.* Government programs are difficult to launch in some sensitive areas. A vocal minority can often veto a government program. The fact that foundations are relatively freer from public pressure allows them to be considerably more venturesome. Foundation work in the birth control field provides an excellent example of this. A growing national acceptance fostered by work supported by foundation funds made it much easier for government to enter this field. More recently—so we have been told—government has

had difficulty supporting research on the effects of various drugs such as marijuana, presumably because it was considered politically dangerous and lacked the sanction of sufficient public support.

Another example would be the national assessment program in education. There is hostility to federal intervention in the operation of local schools. This made it impossible for the federal government to undertake a program which would involve the measurement of the levels of achievement in different school systems throughout the country. It was possible, however, to launch such a program with foundation funds. Once the program was underway the government could get aboard.

Foundation-financed programs may often be acceptable where government-financed programs would be unwelcome. For example, studies of student unrest in the colleges can more readily be conducted with foundation funds than with government money. Similarly, valuable international programs in some nonaligned countries may well have an acceptance if foundations were behind them that would be rejected if the United States government were the sponsor.

3. *Specialized Programs.* The need for government action to gain broad support often makes it difficult for the government to proceed in areas where only a minority has a significant interest. Our earlier discussion of the growth of educational television may illustrate this pattern. In the beginning days of educational television it is unlikely that much enthusiasm could have been generated for government support. Nurtured almost exclusively by Ford Foundation support, then studied by the Carnegie commission under the leadership of James Killian, the concept of public educational television developed in the form of the Corporation for Public Broadcasting.

4. *Filling Niches and Setting New Standards of Excellence.* Government programs rarely cover a field uniformly. Foundations can generally fill niches where special needs or opportunities exist. Thus, for example, while much government money is available for manpower training, foundation funds were able to recognize the need for programs designed to upgrade existing employees at a time when government funding was directed primarily to low-level-entry jobs. We have discussed areas of science and medicine in which inadequate support left a vacuum.

A related point is the understandable, almost inevitable pressure for even-handedness of government support. Foundation support of exceptional talent, with unusual and perhaps more costly approaches, can often set new standards of excellence that later become the standards of broader public programs.

5. *Speed and Flexibility.* The greater flexibility of foundation procedures makes it possible to respond much more quickly to unusual situations than government agencies can. The safeguarding of recreational lands for national parks is an excellent example.

Evaluation of Institutions and Programs—Government and Nongovernment

There is a variety of different kinds of polarization in this country on major public-policy issues. On complex issues, the bureaucrat and the technical administrator in and out of government can sometimes not resist the temptation to engage in a kind of technical sophistry that can confuse and overwhelm the public. Indeed, this tendency often complicates simple policy issues that could be grasped by an intelligent and reasonably informed citizen. For example, students of the national defense decision-making process are agreed that some searching questions of fundamental importance to our country's basic strategic policies are not asked, largely because of the maze of technical verbiage that obscures the central issues.

We see searching questions being asked about some of our most sacred establishments. Who appoints the establishment, we are asked? Who evaluates it? A free press is one such mechanism, but it is probably fair to say that the press is much more likely to focus its energies on incidents of abuse or scandal which can readily be publicized than on complex issues where original and refined research is needed. Traditionally, government agencies are more concerned with selling and implementing their programs than with critical and independent appraisals of their existing activities. Congress has all too limited research staffs. Nor is this limitation restricted to the federal level. Close observers find our local governments inadequately financed, fractionated, and virtually ungovernable.

For these reasons, we believe that foundation sponsorship of impartial appraisals of government policies and programs could become one of their unique contributions to the cause of constructive change. Such appraisals require great sensitivity to the emerging public-policy issues that deserve scrutiny, and an ability to identify and support the best people in the country to perform the requisite research.

Such appraisals also take money, and foundations are among the very few institutions with sufficient pools of capital to finance the studies. This commission, in focusing its fund-raising efforts on nonfoundation sources, has learned firsthand and not without anguish how hard it is to find any such support.

Institutions other than the federal government need constructive, independent appraisal. We all have firsthand knowledge of all kinds of American institutions that are operating with outdated value systems and approaches, without the discipline of the market place or external forces to provide the stimulus of self-correction. For example, business, of all institutions, was one in which success could be measured in a straight-forward way—as absolute as the members in the profit and loss column. The discipline of the market place, some said, was nearly absolute. Productivity and progress were linked as in a chain; today, the young observe they can be the two edges of a sword. Technological "progress," they find, assumes some of the dual character of Dr. Jekyl and Mr. Hyde. Society, it seems, must prepare its own profit-and-loss statement, viewed in terms of its larger effects on society.

It is worth recalling that some of the most notable achievements of foundations involve the study of aspects of American society, including the Flexner report on medical education, Gunnar Myrdal's *An American Dilemma*, and more recent work, especially in the field of education. We would suggest that there are a host of American institutions and problems that could benefit immensely from the corrective insights of outside evaluations.

The importance of this evaluating function is indicated by the widespread feeling of young people—moderates as well as revolutionaries—that the Establishment is not listening to them and is unwilling to reconsider timeworn patterns. Many young people believe that there is a settled policy on the part of institutions to prevent reevaluation of their traditional ways, whether dealing with problems of national defense, of poverty, of social structure, of environmental pollution, or of race relations. Even though foundations are frequently regarded as part of the Establishment, they have the opportunity to rise to this challenge offered by the young.

The task of reevaluating and revitalizing our institutions cannot be given too high a priority. We therefore recommend that foundations first explore the American scene in their own way. When they discover important American institutions and programs—government and non-government alike—that might benefit from impartial and constructive scrutiny, they should consider whether their sponsorship of such appraisals would be in public interest.

We also recommend that foundations explore ways in which periodic appraisals of their own performance might best be conducted and shared with the American public. The foundations, with no electorate or competitors and no need to raise money, are subjected to fewer pressures to measure and improve their performance than are most other institutions. Precisely for this reason, some periodic review of foundation performance would help reduce some of the mystery from foundation activities and convey a sensitivity to the public that has not always been present.

Finally, we would encourage other agents of responsible criticism—scholars, writers and the media—to take advantage of new opportunities brought about by wider disclosure of foundation activities to bring their own critical scrutiny of foundations to the attention of foundations and public alike.

II. IMPROVED PLANNING AND STAFF RESOURCES

The definition of the projects unlikely to be performed as well by the government or others, the selection of the best people to do them, and the evaluation of results require a wide-angle lens and a sense of commitment if foundations are to make distinctive contributions. To the same end, planning and staff resources are required. Many foundations which stand in great need of some expert help are probably too small to utilize full-time staff. For example, the vast majority of foundations make annual grants of an amount that is too small to justify a single, full-time administrator. This perhaps helps explain why so many of the significant grants are made by the few major foundations.

We would urge the leaders of the foundation field to stimulate a variety of approaches to bring more expertness and a sense of mission to foundation programs. The following are only a few suggestions:

1. Encourage foundations in appropriate cases to consider merging into existing community foundations, which often have expert staff.

2. Encourage small and medium-size foundations to pool their resources to share the services of a professional administrator.

3. Form associations of foundations interested in a similar program area and jointly hire an expert in this area.

4. Explore the part-time hiring of experts from universities and other institutions as consultants.

5. Provide much broadened consulting help to small foundations to assist them in defining and carrying out their programs.

6. Explore ways to increase the *geographic diversity* of foundations and in particular the strength of foundations as a central force in energizing local initiatives in urban areas that need but do not have effective foundations. For example, both the foundation field and society might

benefit from consortia of foundations in major urban areas and other regions. They could use common program planning resources and jointly fund those projects which they individually want to support.

We would hope that a few of the large foundations might consider taking the initiative for developing strong foundations in key geographic areas, using either incentive grants or, if necessary, outright grants. We recognize the force of the reasons why so many large foundations clustered in New York. Yet we do not believe the highest interests of the public or of the foundations themselves are well served by this concentration. We suggest that new foundations think twice before deciding to locate in New York. We suggest that some existing foundations might even wish to consider relocating.

In suggesting that more foundations develop expertise and a sense of mission, we do not suggest that the only worthwhile foundation is the innovative one. In much the same way, it is not true that the only good foundation programs are new programs. Sustaining the good works of existing institutions is certainly no less essential than stimulating new programs and new institutions. A delicate balance between stability and change is required.

As vital as innovation is, we should not be unaware of the dangers of its overemphasis. Innovation should not become an end in itself, without adequate attention to whether yesterday's innovation has been assimilated. The search for innovation should not compel grant applicants to design "innovative" programs to which they are not committed or force them to dress an old program in new clothes. Our plea is not for innovation for its own sake, but for foundations to think through their own "comparative advantage," their own areas of concentration and special competence. We only urge that foundations bring fresh relevance to the role of pluralism in a modern, responsive society. In so doing, foundations can make a meaningful contribution to rebuilding the society's faith in independent action.

III. MORE THOUGHTFUL AND CONSISTENT MONITORING AND EVALUATION OF FOUNDATION GRANTS.

Our research makes clear that the follow-up and grant-monitoring procedures of many foundations are simply not adequate. We recognize, of course, that foundations should not and cannot become guarantors against all possible abuses by their grantees. Foundations should, however, be able to demonstrate that they took reasonable steps to avoid fiscal irregularities and should be able to provide reasonable assurance that philanthropic purposes are being served. Such steps should, of course, depend on the subject matter of the grant and the character of the recipient. Thus, a research program dealing with the biochemical properties of cell membranes requires different foundation monitoring procedures from a grant to a street gang in Chicago or a voter registration drive.

For example, the system adopted by the Southern Regional Council to prevent partisan misuse of funds granted for its voter education projects seems to this commission to maintain effective follow-up with organizations receiving grants. A major purpose of the council's undertaking was research into the causes of the low participation, particularly by Negroes, in the political processes in the South. Direct funding of voter registration drives provides a means of determining difficulties voters might encounter. An average grant runs between one and two thousand dollars. A letter to the local organization receiving the grant specifically warns that the money is not to be used in any political campaign or for other partisan use. Both an organizational and a status report is required each week. A field director makes both announced and unannounced visits to the project. Money is advanced on a cash-draw basis, which provides a means of severing support if partisan activity or other irregularity is discovered. These safeguards seem to have been effective in keeping complaints to a minimum.

We believe that it is particularly appropriate for foundations to monitor closely grants which involve experimentation or have important political implications, where we have observed some looseness in foundation practice. The widespread and damaging legislative and public repercussions of a mere handful of small grants on the borderline between politics (or political figures) and charity should remind foundations of both the dangers of and the need for great sensitivity in making and supervising such grants.

Although some foundation "experimentation"—like government "pilot programs"—may only be a euphemism for a limited financial commitment, often a foundation is funding a new approach which, if successful, could be useful elsewhere. (But here again the foundation must take care not to supervise a project so extensively that it stifles the experimentation which was the raison d'être.)

There is much more at stake in foundation surveillance of grants than the mere avoidance of abuse or use of funds for nonphilanthropic purposes. Particularly where experimentation is involved, we cannot forget that the fundamental purpose of the grant may be for society to learn from the experiment. Thus, it is important that the knowledge gained by the grantee—and in some instances knowledge about the new form of organization which *is* the grantee—be made available to the foundation and, through the foundation's own resources or other channels, to those active in the particular field. We believe there is too little of this dissemination.

Also, if society is to learn its full lesson from an important experiment, an in-depth independent evaluation of the results should often be an important part of the total grant program. Normally it should be made by persons other than those who approved the original grant. We have already documented some evidence that indicates that many foundations have not been deeply involved or perhaps even concerned about the results of these kinds of grants—being perhaps more interested in the original conception than the final result.

We also believe that many foundations would benefit by a periodic appraisal of the *process* by which grants are made—the choice of program areas, the choice of institutions and persons, the quality of follow-on effort. In this connection, many universities have found the visiting committee helpful. An honest analysis of successes and failures should serve to improve the foundations' grant-making process in the future. Finally, we would urge that objective processes by which grants are made not only be established and assessed but be communicated fully to all who seek foundation support.

IV. BETTER COMMUNICATIONS

This commission has recommended a legislative requirement of public disclosure of grants, expenditures, and investments and an annual national report that summarizes these individual foundation reports and the results of a much expanded program of Internal Revenue Service audits. These public reports are one very necessary step in helping to overcome suspicion and ignorance about what foundations do with their funds. Yet, if foundations are to have the confidence and independence they will need to tackle some of the major unmet needs of our society, they will need a much broader constituency.

Foundations have been easy and highly vulnerable political targets. It seems to this commission that foundations must somehow build a committed constituency. It is not a matter of convenience, or pleasant relations, or a better "image" for its own sake. Rather, we believe a committed constituency is a necessary prerequisite to the full realization of what foundations can do. Disclosure and audits will not be sufficient to develop a constituency ready to support the institution of foundations in times of real need. Trust and understanding and enthusiasm are needed, and these are rarely the product of statistical reports.

Up to now, it is fair to say that foundations have been reticent. However sincere their rationale for this reticency may be, it has led to an image of disdain and arrogance, and perhaps even reinforced the impression of foundations as "tax dodges" with something to hide. We think it is reasonable that every foundation should have some kind of annual report, even if only a few mimeographed pages. The commission has been deeply dismayed that only a tiny fraction of foundations—probably less than 1 percent—have voluntarily issued any report. Annual reports are published by a variety of profit and nonprofit institutions and fill a purpose above and beyond communication with the outside world. A report on its stewardship encourages an institution to look inward, to reassess goals and methods, and to articulate new missions. Properly done, these reports can convey a qualitative sense of what the foundation is trying to do, clarify the "mysterious" process by which foundations make their decisions. It could help clear the air of suspicions about hidden power in high places, self-serving financial transactions, and the like.

This commission also suggests that foundations explore the potential of a more candid program of communications. A reading of a sample of foundation annual reports suggests that foundations have not overcome the all too human tendency to dwell on successes and to ignore failures. It is, of course, entirely possible that the number of failures has been relatively small simply because most foundation grants seem to involve very low orders of risk. Nonetheless, the reluctance to discuss failures is inappropriate for at least two reasons. First, "failures" in an experimental institution are also learning experiences and should be shared. Second, the candid discussion of disappointments would serve to reduce the impression of assumed omniscience for which foundations are often criticized.

Earlier we discussed our view that too few foundations spend time and resources evaluating their grants or their overall programs. While we are aware that public criticisms of individual grantees might have unfortunate side effects, we would suggest this is not nearly as true of overall evaluations of a foundation's programs. The findings of such evaluations would often be useful in a foundation report of its activities.

The committed constituencies that foundations need will likely come, not from communication to the general public, but from a variety of separate publics whose primary interest is in their own specific fields of work. Difficult though it may be, these publics must be made aware of grants of genuine significance in their fields. Building awareness, understanding, and acceptance of experimental work is not merely communication for its own sake—it is at the heart of the process by which an invention or idea is actually multiplied into widespread use by the society. The dissemination of information about the innovation and the effort to explain it and stimulate field trials are less exciting than the original conception but are absolutely essential in the innovation process. By way of illustration, agricultural innovation is considered one of the outstanding examples of translating research into widely applied practice. The remarkable success of American agriculture is due not so much to superior invention as to superior dissemination and implementation of research results, largely through the work of field agents who showed individual farmers what new inventions and practices could mean to them.

Foundations are hardly alone among our intellectual institutions in neglecting the difficult and costly task of rigorous evaluation and dissemination of the results of experimental work. More attention devoted to these aspects of research will increase the effectiveness of some foundation grants—and, incidentally, minimize the unconscious duplication that occurs from time to time in the foundation field. It will also inform interested groups, in a natural, educational way, of the work of foundations.

Dissemination can often be handled most efficiently and effectively if it is organized to cover the foundation movement as a whole rather than by and for individual foundations. For example, the virtue of *digests* of key developments has been shown in many fields. We believe many interested publics—legislators, administrators, scholars, and others—would benefit from such reviews of foundation-supported programs. A widely distributed magazine on foundations describing how they work and what they are doing, awards for outstanding grants in various fields, and so forth might also serve to fill this communications void.[1] Finally, the local and regional character of the grants of most foundations suggests that the public and interested recipients would benefit from more "regionalizing" information on foundations.

This commission recommends to foundations that they shed some of

1. We think it is significant that television, which has produced hundreds of social documentaries, has not (to our knowledge) produced a single analysis of foundations and their work.

their reluctance to communicate and increase the priority of building greater understanding, trust, and enthusiasm for them and their work. Both the foundations and society could benefit from a more intensive program of communication and education.

V. Improved Investment Performance of Foundation Assets

While we do not have all the evidence we would like concerning investment performance of foundations, everything we have seen points strongly in the direction of a need for great improvement.

With the requirement of a high payout, new legislative disincentives to creating foundations, and the growing financial crises of charitable organizations, there are a large number of converging reasons for foundations to improve their investment performance and improve it significantly. This is not a trifling matter. An improvement of 2 percent in foundation investment returns would make available more than half a billion additional dollars each year for philanthropic purposes. While this commission strongly reaffirms the principle of individual choice of philanthropic programs, we also believe that the privilege of an immediate charitable tax deduction for a long-term capital investment in philanthropy carries with it the responsibility to invest that capital productively.

While the payout requirement in the new law will obviously serve as a goad, the solution to this problem depends on the attitudes and interests of the foundation's managers and trustees. They must recognize the importance of their responsibility to invest the foundation's assets productively. Too often this responsibility has had a low priority. Also, there is the possible impact of over-restrictive interpretations of the legal dangers of jeopardizing investments (the prudent man rule).

Foundations should do what many others with pools of capital, such as profit sharing trusts, retirement pension funds, and educational endowment funds, have done and in rapidly increasing numbers are doing—seek out the best advisory help they can find. The public interest would be well served by a vigorous exploration of investment alternatives and the improved investment performance we are confident would result.

VI. More Diversity in Foundation Boards of Trustees

We reported earlier that the boards of trustees of America's largest foundations, distinguished though they are, represent a very narrow range of backgrounds. The boards can accurately be characterized as consisting largely of businessmen, lawyers, or bankers, educated in eastern Ivy League schools, white, and Protestant. There is scant representation of the young, women, blacks, Catholics, and Jews and none from organized labor. It is fair to say that these boards lack diversity.

We suggest that added diversity could have two advantages. It might provide added perspective to the insights of the boards. This would be valuable in view of the enormous range of new problems our society faces. Also, it might allay some of the public suspicion of privatism and disdain. There is an obvious contradiction in claiming to represent the interests of pluralism in our society and yet practicing monism in the selection of trustees. We have great respect for the abilities of the best trustees. Added diversity need not come at the cost of quality.

We also recommend that foundations seriously explore steps to improve the extent and quality of the involvement of trustees in the direction foundations are taking. We applaud the deep involvement of able trustees in a few cases but are dismayed by our finding that foundation trustees much more often appear to play a limited, haphazard role. Deeper involvement might have prevented a few of the spectacular and certainly harmful cases of foundation abuse and bad judgment. One of the problems is lack of knowledge of, and ambiguity about, the appropriate responsibilities and roles of foundation trustees. We believe a foundation effort to define a code of responsibilities and standards for trustees, widely disseminated to members of foundation boards, would improve the contribution of trustees.

Various proposals have been made that foundation boards be required to include one or more trustees unrelated to the donor. Some suggest that there be a majority of independent trustees, at least after a given period in the foundation's history. We do not believe that this is an appropriate matter for legislation; the effect of donor control cannot be assessed on an overall basis. Some of the most productive foundations have been controlled by a single family; some of the least imaginative have had broadly based boards. There is no particular abuse associated with donor domination of the board, provided that self-dealing is stringently regulated. It is obvious also that an "outside" trustee could easily be selected who would behave very much like an "inside" trustee.

Although we oppose a legislative requirement, we do consider it appropriate for foundations themselves to consider seriously the advantages of having independent trustees. The need for independent trustees will vary depending on the nature of the foundation and its program. For a small family foundation which limits its grants to local qualified charitable institutions, an "outside" trustee would probably be an artificial formality. The addition of some independent trustees becomes more desirable the more ambitious or controversial a foundation's program becomes. The considerations in this connection are not very different from the argument about "outside directors" on corporate boards.

A related problem is representation of foundation recipients on the board of the foundation. Such board membership may result in an appearance of conflict of interest. Often the member's voluntary abstention from participation in board consideration of grant requests by his organization, and independent appraisals of such grants, will be sufficient solutions to this problem. A blanket rule seems inappropriate, since the individual associated with the recipient may be exceptionally capable and contribute valuably to the board's deliberations. Also, a blanket rule might eliminate such crucial fields as higher education and civil rights from representation on the board since the most worthwhile and attractive board representatives could often be from one of the most likely and attractive recipient organizations in this field.

VII. ORGANIZATION FOR THE FOUNDATION FIELD

One of the lessons of the year 1969 is that foundations have only limited popular acceptance and even less popular support. Because we believe that the most distinctive and useful role of foundations will require them to be active in controversial areas, improved public support is essential to their effectiveness.

We do not believe that steps taken by foundations individually can do enough to improve their public acceptance. We suspect that only organized action on behalf of foundations as a group can accomplish what is needed.

We now propose a new organization devoted to improved performance and broadened public understanding of foundations. It should have a name that makes it clear to everyone that the focus of its work is American foundations.

We propose this organization for a number of reasons. It is neither fitting nor proper for individual foundations to trumpet their own virtues beyond the issuance of a descriptive annual report. In the case of individual foundations, as in the case of individuals, virtue speaks best through the medium of the deed. There is something timelessly offensive about the Pharisee praying loudly in the corner to call attention to his holiness. Moreover, most individual foundations are much too small to engage in any major effort at improving public understanding. While a few large foundations are in a position to do so, it is questionable how effectively they would represent the whole foundation field.

The effort to achieve improved public acceptance of the foundations would be useless if it became a conventional drill in what is known as "public relations." The best mode of public persuasion requires an improved standard of performance for the whole foundation field, including more cooperative efforts among them. It requires more effective working relationships with a variety of specialized constituencies, and a much more open relationship with government agencies. In all these areas, the results which can be achieved by a go-it-alone approach on the part of individual foundations seem quite limited.

The experience of the past year indicates that the existing organizational efforts within the foundation field are on too limited a scale to accomplish the job of achieving better public acceptance. We therefore recommend a reexamination of the existing organizational structure with the objective of establishing a much stronger and more broadly based organization. While an effective organization can only be established through the initiative of its constituents, we hope that a few observations regarding the scope and function of the organization may be useful.

Scope and Function. The organization should provide a vehicle for the top people in the foundation field, enabling them to work together on the major problems affecting philanthropy. It should provide a forum for dealing with the internal problems of the foundation field— the problems of how they can achieve their fullest potential of usefulness to our society.

A strong and independent organization should also be able to act as a two-way interpreter of government agencies to the foundations, and of foundations to government agencies. There is ample precedent for such a role in a variety of other fields. The foundation field would seem particularly suitable for such an intermediary function because it is made up of a small number of large entities which have some political vulnerability, and a "silent majority" of small units which are too small to be effective on their own. If experience in other fields is any guide, a government agency is more likely to carry on informal exchanges with an independent organization than it would with representatives of particular foundations.

The need for improved understanding and relations between the foundations and government is not limited to regulatory bodies. In many areas of foundation grant-making activity, government agencies are also active, generally on a considerably larger scale. In order to assure that foundation programs are productive, cooperation with interested government agencies is desirable. The increased complexity which the Tax Reform Act has introduced into the relationships between foundations and government agencies enhances the usefulness of the proposed organization in improving these relationships.

The need for cooperation is not confined to the federal government but exists also on the state and local level.

Another important task is the development of effective relations with a variety of private organizations with which foundations deal. In each of the major areas of foundation activity—education, health, civil rights, the environment—there are professional, technical, and other bodies which have an interest in foundation activities. An organization working for the whole foundation field could do a more effective job of establishing relations with such organizations than individual foundations can. Such relations are of considerable importance both to effective grant making and to the public acceptance of foundations, because support for foundations is more likely to come from the specialized "publics," on which foundations have a direct impact, rather than from the general public which foundations affect only indirectly and intermittently.

The effectiveness of foundation work would undoubtedly be enhanced if there were more pooling of foundation resources and other forms of cooperation on projects of common interest. There are no legal objections to such cooperation, and we know of no legitimate policy reasons why there should not be increased cooperation. We believe the proposed organization can fulfill an important need in encouraging, and perhaps even sponsoring, a variety of formal and informal cooperative projects. At the present time there does not appear to be any effective mechanism for this.

The organization should also deal with the large range of internal problems in the foundation field that have already been mentioned— the need for mutual consultation, the need for local cooperative efforts, studies of the role and responsibilities of foundation staffs and trustees, training of foundation staffs, reviews of alternative planning and grant-making processes, studies of investment performance and methods of improving it, grant supervision and evaluation techniques, and the like—all with the object of raising the standards of foundation performance. It should enable foundations to benefit from common experience both in grant-making activities and in administrative matters. However, we question the desirability of taking on the job of foundation "self-regulation." Regulation in the sense of policing the foundations is a job better left to the government for a number of persuasive reasons. Furthermore, the attempt to carry out a regulatory role could well reduce the support from within the foundation field which the organization needs.

The proposed organization can help to fill the "information gap" regarding foundations on which we have commented elsewhere in this report. The organization could undertake to have research work done on a range of public policy issues affecting the foundation field. Many of these have been identified in our report. The information gap is serious enough to require a significant expansion of existing research activities, most notable among which are the studies of foundations and philanthropy conducted by the Russell Sage Foundation. We would also urge broad dissemination of this information. This would require a major expansion of the excellent but limited activities of the Foundation Center. We have commented earlier in this chapter on the need for better communication, and it is clear that subtle and complex issues are involved. The program to improve public understanding of foundations will require much deeper and original thought than that which goes into the typical trade association publicity program.

Structure and Organization. A few observations with respect to structure and organization may also be pertinent.

1. While we believe that both the Foundation Center and the Council on Foundations[2] have been and are doing valuable work, it seems evident that the scope we have outlined for the proposed organization is much broader and more ambitious than that of the existing organizations. We would hope that the talents and resources of both the council and the center can be effectively utilized in building a stronger organization. Depending on the scope of the organization, it might also benefit from the close consultation with the National Council on Philanthropy.

2. The organization should be established in a manner which makes it likely that the largest possible number of foundations will participate in its activities. Foundations are set up to help all of society. It would be wrong for the proposed organization to appear as if it were a private

2. The Council on Foundations is an organization that includes approximately 443 foundations.

club for the benefit of a membership restricted to the large New York–based foundations. Every effort should be made to secure participation by all types of foundations, including community and company foundations, foundations from all parts of the country, and of all sizes.

3. We believe it would not be desirable to include in the membership of the organization other philanthropic organizations such as united funds, or recipient organizations such as universities or museums. The foundation field itself is quite diverse, and the inclusion of other types of organizations would probably result in a diversity of interests so great that cohesive action would be difficult. For certain projects, there may be advantages in the form of greater independence and objectivity and lessened parochialism in more broadly based participation. The organization's information gathering activities, for example, would probably benefit from wide participation by philanthropic organizations.

4. If foundations decided they genuinely wanted outside perspective, the board of the organization itself could usefully include outstanding individuals independent of foundations. These outside board members would give the organization the benefit of an objective and wide-ranging perspective in its deliberations.

5. Wherever the organization is based, it should have as a high priority task the building of much stronger *local* and *regional* organizations to provide the nucleus of local coalitions and cooperative efforts at the local level. To identify this as a high-priority task is not to downgrade the importance of relations with the national government. It is to develop the kind of local counterweight to any tendency to overemphasize federal agencies or exclusively national constituencies.

6. The organization will require forceful and independent leadership. Ideally, it should obtain as its head a person with sufficient public stature to have the respect of the foundation world, of the government officials concerned with philanthropy, and of the various academic professional and other constituencies with which foundations deal. Not the least of the qualities to be looked for in the head of the proposed organization is a person with the organizational and leadership abilities to set up strong and energetic local chapters so as to bring local initiatives more readily to bear on local problems.

We believe it is fair to say that the 1969 legislation leaves foundations the least favored sector of the charitable world. Lady Bountiful has never been a beloved figure; nonetheless, we believe that the foundations' tardy and inadequate response to earlier critiques—such as the Treasury report of 1965—contributed to the unfriendly environment in 1969.

Looking ahead, we believe the foundation world could become the recipient of additional and even more restrictive public and legislative disfavor at both the national and the state level if it does not move with sensitivity and vigor to anticipate abuses and problems that remain, improve its future performance, and broaden the public's understanding of that effort.

16

Recommendations to Government I: Tax Policy and Tax Administration

We recommend that this administration give a high priority to the development of new and better tax incentives for charitable giving.

1. Such new tax incentives should: produce significantly more money for charity—in the range of several billion dollars more annually. The charitable crisis of the 1970s requires more funds in substantial amounts, and the private sector should be encouraged to give more, both to sustain the operation of valued existing charitable institutions and to support crucial new projects and new institutions.

2. Incentives should be compatible with tax equity and prevention of tax avoidance.

3. They should spread the giving among more people, *democratize* philanthropy more, and be less "elitist." It is clear that only the very wealthy can make the really large gifts, and if we are to increase the total flow of funds, they too must be further encouraged. Yet we believe a better tax incentive system would give *more* people an incentive to participate in philanthropic giving and hence to participate in the decisions on how to allocate these funds.

4. Incentives should minimize federal revenue cost, consistent with the preceding guidelines.

5. They should preserve the freedom and diversity of the private sector's charitable efforts and stimulate the will of people to venture new and better approaches to social problems.

No new incentives can be wisely framed until a knowledge gap is first filled. Data in the public realm bearing on the structure of charitable giving and the effects of various incentives are either crude or out of date. Information about the equation between revenue costs and charitable giving now available only in raw form should be refined and made public.

Every expert the commission has talked to agrees that current incentives have serious defects. They also agree on the complexity of the task of designing new approaches to the desired ends. The design of new incentives involves competing policy considerations and requires expertise, imagination, and judgment. There are no "quick and easy" solutions.

We therefore recommend that the present administration assemble a group of the best informed experts in the country and charge them with the responsibility of proposing new tax incentives for philanthropic giving. These proposals should be ready for consideration by the Ninety-second Congress, preferably by the fall of 1971.

The design of a new set of tax incentives for charitable giving should be coordinated at high policy levels of the administration. This would include representatives of those agencies of the federal government such as the Department of Health, Education, and Welfare that are broadly concerned with the financial support of educational, scientific, cultural, and social activities, as well as representatives of the Treasury Department. We commend the Nixon administration for stressing the importance of voluntarism in America, of which philanthropy is, of course, one important part. We hope that the cabinet-level group that has been established to review volunteer and private efforts along social and economic fronts will thoughtfully consider and relate philanthropic tax incentive policy to the total programs and policies of the administration.

We believe that the objective of tax incentives to induce more charitable giving must be coupled with better regulation, resulting in less abuse of these incentives. The American public must have genuine confidence, that charitable giving indeed goes to charity. Without such confidence it will not support or encourage the agencies that will be needed to deal with the added problems of the seventies and to preserve one of America's distinctive, dynamic, and most humane trademarks—the dual partnership of public and private resources.

17

Recommendations to Government II: Regulation of Foundations— Payout, Reporting, and Administrative Expenditures

The commission formulated its own regulatory recommendations while congressional consideration of the Tax Reform Act of 1969 was in process. In some respects our proposals paralleled the legislation that was ultimately enacted. We strongly favored a strict prohibition against self-dealing; limitations on speculative investment, on partisan political expenditures, and on grants to individuals; and an expenditure responsibility provision—all quite similar to those eventually enacted. In some cases, however, we would have preferred a different approach. In two areas covered by the Tax Reform Act of 1969—*payout* and *reporting*—we agree in principle with the new provisions, but believe they require additional refinement. We will deal here with these two matters while reserving for the next chapter three other matters where the commission was in substantial disagreement with the new legislation.

Payout Requirement. This commission recommended to the Senate Finance Committee in October of 1969 that foundations be required to make annual distributions to charity in the range of 6 to 8 percent of their asset market values. The annual total return of a wide variety of balanced investment funds over the previous ten years was about 9 to 10 percent. Allowing for an annual rate of inflation of 2 to 3 percent, we felt that a payout of 6 to 8 percent would permit a reasonably managed foundation to maintain its size in *real* dollars.

We also recommended that the Secretary of the Treasury be authorized to set the payout level in the future, after appropriate hearings, to reflect any significant trends in the overall level of total rate of return of a wide variety of institutional investors—such as would be the case if the trends of 1969 and early 1970 were to continue for any significant period.

We made this payout recommendation because we believe the urgency of philanthropic needs is so great that foundations should not be permitted to increase in size by retaining the return on their assets without making significant distributions for current charitable purposes. The information we obtained on foundation investment performance and distributions to charity convinced us that a prod was needed to bring about substantial improvement in both.

There was agreement in the commission that the payout requirement for foundations should be high enough to insure substantial current charitable distributions and to persuade foundations to invest their funds productively but not so high as to amount to a delayed death sentence. Our criterion for a payout requirement is a percentage which would permit a foundation with average investment performance to maintain its size and stay abreast of changes in the value of the dollar. On this basis, foundations with better-than-average investment performance would grow in real terms, and those with below-average investment performance would see a decline in assets in real terms, though their gross dollar assets might still increase. Obviously, foundations could also still grow in size as a result of new contributions to them.

Selection of an appropriate payout percentage involves a balancing of priorities between the present and the future. Those who view the current problems facing charitable organizations as especially urgent would lean in the direction of a higher annual payout. Those who lean toward the longer-range future might pick a slightly lower number. The commission, for its part, agrees that a significant payout percentage is a central part of the necessary regulation of foundations.

The new legislation requires that a foundation distribute all of its annual net income (excluding long-term capital gains) or a percentage of the value of its assets—whichever is higher. The rate is initially pegged at 6 percent (after a phase-in period for existing foundations) in conformance with a Senate floor amendment which was said to reflect this commission's recommendation. In setting a higher payout figure than that originally proposed in the legislation, Congress was moving in the right direction. Unfortunately, we find the enacted provision deficient in the following respects:

1. We do not believe that foundations should be required to pay out their "income" if it is higher than the required percentage of assets. In measuring a foundation's investment performance, we believe it is inappropriate to distinguish between ordinary income and capital gains income; there are of course no taxes for either type of income for tax-exempt

institutions. We believe the only correct yardstick for measuring investment performance is the *total rate of return*—the measure used by practically all mutual funds, profit sharing funds, pension funds, and other endowments. It includes interest, dividends, realized and unrealized capital gains.

2. One of the purposes of the distribution requirement is to bring about more productive investment of the philanthropic capital held by foundations. The income payout test, however, introduces a new factor into foundation investment decisions which may be at odds with the achievement of this purpose. It makes some forms of investment return more attractive to foundations than others. To maintain maximum flexibility over the amount of their annual expenditures, foundations will be inclined to seek economic return in forms which are not "income" as defined for purposes of the payout. Under the definition in the new law, this means long-term capital gains. Thus, the income test will tend to cause foundations to invest in growth stocks or other appreciating assets in order to receive return in a form which is not "income." Including long-term capital gains as income would simply make foundations more reluctant to sell assets which might have appreciated in value even when proper investment management might make this appropriate.

A distribution requirement based solely on asset size would not produce these distortions. It would put the emphasis where it belongs: on the overall investment performance of the foundation, not on the form of the return it receives.

3. The new law requires the Treasury Department to set the annual payout percentage (the minimum investment return) at a figure which bears the same relationship to 6 percent as future "money rates and investment yields" bear to those in 1969. The Treasury will undoubtedly have some latitude in determining the factors to be included in this formula. Unfortunately, however, the two types of factors to be included—money rates and investment yields—may suggest to some that the figure is intended to place more emphasis on current income return from investments (dividend and interest rates) than on capital appreciation. Because of the abnormally high interest rates in 1969, this interpretation could lead to a reduction in the "minimum investment return" percentage in the future at a time when other measures of investment performance such as unrealized capital gains are increasing. A lowering of interest rates and a decrease in dividends as a percentage of asset values may well accompany a rapidly rising stock market, which could substantially increase the total return on foundation holdings.

We believe that the most appropriate standard for comparison is the investment performance of a variety of types of institutional investors (such as balanced mutual funds, pension trusts, profit sharing plans, and the like) adjusted to recognize the impact of inflation and the need of foundations to maintain an appropriate proportion of their assets in relatively liquid form. We hope that the Secretary of the Treasury will feel free to implement this type of standard in administering the law. If not, we would favor amendment to clarify the basis for adjustment of the payout percentage.

In several other respects—mostly minor—the views of this commission differ from the enacted legislation bearing on payouts. We would prefer a payout based on a two- or three-year moving average of asset values rather than a single year's valuation. This would avoid fluctuations reflecting short-term changes in asset values. A still longer averaging period might be appropriate for new foundations and those receiving substantial new contributions.

In addition, we believe that the Internal Revenue Service should have the discretion to provide extra time to those foundations which have difficulty meeting the payout requirement because divesture or diversification of assets proves especially difficult. The new law provides a gradual phase-in of the payout percentage, which should be sufficient to meet many existing situations of this type. New foundations, however, are not allowed any phase-in period. The law also permits sale of foundation-owned stock in a business back to the donor (or another party related to the foundation), despite the new prohibition on self-dealing, in situations where the stock constitutes prohibited excess business holdings (or would, except for special transition rules for existing holdings). Corporations are specifically permitted to accumulate funds to redeem their existing business holdings of existing foundations without incurring possible accumulated earnings tax liability. Although these provisions are not designed to meet payout problems, it will be of assistance in some cases where diversification is needed to obtain an adequate return.

More flexibility, both in timing and procedures, however, may be needed by some foundations. We believe it should be provided, subject to two requirements. First, the foundation should receive fair market value where it disposes of assets to diversify. To insure this, independent appraisals should be required for sales to related parties under any additional exception to self-dealing rules. Second, where foundations are granted additional time to dispose of assets, they should be required to make up the deficiency in their payouts after the appropriate reinvestments have been made.

Provision of this kind of flexibility probably will require amendment of the law. Foundations themselves must also consider methods by which they can dispose of unproductive assets in an orderly fashion. While the new provision is not altogether clear, the legislative history indicates that qualifying distributions may be made in the form of property, including low-yield assets. Of course, these distributions must be valued fairly. Foundations may also wish to consider the possibility of merger into community foundations or other entities.

In summary of our payout recommendations, the commission believes that foundations represent a huge capital investment in philanthropy, probably somewhere between twenty and thirty billion dollars. This capitalized philanthropy has been jointly funded by the donor and by society through a full and immediate tax deduction. Thus, the public has every reason to be interested in a satisfactory return on the investment, in both the short and the long run.

We have observed a number of foundations which may have lost sight of the fundamental point that the tax deduction for the donors and their own tax-favored status were granted in order to benefit charity. This is reflected in the low payout rate of some foundations and in the pride of others in the growth of market value of assets without reference to their contributions to charity. We believe that a high payout requirement will not only increase short-term payout to charity but will also increase the long-term payout by stimulating better investment return while refocusing the energies of foundations on their primary purpose—the support of charity.[1]

Reporting and Disclosure. The new law requires a revision of the Form 990-A to include a listing of substantial contributors, foundation managers, and highly compensated employees, and the compensation and payments to these persons. This additional information will be included on the copy of the return which is available to the public. The new law also requires foundations to submit an annual report giving substantial information on their activities. Each foundation must make the report available for public inspection at its office and publish a notice in a newspaper of general circulation informing the public of its availability.

Prior to the passage of the act, this commission considered the question of foundation reporting and disclosure, drawing heavily on the work of a

1. One member of the commission disagreed with these payout recommendations. For Mr. Austin's dissenting view, see pp. 158–59.

task force on this subject.[2] The commission's recommendations cover three areas: the development of uniform accounting standards; improved reporting of both financial and program activities, and increased efforts to collect, organize, and disseminate information about foundations. The new law has an impact on the second and third areas, but much more remains to be done.

Uniform Standards of Financial Reporting. We are concerned by the absence of uniform standards for financial reporting by foundations. Financial reports may be used for three purposes: to show the financial position and results of operations of a single foundation standing alone, to compare the results of several foundations, or to compile overall statistical data on foundations. Uniformity of definitions, bases of measurement, and reporting practices is essential in order to permit comparisons between foundations or to compile meaningful statistical information.

A sampling of foundation financial reports by a commission task force revealed many reporting differences. Lack of uniformity can produce material misconceptions as to asset value, annual income, level of grant activity, and administrative costs. The task force noted variations in the basis of accounting (cash versus accrual), in allocation of current contributions, and in the treatment of realized and unrealized capital gains or losses.

Variations in accounting practices also have significant influence on the reporting of income and expense. Existing practices range from recording a "grant" at the time of approval of an area of interest and a general dollar allocation, through the various steps of project development and approval, to the actual payment of grant funds.

The total value of assets owned by foundations collectively is highly relevant to the formulation of public policy. Any payout requirement must rest on a consistent basis for determining both asset values and grant payments.

The variations in foundation accounting detailed in the task force report reflect, in part, the exclusion of nonprofit organizations from the considerable body of opinions issued by the American Institute of Certified Public Accountants and its Accounting Principles Board. In recommending uniform standards of accounting for foundations, we suggest

2. This task force consisted of Morton Moskin, Daniel Robinson, and Carmel P. Ebb. Mr. Moskin is a partner in the law firm of White and Case; Mr. Robinson is a partner in the accounting firm of Peat, Marwick, Mitchell and Co. and is in charge of the firm's institutions and nonprofit organizations; Mrs. Ebb is associate editor of the *Review of Securities Regulation.*

changing their position from one step behind to one step ahead of corporate accounting. We believe that the public trust implicit in the philanthropic commitment justifies the higher standard of responsible accounting.

Experience with uniform accounting standards for educational institutions and for voluntary health and welfare organizations has demonstrated their value to those institutions. Accordingly, we recommend that AICPA establish a research study group, in cooperation with representatives of both large and small foundations and the Internal Revenue Service, to develop and propose uniform standards for accounting and financial reporting of foundation operations.

Improved Reporting of Financial and Program Activities. The new law will substantially increase the amount of information foundations must report. To some extent, the information required for the public report will duplicate that in the Form 990-A, but it will also include additional information. Most notably, it will include an itemized statement of all securities and other assets held by the foundation at the close of the year (showing both book and market value), a statement of the relationship between foundation managers or substantial contributors and any individual recipient of a grant, and a listing of foundation managers who are also substantial contributors or who own a 10 percent or larger interest in a business in which the foundation also owns 10 percent. For our purposes, we will treat the two forms as though they were consolidated, as hopefully they will be, in order to avoid repetition and confusion.

These forms will serve as the basis for federal and many state regulatory programs, as has the existing Form 990-A. Even the present Form 990-A, properly completed, with all its accompanying schedules filled in, elicits a substantial amount of information about a foundation's activities, expenditures, contributors, and beneficiaries. However, 990-A is essentially an attempt to compress into a standard two-page tax form a broad range of inquiries directed to a disparate group of exempt organizations.

The new requirements do not indicate any congressional consideration of the need to eliminate the confusion in the Form 990-A. The additional report, while required only of foundations, will be limited in its usefulness in some important respects. While it is an encouraging step forward, it does not go far enough. Unfortunately, by prescribing with great precision the items to be included, Congress has not provided an impetus for the development of more useful and less confusing reporting forms.

We believe that the Internal Revenue Service must design new and comprehensive reporting forms. If legislative authority to seek additional information is required, it should be granted. The goal should be a single, public report which informs both regulators and the public. While we would not like to see foundations engulfed in paperwork,[3] this report should be sufficiently comprehensive to achieve this goal. This will doubtless require more detailed reporting of investment activities, for example, than is specifically required in the disclosure provisions of the new law, covering not only assets at the end of the year but also transactions during the year.

In the grant-making area, the report should provide a fuller description of grant purposes (perhaps of all grants over a certain amount) than is presently provided on Form 990-A. Procedures for awarding grants, especially to individuals, should be described, as should be the procedures for determining that the funds have been used for grant purposes.

It would be extremely helpful if uniform classification of grants were developed so that the activities of foundations could be readily compiled for statistical purposes. Also, as the public interest in specific kinds of grants warranted it (such as voter registration grants) special categories could be added. The 1969 legislative experience demonstrated to this commission that key policy makers had substantial misconceptions about the pattern of foundation grants.

Dissemination of Information. The new law greatly changes the prior disclosure rules. Before the passage of the new Act, Form 990-A's were ostensibly available from the IRS for inspection. But they have since been collected, along with the returns of all other exempt organizations, in a central depository in Philadelphia. Reproduction of a form costs one dollar per page. The new law will make every foundation's annual report available for inspection at its offices.

Some foundations will probably provide copies to any member of the public who asks for them. Some may use the opportunity to accompany the required report with a narrative statement of the foundations' activities; foundations should be strongly encouraged to do so. This kind of annual report, which only a small number of foundations now issue, could greatly improve public attitudes about foundations as well as sharpen a foundation's own focus on its mission. The sense of privatism

3. For very small foundations, the requirements for legal, accounting, and editorial help in preparation of reports could present some serious practical or cost problems.

which many foundations have displayed serves neither the public interest nor their own. One element underlying the current concern about foundations is a feeling of unease about activities behind the scenes; a suspicion nurtured by the paucity of available information.

Even with annual reporting by foundations, it is important to improve the dissemination of aggregate information. The availability of annual reports at the thirty thousand foundation offices is little improvement over the present system when it comes to making available a convenient compilation of the significant information about foundations as a group.

For some years, the Foundation Center—a nonprofit organization supported by a number of major foundations—has collected and reproduced foundation Form 990-A's and kept them available in its files. The center's files in New York and Washington are open to the public as are the smaller repositories it maintains in six locations throughout the nation. The center also publishes a triennial Foundation Directory. This volume, based on the Form 990-A and a center questionnaire which is circulated in an effort to flesh out the 990-A, contains a classification of foundations by areas of interest and useful descriptive material.

The services of the Foundation Center are of great value. But the 990-A's are basically tax records, and there has been a substantial time lag in their availability. Lack of voluntary cooperation on the part of many foundations has been an added handicap to the work of the center.

A greater effort to assure adequate compilation and distribution of necessary information is needed. Public reporting should recognize there are several publics which should be informed about foundations: the public composed of the legislative and executive policy makers; the publics composed of charitable organizations of various types and scholars in allied fields who should have full information and easier access to foundations; and, finally, the general public.

We recommend that the Internal Revenue Service publish annually a statistical report on foundations and their activities, being careful to distinguish between grant-making foundations and operating foundations.[4] The report should include such items as dollar level of grants, allocation of these grants to various purposes, assets, investment practices and results, administrative expense levels, level of new foundation contributions and formation of new foundations including the form of these

---

4. While we are sensitive to the point that some might interpret a special report on foundations as further evidence of "second-class" status, we believe on balance that the information gap on foundations is sufficiently serious at the present time to warrant such a report.

contributions. This report should include the results of a much expanded audit that would report the level and nature of abuses encountered.

We recommend that methods be explored by which interested members of the general public and of charitable organizations could conveniently locate significant reports of foundation activity, both in their areas of interest and in their geographic areas. These reports should be available in locations throughout the country such as libraries, government offices, and so forth. The economics of this kind of dissemination of information needs of course to be studied. It would seem appropriate to consider a charge by the IRS for these special reports and IRS cooperation with private service organizations which might provide special indices and abstracts as they have done effectively in the fields of law, commerce, science, and government regulation.

Limitation on Administrative Expenditures. The new law permits only reasonable administrative expenditures to be included as qualifying distributions for purposes of the payout requirement. And it limits compensation to foundation managers to "reasonable amounts." Neither of these provisions, however, provides a complete prohibition upon unreasonable administrative expenses.[5] The commission favors a general prohibition on payment of excessive or unnecessary compensation, consultant fees, or other administrative expenditures. Such a prohibition would be comparable with the limitation to "ordinary and necessary" amounts of business-expense deductions by taxpaying entities.

Total expenditures for administrative costs should bear some relationship to the amount of funds being expended for charitable purposes. Examples of expenditures which call for regulation are the payment of excessive consultant fees and the use of a foundation's administrative budget to finance personal amenities for donors, foundation managers, or their families. We believe that a requirement of the kind indicated about administrative costs would tend to remove temptations for abuse and build public confidence. There is, of course, no fixed formula for determining what is "excessive or unreasonable." As in the application of the "ordinary and necessary" limitation on business expenses, the determination must be made on a case-by-case basis.

5. It might be argued that the new law's catch-all prohibition against expenditures not in furtherance of exempt purposes can be used to serve this purpose. Whether or not such an interpretation is possible, this argument misses the essential point that what is needed is a clear prohibition in order to remind foundation officials of the legal framework in which they operate. We should remind the reader that we have found little evidence of serious abuse in administrative expenditures.

In applying any restriction on administrative expenses, *great care should be taken not to interfere with the development of expertise by grant-making organizations in selecting recipients, overseeing their activities, and evaluating their accomplishments.* As our discussion regarding relationships with grantees indicates, we believe that, particularly in controversial areas, increased supervision by foundations of the work of their recipients is desirable. In addition, foundations should not be prevented from making reasonable expenditures to inform the public of their activities and to disseminate the results of projects they have supported. Furthermore, some foundations engage in the direct operation of charitable, educational, or scientific programs, thus increasing the percentage of their budgets for administration as opposed to grants. In-house activities by foundations should not be discouraged.

We recommend that the prohibition on excessive administrative expenses be applied only in clear cases of abuse. However, we are confident that such application will have a much broader prophylactic effect on foundation practices. And in any event such a legal prohibition is not a substitute for persistent surveillance by foundation trustees and managers to insure that economy of administration is a basic operating principle of all foundations.

Sanctions for violations. The development of effective sanctions is essential to any regulatory system. In the past, loss of tax exemption was the principal sanction against foundations available to the Internal Revenue. This was so drastic as to be useless except in the most extreme cases.

While we support the general bent of the 1969 Tax Bill in providing more specific penalties, we would prefer other approaches and emphasis.

1. The objective of the system of sanctions should be to get charity back on its proper rails, not to increase the collection of taxes. As a general rule, penalties should be levied not against the assets of the foundations but rather against the individuals responsible for the violation. An individual who has enriched himself at the expense of the foundation should be required to repair the damage done to it.

2. Fines should only be levied where the prohibited conduct can be defined in an unambiguous manner. In particular, fines should not be imposed in areas where there are difficult questions of judgment, as may arise, in connection with certain investment-policy and grant-making decisions. To do so would have a severe *in terrorem* effect in areas where foundation activities are essential.

3. Sanctions should reflect the seriousness of the violation and whether it is willful or inadvertent. For minor or technical violations, a warning with an opportunity to make corrections may often be sufficient. In other cases monetary penalties will be necessary. Such penalties should increase in the event of repeated violations. Effective sanctions need not be draconian. They should be designed to deter illegal activity, not to make it difficult for foundations to attract much-needed trustees and staff.

DISSENTING VIEW BY COMMISSION MEMBER J. PAUL AUSTIN, CHAIRMAN, THE COCA-COLA COMPANY

The commission recommendation that foundations be required to make annual distributions to charity in the range of 6–8 percent of their asset market values violates a long-established legal concept and contradicts two commission positions supported elsewhere in the report. I am opposed to this recommendation, as I am to the provision in the Tax Reform Act of 1969 requiring a payout of 6 percent initially (after a phase-in period for existing foundations), which was influenced in part by this recommendation.

It has been a long tradition in law and in practice that charitable trusts and endowments established to preserve an investment corpus for production of income for charitable purposes be held inviolate, subject only to conditions of the donor. Capital appreciation, realized and unrealized, as well as capital depreciation, has traditionally been attributable to the corpus and not to income, whereas normal income has been generally considered fully expendable and not available for addition to capital. The commission arbitrarily equates capital gains with ordinary income for charitable endowments, which position may properly be applicable to mutual funds and other profit-sharing funds but represents a violation of trust when enforced against legally constituted charitable endowments.

The commission report properly makes a strong case for both current and future philanthropic support of eligible charitable purposes. However, it arbitrarily opts for current charitable support, at the expense of future support, by advocating enforced payout of foundation capital, thus negating, to the extent capital is currently invaded, the discretion of donors as to future support of charitable needs through the foundation.

Also, the commission properly supports a dual system of private giving and government funding as a better way to allocate resources for the general welfare than the alternative of relying solely on governmental allocations, and proposes that government stimulate an increased flow of private resources to philanthropy by offering higher government inducements to contributors. A donor who prefers to provide an ongoing fund from which income could support eligible charities according to changing needs—the grant-making foundation—would certainly be deterred from such legitimate social purpose by a tax policy which would require liquidation of the capital fund, however gradual, by enforced payout beyond normal income. Such policy is an arbitrary and special deterrent to foundations, since comparable payout is not required from capital funds held as endowments by operating charities such as colleges, hospitals, and orphanages. This restrictive policy is inconsistent with the commission's position of encouraging better tax incentives for charitable giving.

18

Recommendations to Government III: The New Law— Legislative Activities of Foundations and the Birth Rate of New Foundations

An allusion was made in the preceding chapter to three issues on which the commission was in substantial disagreement with the provisions of the Tax Reform Act of 1969 as they affect foundations. These are, first, the provisions banning so-called "legislative activities" by foundations; second, the provisions affecting the creation of new foundations, and third, the imposition of an excise tax on foundation income.

Studies of public issues and the legislative process. The Tax Reform Act of 1969 prohibits any attempt by foundations to sponsor so-called "grass roots campaigns" in the course of which members of the public are urged to contact their legislators in support of or in opposition to a specific piece of legislation.

The commission agrees with this general prohibition, taken by itself. Where the objective is political pressure rather than dissemination of information and ideas, foundation involvement becomes improper. We recognize that this distinction is more easily stated in the abstract than applied in practice, yet the fact that there may be some difficult borderline cases is no reason for ignoring the underlying principle.

Unfortunately, the prohibition on grass roots campaigns in the new legislation is accompanied by a legislative history which is confusing. Some may believe that the legislation could in fact be used to stifle foundation-financed studies of public policy issues. By providing an exception for "making available the results of nonpartisan analysis, study or research," the legislation could be read to prohibit foundation-financed studies which do not qualify as "nonpartisan" within a particular interpretation of this highly ambiguous word. It is true that the Conference Committee of the Senate and House indicated that the provision was not meant to prevent the examination of broad problems of the sort that government may be expected to deal with ultimately; but the committee added the qualifying statement that "lobbying on matters which have been proposed for legislative action" would not be permitted.

The line between the permissible and impermissible in this area is not always easy to draw. We presume that by contrasting "examination" of broad issues with "lobbying" on matters proposed for legislation, the Conference Committee was indicating that the prohibition does not apply unless the activity constitutes specific advocacy focused on the legislative process and directed at the particulars of a pending bill. The restriction should not apply to the analysis of the broad issue to which the bill relates.

In administering the act, we hope that the Internal Revenue Service recognizes that the common sense purpose of this provision is to prevent lobbying by foundations. It is not to impede foundations in legitimate public-policy studies simply because the studies may have an impact on an item of legislation pending in a local or state legislature or in Congress. "Nonpartisan" should not be taken to mean that no final conclusion is drawn. To draw no conclusions would destroy the underlying purpose for which most studies are undertaken. Nor should it be taken to mean that a study must be free from any impact on partisan politics; any significant public question can become a partisan issue in the future.

The new act also prohibits attempts to influence legislation through communications with legislators or government officials who may participate in the formulation of the legislation, again excepting "making available the results of nonpartisan analysis, study or research." As a restriction on direct lobbying activities on specific legislation, this provision may be justifiable. But it, too, should be interpreted narrowly to avoid deterring socially useful activities by foundations or their grantees which are not intended to result in pressure on legislators on specific bills.

We consider it both unnecessary and undesirable to shield legislators or their staffs from groups engaged in studies of issues which are of legislative interest. Exchange of ideas between private individuals and members of legislatures and their staffs are, of course, mutually beneficial. On many issues, legislators and members of legislative staffs are among the experts who should be consulted in a serious study. One member of our commission who has had extensive congressional experience points out that the executive branch's vast input into the legislative process makes it particularly useful that there be well-conceived and well-organized private contributions to congressional deliberations. To require that the foundation or its grantee receive a written request from a congressional committee before it can render technical assistance or advice to that committee will needlessly confine private contributions to congressional deliberations.

We recognize the genuine sensitivity of what is involved here. The commission favors the controlling force of prompt and full advance disclosure of any foundation-financed study likely to involve any substantial number of contacts with members of legislatures or their staffs. This approach is preferable to statutory prohibitions on such contacts.

As to influencing public opinion on public policy issues, we have stated our view that a legitimate function of foundations is education. But here again, the definition of what is permissible education and what constitutes prohibited propagandizing is not easy to state. We do not believe that an appropriate test of permissibility should be whether "both sides" are presented in an impartial manner, or whether conclusions are drawn from a study. The line between propaganda and education should not provide a basis for the censorship of ideas. Only in absolutely clear-cut cases, such as "hate material," which no reasonable man could consider educational, should the restriction on propaganda be invoked.

The commission is concerned over the possibility that the new law might impair desirable activities of private foundations. To minimize any unfavorable impact of the law we believe that the Treasury Department should frame regulations for the guidance of foundations which display a sensitivity to the difficulties in this area. We therefore urge the Treasury to issue such regulations as promptly as possible and, in doing so, to obtain the advice of individuals who are aware of the complexities involved.

This commission would have preferred far narrower legislation in the area where education and government policy meet on a common frontier. We do not believe it is possible to draw a line between the fields of interest of foundations and those of governments. Practically every area of significant foundation activity is one in which federal, state, and local governments are also active, generally on a much larger scale. This is true both of the conventional fields of philanthropy—health, education, welfare, science, and technology—and of such newer areas as urban problems, civil rights, the arts, the environment, and population control. It is thus unrealistic to expect that foundation programs should not have direct impact on government programs.

Far from deploring this intertwining of the private and the public sectors, we consider it one of the healthy features of American society. In the development and formulation of public policy it forms an essential part of the democratic process. The larger and more complex government becomes, the greater the need for private inputs into the decision-making process. The complexity of the problems, however, makes it much more difficult for private individuals to make meaningful contributions. As the work of our own commission illustrates, private individuals can deal adequately with even a relatively limited subject only after extensive study and analysis including substantial fact-gathering. This is not only time-consuming but can be quite costly, even where persons serve without compensation.

The difficulty we experienced in attempting to conduct our study without requesting foundation funds confirms the widely held view that foundations are by far the best source of funds for private efforts to study significant policy issues. A legal restriction on the availability of foundation funds for policy studies cannot help impairing private contributions to the decision-making process. Accordingly, we recommend that the IRS avoid overzealous interpretation and execution of these provisions of the law, and thereby avoid hamstringing foundation-financed public policy studies.

The commission urges that IRS also show a high order of common-sense judgment in two other matters covered by provisions in the new tax law: elective politics and grants to individuals.

We fully endorse the law's prohibitions on foundation involvement in elective politics. Charitable funds should not be used in election campaigns, whether to support the election of candidates or the passage of measures voted on in referendums. Yet we believe that a ban on foundation involvement in political activities connected with a specific election or referendum is most sensibly applied when it is subject to a test based on intent, not simply on the nature of the activity involved. For example, we do not believe that foundation support of a voter education campaign should be prohibited unless the foundation managers know or reasonably should know that the activity will be conducted in a partisan manner.

The proper approach to the use of the proposed test necessarily involves weighing all the facts and circumstances in an individual case. The relevant factors used in determining whether an intent is to benefit a particular party or candidate in an election can be seen in the overall pattern of the foundation activity, the nature and location of the recipient of the grant, the purpose of the grant, its timing, and the method by which it is made.

Because we do not believe a precise definition of partisan activity can be fashioned, we do not believe that the new law's precise criteria for permissible voter registration campaigns is the best solution to the vexing problem of determining whether a grant for voter registration is intended to influence the outcome of a specific election.

As to grants to individuals: these have been among the most productive of foundation activities. They do, however, raise the danger of cronyism. Provisions to insure that individual grants are made on an objective and nondiscriminatory basis, such as those contained in the new law, are obviously desirable. At the same time, the commission questions the new law's requirement of advance approval by the Internal Revenue Service of individual grant programs. We have proposed instead that foundations should be required to develop written procedures defining the criteria for making grants to individuals, including methods of assuring objectivity such as use of independent experts and the formulation of ground rules to avoid conflicts of interest. Such procedures could either be filed with the IRS or be kept available for an inspection. We would encourage the IRS to establish general criteria on a permanent basis, as it has done temporarily, to minimize the need for case-by-case approvals.

Guidelines for Foundation Grant Making in Sensitive Areas. Some have wished that the commission itself could have drafted neat, categorical, easily administered guidelines, applicable in all cases, that would sharply distinguish between grants that are charitable or noncharitable, partisan or nonpartisan, for education or for propaganda. Yet no drafting zeal on our part has overcome the fundamental fact that the boundaries lie in twilight zones. Simple, mechanistic guidelines, while easily applied, either may miss the subtle distinctions or can be easily evaded. Thus, to "simplify" these distinctions is to oversimplify them.

Our recommendations on grant making, therefore, are confined to statements of principles that should govern the drawing of distinctions between grants that are charitable and those that are not. We also recommend an increased emphasis on *processes* by which facts and circumstances in each case are determined and weighed. In consequence, we believe that some of the following steps should be given serious consideration.

1. Accelerated disclosure procedures for grants in specified sensitive areas. Early disclosure of sensitive grants exposes them not only to administrative scrutiny but to public examination. The injury done by a partisan political grant cannot be measured solely by the loss of dollars that might otherwise have been given to legitimate charitable purposes. The damage is in the potential harm to those against whom the partisan activity is directed, and to the entire credibility and integrity of the tax incentive system for charity.

2. We commend the IRS's broadened utilization of trained specialists to decide whether or not to proceed against a questionable grant that has been detected in the normal audit. The training required to audit foundation financial activities and conventional foundation grants to a public charity is quite different and certainly less sophisticated than determining, for example, whether a grant is or is not partisan.

3. Provision for promptly enjoining improper activities, rather than simply penalizing them after they have occurred. We recommend providing equity jurisdiction in the federal courts so that improper foundation activities can be enjoined. This can be provided by congressional action; we see no basic constitutional problem. We believe that federal equity jurisdiction would provide a very useful additional tool for the regulation of foundations.[1] Action in the federal courts could be initiated by the United States attorney general. Such actions could be brought at the request of the Internal Revenue Service. An injunction suit would be particularly appropriate in preventing questionable activities in the political or legislative area where legal remedies such as fines could be too little or too late.

The successful development of equity remedies might well be a much more effective way to deal with controversial and difficult cases than are present administrative procedures. Particularly where sensitive issues are raised, such as drawing the line between proper educational activities and improper political activities, we believe that the courts are uniquely qualified to provide prompt and effective relief.

Birth Rate of New Foundations and New Foundation Contributions. Contributions to grant-making foundations in the future will be discouraged by provisions in the tax law—this because the provisions make contributions to a grant-making foundation a less attractive prospect for a wealthy individual than it has been in the past. The rea-

1. In a broader study of the regulation of exempt organizations it may be worth considering how this tool might apply to other organizations.

sons why the new law could significantly reduce private giving—at a time when we believe the thrust of national policy should be to encourage private giving—include the following:

1. The new law increases the disparity in tax incentives for contributions to grant-making foundations as opposed to other charitable organizations. Lifetime contributions of long-term capital gain property to endow a private nonoperating foundation receive less favorable income tax treatment than such gifts to other charitable organizations. This type of property has accounted for the bulk of all contributions to private foundations in the past.

2. The new law discourages future lifetime or estate contributions of "control" stock in a corporation by requiring that the foundation dispose of the holdings within five years. The history of foundations, particularly of the larger foundations, indicates that they were often started with gifts of stock, usually controlling blocks, of a business which the donor had developed during his lifetime. Our data indicate that over two-fifths of all contributions to foundations were in the form of control stock. Blocks of control stock, of course, have a very high appreciation component; so lifetime contributions of them would be affected by the appreciated property provision as well as the limitation on foundation business holdings.

3. There is the problem of complexity in the law. The combination of regulatory provisions affecting foundations might discourage their establishment simply because of the time and effort involved in assuring that the foundation complies with them. An inevitable result of regulating one form of charitable organization extensively while not imposing new regulation on others is to create a climate in which the regulated organizations are considered less attractive, second-class charities. Additional regulation affecting the less-favored class of charities may be feared once the disparity is introduced into the law. The establishment of a foundation is often motivated in part by estate-planning considerations; uncertainty about the legal standards which will govern the contributions may cause individuals to formulate alternative testamentary plans, perhaps placing far less emphasis on charitable contributions.

Other provisions in the new law may also discourage the establishment of new foundations. It should first be said, however, that the commission endorsed the imposition of an audit fee on the foundations for a three-year period. The fee would be used to cover the costs of stepped-up regulatory activity to determine the nature and level of abuse, to bolster public confidence in the legality of foundation activities, and to assess future regulatory activity on the basis of concrete facts rather than isolated incidents.

At the same time, the commission opposed the tax on foundation investment income. The initial tax rate set by the law is low. Yet it creates a bad precedent, since the rate could easily be increased in a moment of disfavor and could be broadened to include other charitable organizations. It seems inconsistent and counterproductive to encourage giving to charitable organizations and then to impose a tax on foundation income which inevitably reduces the flow of funds to these organizations by diminishing the amount available for foundation grants. The impact of the new tax will be felt by potential grant recipients—primarily charitable organizations—far more than by foundations themselves. Moreover, because the tax flows into general government funds and is not earmarked for improved regulation of foundations, it cannot be justified as a regulatory instrument.

We also objected to the way the new law limits foundation ownership of corporate control stock. One of the major and understandable concerns about foundation holdings of such blocks of stock has been that they may be given to foundations for reasons such as protecting the donor's control of the corporation, which have nothing to do with their desirability from an investment standpoint and the best long-term interests of charity. In our view, this concern is substantially reduced when such holdings must make a significant, annual contribution to charity. A high payout requirement, prohibitions on self-dealing, and greater disclosure—all required by the new law—seem to us to provide a better solution than an arbitrary limit on percentage of ownership, especially if coupled with greatly improved government supervision of foundations. We believe that this provision could easily retard the flow of large pools of capital into philanthropy.

The discrepancy between incentives for contributing to grant-making foundations and incentives for contributing to other charitable organizations seems to us unfortunate, given the present tax treatment of appreciation in value of property.[2] We believe that it is important that new

2. The tax treatment of the appreciation component in gifts of property to charity is but one element of the tax law concerning such property (including, for example, its treatment at the death of the taxpayer). Because of the complexities of the subject, including its relationship both to other elements of tax policy and to the entire system of tax incentives for charitable contributions, the commission has taken no position on whether the tax treatment of contributions of appreciated property should be revised.

foundations be created. This would not only increase total philanthropic assets but would increase the diversity within the foundation field. In particular, it would probably result in a better national distribution of foundations, as the more recently acquired wealth outside the Northeast became reflected in the creation of foundations which might be expected to maintain their base of operations in these areas.

The commission strongly recommends that the possible effects of the new law on the creation of new foundations and on the total level of giving to and through foundations be thoroughly thought through. The principle that broadly supported operating charitable organizations should be given relatively more encouragement than narrowly supported charitable endowments has a certain appeal. But this policy may result in the undervaluing of the unique attributes of grant-making organizations. It may also be that broad support is not a reliable indicator of the value of a charitable enterprise.

We would recommend that Congress review the impact of the 1969 law within three years in order to determine whether the differences in the treatment of appreciated property and control stock as between foundations and other charitable organizations is really in the public interest.[3] More generally, we also recommend (see chapter 16) an advisory group of tax experts to review the whole situation of incentives for philanthropic support.

3. For example, it would be worthwhile to determine to what extent other charitable organizations not subject to business holdings and the self-dealing prohibition, such as schools and churches, are receiving contributions of "control stock" and, if so, what issues such a finding would raise.

19

Federal Regulations of Foundations: Further Considerations and Summary

The commission heard and debated proposals for a new federal agency to regulate foundations or for a Commissioner of Foundations or a Commissioner of Philanthropy.

We do have some doubts about the wisdom of regulating the operations of foundations through the Internal Revenue Service, an agency whose primary objective is collection of tax revenues. From a conceptual standpoint, it would probably be preferable to divorce administrative responsibilities for the regulation of tax-exempt organizations from the enforcement of the revenue laws. The separate regulatory responsibility, however, should cover *all* exempt organizations (or at least all charitable organizations) to provide for a sensible division of labors between the IRS and another agency. A separate agency charged with regulating foundations would find much of its work overlapping that of the IRS. The determination of whether an activity is partisan or charitable or educational requires the same type of inquiry when a broadly supported organization is at issue as when a foundation is.

A separate regulatory agency within the federal government, whether for foundations or for all tax-exempt charitable organizations, might fall prey to the familiar dual dangers displayed by some other regulatory agencies: bureaucratic empire building and the capture of the agency by the interests it is supposed to regulate. Neither trait would be desirable in an agency regulating as sensitive a segment of our society as charitable organizations. Ineffective regulation in the short run might lead to abuse of the privilege of tax exemption. By the iron law of compensation which works in the long run, it could readily result in far more drastic legislation. Overzealous regulation by an expansionist agency, or simply an agency attempting to justify annual appropriation requests, might stifle the diversity and the private initiative which are the primary values of private philanthropic activity. We are particularly concerned about the danger of a government agency's dominating the formation of policy for a group of private organizations, one of whose main reasons for existence is to provide alternate and perhaps contrasting approaches to those of the government. We are, to repeat, in favor of regulation designed to prevent financial and other abuses. However, government involvement in the area of grant-making policies contradicts the basic principle that a large measure of freedom for these organizations is very much in the public interest.

The Internal Revenue Service. For the time being, the commission accepts continued reliance on the Internal Revenue Service as the primary regulatory agency at the federal level. The commission believes, however, that the IRS's performance in this area must be improved. Not the least of the reasons why is a general lack of public confidence in the foundation as an institution. In point of fact, evidence gathered by the commission shows that the vast majority of foundations do not engage in any of the activities which form the core of the current concern. But to eliminate those abuses which do exist, and as a take-off point for the restoration of public confidence in foundations, greatly intensified auditing by the Internal Revenue Service is desirable.

We are informed that IRS has already taken steps in this direction by increasing the number of agents assigned to audit charitable foundations and giving them special training. The move is laudable. We do not believe, however, that merely increasing audit activity to 10 or 15 percent coverage is enough.

We therefore recommend the inauguration of a program to insure that *every foundation will receive an Internal Revenue Service audit at some time before 1973.* Once full coverage is achieved, it will probably be possible to decrease audit activity. As part of this program, the Internal Revenue Service should annually report the results of the increased audit program, including the nature and incidence of abuses. Given present doubts about the legitimacy of foundations, we believe that this expanded effort on the side of auditing and reporting alike is needed if public confidence is to be restored in foundations' integrity and the value of their charitable activities. The expanded effort will call for increased appropriations for the IRS. We believe that the appropriations should be increased, especially since foundations are now subject to an excise tax on their income which will provide additional federal revenue.

The Relationship between Federal and State Regulation. Both the state in which a foundation is established and the federal government have a valid interest in the foundation's operation. The interest of the state is twofold: the foundation is created under state law, and the state must take care that the privilege it has granted is not abused and that funds dedicated to charity are used for the purposes stated in the governing instrument; the state also has a revenue interest in the foundation because of deductions and exemptions from state taxes. Federal involvement is based primarily on the federal government's revenue interests; logically, then, it should be limited to prescribing the tax privileges foundations enjoy and defining the conditions under which they qualify for these privileges.

As between the two levels of government, however, federal regulation has been far more significant than state regulation, in part because the tax consequences are greater in magnitude, but mainly because state enforcement has been lax. Even if state laws were locally strengthened and these enforced everywhere in the nation, the gross lack of uniformity in the laws could result in the large-scale migration of foundations to states with the most advantageous law. Another serious consequence of the lack of uniformity is that it could hamper the operations of national foundations, which might, for example, face varying definitions of permissible charitable activities.

The desultory performance of the states suggests that if we are to rely on state regulation, at least in the near future, we shall have, in effect, no regulation at all for foundations in many parts of the country.

Suggestions have been made for federal action to spur state regulation. This could take several forms, from denial of federal tax exemption to foundations in states without a regulatory program which meets minimum federal standards, to exempting foundations in states with a qualifying regulatory program from more stringent federal regulations. Some have suggested financial aid to the states—perhaps a share of the proceeds of a federal auditing fee—to establish such programs. When these suggestions, however, are viewed in the light of the feeble regulatory performance of many states, they seem unrealistic for the time being. Some minor steps to improve state regulation do seem feasible; they are provided for in the Tax Reform Act. These include the sharing of information from federal tax returns (and other reports) with the states, deferral to state enforcement prior to the imposition of certain sanctions, and a requirement that foundations include the provisions of federal law in their charters or trust instruments (thereby making them enforceable by state as well as federal authorities). These provisions should permit more states to develop active regulatory programs. The commission encourages states to play a far more active role in the realm of foundations.

Perpetual Existence. As the Congress has done, the commission has considered proposals that the life of foundations should be limited to a fixed term, or, to produce the same result by an indirect route, that a foundation's tax exemption be revoked after a given number of years. In the Congress itself, a proposed forty-year limitation on the tax-exempt life of foundations was decisively rejected. This, however, was but a defensive action. The vote cannot be construed to mean that foundations have a broad constituency prepared in any positive sense to support an expansion of the scope of foundations' works.

The commission did not feel that restrictions on the life of the foundations should be enacted. At the same time, it recognized that proposals to this effect reflect a wide variety of concerns. Among them are the distrust of institutions without clearly defined public accountability; concern about the legitimacy of self-perpetuating boards of trustees, and a fear that the "dead hand" of the past will cause foundations to devote themselves to obsolete objectives or become moribund.

In our view, the perpetuity problem should be placed in broader context. The special privilege of perpetual life was once granted to entities only in exceptional circumstances. It is no longer a novelty. Each year, thousands of business corporations and other organizations are routinely granted perpetual existence. The rationale seems to be that an organization which serves a continuing need should have continuing existence. We see little reason why, in this respect, stricter standards should be applied to foundations than to other institutions.

We believe that a high payout requirement provides a satisfactory answer to the concern that foundations become listless and inactive after the death of the original donor. Such a requirement means, in effect, that the right to perpetual life must be earned and will not be conferred as an automatic privilege. A foundation's ability to continue to make a high payout to charity—and not the fact that it has reached its twenty-fifth or fortieth birthday—provides one rational basis for distinguishing between those foundations which should be permitted to continue and those which should be phased out of existence. It might be added that a continuing payout requirement is a tougher standard of performance than is imposed on other organizations, whose perpetual existence is continued as a matter of course.

We do not believe that there is real ground for concern about the "dead hand" of the past. We have seen little evidence that the older foundations spend money on outmoded objectives, and we have cited instances of updated aims. From the legal standpoint, foundations are generally organized for broadly stated purposes. (It is very common to draft the "purposes" clause of foundation charters using the broad language of section 501 [c] [3] of the Internal Revenue Code.) Where language too narrow has been used, the courts have generally been liberal in applying the doctrine of *cy pres* to reform outmoded foundation charters.

By their nature, grant-making foundations are more likely to be flexible in adapting to new challenges than are operating organizations endowed for specific purposes. Thus a rule against perpetual existence which would cause foundations either to turn themselves into operating organizations or to give their funds to operating organizations could well reduce rather than enhance the ability of our society to deal with newly emerging problems. To force this result because of concerns about the "dead hand" of the past would be ironical.

The evidence with respect to the detrimental effect of continued existence of foundations is largely conjectural. Particularly with the larger foundations, there are indications that many which started out under close control of an individual donor or his family have, over time, become independent of such control.

We suspect that limited life might well have a discouraging effect on the birth rate of new foundations. The ability to create an institution bearing the donor's name and having perpetual life may be a very significant psychological incentive for the creation of a foundation. Besides, foundations offer an institutional framework in which skilled staff people can both make substantial contributions to society and plan meaningful careers on the same long-term basis as those who decide to work for a business, a university, or a hospital. The certain knowledge of the death of the foundation could be expected in its middle and later years to discourage talented staff from working for it. For example, to most people a retirement plan is more than just a fringe benefit. It is a necessity.

In sum, we believe that a high burden of proof should be met before an arbitrary life term is established for foundations. The arguments for limited life are not sufficiently persuasive to make such a drastic step appropriate. As long as a high payout requirement assures that foundations will continue to be productive, a mandatory death sentence is not justified.

Our recommendation against a fixed term for foundations is directed solely to the desirability of a statutory restriction. This does not mean that all foundations should be set up on a perpetual basis. It might well be desirable for the example of Julius Rosenwald, who required his foundation to expend its funds within twenty-five years of his death, to be followed more widely. Our only point is that the arguments for a fixed term are not persuasive enough to justify its enforcement as a legal rule.

Classification of Foundations for Purposes of Regulation. While we agree that the treatment of foundations as a homogenous class has some unfortunate effects, we have not been able to distinguish between foundations in a way that would provide for differing regulation. We have explored the kinds of distinction that follow and find them wanting.

Many people associate quality of foundation performance with various characteristics, including their size, the presence or absence of a professional staff, and the independence of a majority of the board from the donors to the foundation. From our own observation we would agree that foundations of at least moderate size, with staff assistance and without donor control, have, on the whole, been more productive than other foundations. They also appear to have less potential for certain forms of financial abuse.

It is tempting to translate this observation into a legislative classification of foundations, subjecting these "better" foundations to less stringent forms of regulation. Prior to the enactment of the 1969 tax law, some observers of the foundation field proposed just such a two-tier system of foundation regulation (for example, foundations with and without independent boards). Presumably the new law has made this suggestion obsolete, since it has subjected all foundations to the same legal standards.

We agree with this uniform treatment. Legislative classification of foundations, subjecting "good" foundations to less stringent regulation than others, while tempting in theory, is not desirable in practice. It adds yet another layer of complexity to what, as the tax law demonstrates, is necessarily a complicated legal superstructure. It involves arbitrary assumptions about the correlation of definable organizational characteristics with the potential for detrimental activity, assumptions which presume a casual relationship where none may exist. Finally, almost any feasible criterion for dividing the foundation field may be avoided by a foundation intent on escaping more rigorous regulation, generally by relatively simple formal steps.

In another form, however, the suggestion for differentiation may be worth pursuing. If foundations with professional staffs and independent boards are better, should all foundations be required to have them? Our answer is no. Quality cannot be legislated, and it is fruitless to try. There is no profession of foundation administrators. Professional staff members of foundations have been drawn from a broad spectrum of occupations; turnover is high. It is extremely doubtful that any standards could be devised for ascertaining whether a staff member is a "professional." Requiring a staff is simply requiring the foundation to pay salaries, hardly a useful endeavor.

An "independent" board requirement could also be easily evaded by a donor who wished to do so. Moreover, an independent board is not necessarily a better board. A narrowly based, cohesive board may in some instances make better decisions than a broadly based, representative one. A blanket mandate would impose management by a representative committee, and there is no guarantee that this would improve foundation performance. We would leave the matter for decision by the foundations themselves.

The commission considered the feasibility of a requirement that foundations be of a minimum size, which might reduce inefficiency. Such a requirement would have two effects. First, small foundations would be forced to pool their assets, a result we would encourage (and urge them to consider without respect to a legislative requirement). Second, and more significant from a policy standpoint, personal foundations could be established in the future only by those with sufficient wealth to endow a foundation of the requisite size. This would have the effect of restricting the tax benefits available from foundations, which already increase with wealth, to the very rich—hardly consistent with our broad policy objectives of democratizing private giving.

Finally, we have also explored the possible classifying of foundations for regulation purposes according to whether they make grants only to "public charities" or whether they also make "sensitive" grants to individuals, foreign organizations, etc. While we believe this may be a useful basis for determining the level and kind of auditing, we would not want to encourage a "public charity" foundation to stay that way to avoid regulation.

Conclusion. This commission does not countenance the use of foundations for tax avoidance purposes or for the personal pecuniary benefit of those associated with foundations. Accordingly, we have supported a high payout requirement to insure that charity receives a current benefit from foundation resources, a prohibition on transactions between donors or foundation insiders and their foundations (including indirect transactions for the benefit of donors or insiders), and restrictions on undue speculation and other improper investment of foundation assets. We also favor prohibitions on certain kinds of foundation expenditures or grants—for partisan political activities, for "grass roots" legislative activities, and for individual grants not awarded under objective procedures. In addition, we have supported the imposition of "expenditure responsibility" on some grants, requiring the foundation to take reasonable steps to verify that the funds are spent solely for permissible charitable purposes. We have also proposed some processes by which facts and circumstances in questionable grants of foundations could be determined and weighed. We favor increased disclosure of foundation activities, including dissemination of data and information about foundations. We strongly urge increased surveillance and enforcement of these and other regulatory provisions by the Internal Revenue Service and efforts by the states to implement regulatory programs.

These measures will, we believe, curb the abuses of foundations which have been discovered without hampering the legitimate and beneficial activities of the vast majority of foundations. They represent a desirable balancing, in our view, of the need to eliminate abuse with the desirability of maximizing the public benefits from foundations.

This commission rejects the notion that the foundation is a second-class charity which should be abolished, discouraged, or merely tolerated by society. We are seriously concerned that some provisions of the Tax Reform Act of 1969—the restriction on foundation ownership of control stock in corporations, the comparatively less favorable treatment accorded contributions of appreciated property to foundations than to other charitable organizations, the excise tax on foundation income, and monetary sanctions imposed against the charitable assets of a foundation—will materially inhibit new contributions to foundations and, as a result, reduce the flow of private funds into philanthropic activities. We hope that these provisions will be reassessed. We are also seriously concerned that the uncertainty surrounding the new prohibition on partisan activities by foundations in support of or in opposition to specific legislation will inhibit valuable and legitimate grant-making activities at a time when public policy research is badly needed in a variety of fields. We urge the Internal Revenue Service to act promptly to develop regulations which will not have this effect.

At the same time, we are concerned that some foundations may have overreacted to the new law. It is true that it contains some provisions which we consider unwise and others which could have a harmful effect if highly restrictive regulations are enforced. But foundations themselves have an opportunity to minimize the latter possibility by working closely with IRS in the drafting process. And in general we believe that the new law provides a framework in which foundations can continue to make significant contributions to the improvement of our society.

DISSENTING VIEW BY COMMISSION MEMBER LANE KIRKLAND, SECRETARY-TREASURER, AFL-CIO

While I do agree with some of the commission's recommendations, there are some I do not agree with, and I take strong exception to the overall thrust and tone of the report.

Private foundations and their donors enjoy special privileges under the federal income tax law. When certain individuals or institutions receive preferential tax treatment, the public sector is relinquishing funds it would otherwise receive. Such preferences are justifiable only if it can be established conclusively that such tax privileges serve to forward the interests of the public. And the burden of proof rests with those who are the recipients of the tax privileges. In my judgment, the evidence uncovered by the commission and presented in the report falls short of this burden of proof.

The study seems based on the premise that private foundations are desirable and their growth should be encouraged and stimulated. And the *need* for the private allocation of public funds through tax-exempt entities "standing outside the frame of government" is taken for granted.

In my opinion, the major task of this commission was to explore this very issue and subject it to challenge and critical appraisal.

The report recognizes the advantages of a dual system of government funding and private giving. But immediately the issue is polarized erroneously by noting that such a "dual system . . . is a better way to allocate resources for the general welfare than the alternative of relying *solely* on government allocations" (emphasis added). What is more, the report fails to recognize that such a "dual" system would exist even if there were no foundations. Most "general welfare" needs have traditionally been met by means other than "government allocations."

Similarly the first four chapters of the report are devoted almost exclusively to a discussion of the virtues of charitable giving. These virtues are then equated with the need for encouraging and stimulating the growth of *private* foundations; the transition is made by defining a foundation as "an intermediate entity between a donor and the recipients of his philanthropic giving." The only hint to a lay reader of the report that private foundations are not the only types of charitable organizations is found in a brief section summarizing the Tax Reform Act of 1969. Here the report notes that the act distinguishes (and discriminates) between private foundations and "other charitable organizations," and a brief mention is made of the existence of "publicly supported community foundations."

Much of the reasoning underlying the conclusion that the growth of foundations must be encouraged stems from a prognosis of an impending "charitable crisis of the 1970s." The conclusion that there is in fact such a crisis stems from a survey of foundations' executives and specialists in medicine, education, and the like. Although such a survey doubtless reflects the *aspirations* of this group, it does not necessarily support a conclusion that "we will feel the full force of what can be called in advance the *charitable crisis of the 1970s.*" Nor is it demonstrated that, if such a crisis exists, it can be met best by promoting the growth of foundations per se, as preferable to all other forms of charitable giving.

Similarly, many other conclusions and assumptions stem from generalizations and, unfortunately, polemics. For example, I do not feel that the very important question of cost-benefit assessments of foundations (tax loss versus social benefits achieved) can be dismissed by merely noting the development of the polio vaccine and asking the question: "How do we measure the 'benefit,' its value to society?"

One could also ask to what extent the tax loss resulting from the tendency of the rich to endow universities limits the public funds available for improving elementary and secondary educational facilities.

"Evidence" such as the above does not lend itself to conclusive statements that "foundations, in a word, can be one of our preeminent institutions of reform." What is more, depending on their orientation, it is equally true that foundations could be one of our preeminent institutions of *reaction*. What has either necessarily to do with "charity" per se, in the general understanding of that term?

Thus, I cannot agree with two of the "three great ends we have in view":

1. "We want to stimulate an increase in funds available and actively devoted to philanthropy. We have presented evidence showing that charitable needs will continue to rise rapidly in the 1970s, and we have stated the reasons why private philanthropy should be encouraged to help meet these needs."

2. Since such an increase would in the main be stimulated through increased tax incentives, there is necessarily a trade-off between availability of funds for public programs to meet public needs and private funds to meet such needs. (The case is not made in the report.)

3. "We want not only to increase but to diversify philanthropic efforts in the private sector so that more foundations can fulfill their inherent potential as a source of unique contributions to the general welfare. If foundations are to be the way-showing institutions of social modernization and orderly change, they can be that only if they build for themselves a far broader base of public understanding, trust, and enthusiastic loyalty."

Again, the truth of the premise underlying this third conclusion has not been demonstrated. Moreover, such a statement runs counter to the view expressed earlier in the report that charity should become less "elitist" and more democratic.

There are a number of commission recommendations which I deem appropriate. For example, I support those recommendations calling for a better definition of the foundations' mission and increased public disclosure of foundation activities and finances. I support the recommendation of 100 percent auditing of foundations over the next three years and the tightening up of regulation of foundation administrative expenditures.

In addition, I agree with the majority that the investment performance of many foundations leaves much to be desired. And I support in principle the report's recommendation for legislation which would require payments high enough to ensure substantial distributions of foundations' funds to charity. Nor would I object to the need for a foundation organization and an Advisory Board on Philanthropic Policy.

I do not feel, however, that the evidence uncovered by the commission supports a recommendation for "new and better tax incentives." While I believe the "democratization" of philanthropic giving is an appropriate goal, I would be suspicious of new tax incentives as a means to that end. Nor do I share the majority's view that the 1969 tax law provisions which "make contributions to a grant-making foundation a less attractive prospect for a wealthy individual" are objectionable. I also feel that the law's limitation on the amount of controlling stock of a corporation that a foundation can own is appropriate.

In conclusion, I fully recognize that a salutary role can be played by institutions working outside the framework of government, even though they are supported by tax-exempt funds. Nevertheless, private foundations have grown and proliferated, and their known abuses have been many. The questions that must be answered first are: (1) What is the appropriate balance between the amounts of *publicly* controlled *public* funds available for social purposes and privately controlled public funds? And, perhaps more important: (2) What is the appropriate balance between the role of a democratically chosen government, in affecting social change, and that of private institutions supported through the willingness of government to relinquish funds which would otherwise be part of the public domain?

20

For the Future: An Advisory Board on Philanthropic Policy

Government policy toward philanthropy and charitable organizations has developed haphazardly. It has not been reviewed from the perspective of the values of philanthropy, the needs of the charitable sector, or other national policies. Because regulation and incentives for the charitable sector are part of the tax law, they tend to be considered primarily from the viewpoint of tax policy and revenue costs. Equally important—indeed, in many respects more important—considerations of the effects of the law on private giving and in turn philanthropy's qualitative effect on the nature of our society are often ignored. The tax impact of revisions or reforms in the law are reviewed, but not the impact of these revisions on the affected institutions. Many of the judgments have been reached emotionally in response to an ill-informed outcry. Long-range conclusions about an invaluable institution often seem to rest on a public mood, often short-term anger, rather than on meticulous study. Decisions concerning charitable organizations, even though they are included in the tax code, should reflect the broadest considerations of public policy.

We believe that philanthropy is a sufficiently important aspect of American life that its needs and problems deserve to be articulated within government. Public policy affecting philanthropy requires continuing reassessment.

Accordingly, we recommend the creation of an Advisory Board on Philanthropic Policy.

1. This board will need certain governmental powers—primarily the power to obtain information concerning philanthropy from private organizations and state and federal agencies. But because this new board will be concerned with important policy questions concerning the

proper mix of governmental and private efforts, we believe it is essential that the board be separate from existing departments or agencies. While the board might receive a federal charter, as other federally chartered private groups have done, it should be as independent of government as possible. Its funding might come from both private and public sources in order to encourage this independence.

2. We envisage a board composed of from ten to fifteen outstanding private citizens selected from the leadership segments of society that are concerned with social and philanthropic programs—public and private. We prefer presidential appointment and Senate confirmation of its members. While we do not believe any members of this board should be government officials, we believe that this all-private-citizens group should be given a specific legislative mandate to advise the Secretary of the Treasury, with whom the advisory board should probably maintain its principal liaison, the Secretary of Health, Education, and Welfare, and other appropriate governmental agencies or groups (such as the President's Cabinet Committee and Task Force on Volunteer Efforts) on the needs of the private philanthropic sector and how they may relate to government programs and policies.

3. The board should be a continuing body, not a one-time commission. Its members should be appointed for staggered fixed terms after the initial appointment, perhaps for four years. The board should meet on a periodic basis, perhaps four to ten times per year. It should have a small, full-time staff and also be authorized to arrange for studies by consultants and organizations.

4. The board's concern would not be foundations alone but philanthropy as a whole. Many of the problems of foundations are really problems of philanthropy, which require consideration from a broader perspective.

It would be presumptuous for us to do more than suggest a preliminary agenda for this board, simply to illustrate how much work needs to be done. There are many complex issues we have identified which we have been unable to explore, because our main concern was foundations and because our schedule and staff resources were limited. Continuing tasks that such a board might undertake include the following.

Providing Information about Philanthropy. This function, of course, requires the collection and classification of appropriate data. It also requires effective analysis and dissemination of data.

The board could use a variety of approaches to achieve this. One could be an annual report to Congress, the president, and the public on the needs and the state of philanthropy and charitable organizations. It could provide interpretation and broader dissemination of statistical reports by the Internal Revenue Service on levels of private giving and its recipients.

It could prepare reports on foundations, including such data as the number of foundations; assets; investment practices and returns; amount, recipients, and purposes of grants. We believe the fine library efforts of the Foundation Center should be supplemented by the establishment of more repositories at locations around the country where information about foundations and other charitable organizations would be readily available to anyone interested. For example, the information about foundations in such a repository could be organized in a manner which would enable a prospective grantee to determine which foundations were active in his field of interest and provide for an interchange of information between foundations to reduce useless overlapping of foundation programs.

Continuing Evaluation of the Regulation of Charitable Organizations. This could include continuing assessment of the Internal Revenue Service's program to audit foundations and other charitable organizations, including the reporting of the results of this audit program. The board could consider the question whether the level and intensity of auditing is sufficient to discover abuse, and thus reassure the public.

The task would also involve evaluation of the procedures for determining the borderline between charitable and noncharitable activities, including an assessment of administrative rulings to see how this borderline is being drawn in practice, the procedures for qualifying a charitable organization, etc.

Continuing Review of the Effectiveness and Current Operation of the Tax Incentive System. With appropriate liaison with the Treasury Department to obtain the data that are needed for such a review, the board should be able to assess the impact of tax incentives for charitable giving, including not only who gives and what the revenue cost to the government is, but also the efficiency of the incentives in increasing charitable giving.

This continuing assessment and reporting of the philanthropic situation, including a review of the regulation of philanthropy, are necessary. However, there are some fundamental, long-range issues which also require analysis and action by an independent, top-level group with full access to the data it needs to make comprehensive recommendations.

In 1969, foundations were singled out as a target for legislation. Some good and some bad has resulted. Some of the unfortunate decisions were triggered in our view by equally unfortunate, but atypical, incidents which received broad publicity.

Next year's philanthropic target could be one of a variety of other charitable organizations and practices. While our study of these other areas has not been extensive, we have not been totally reassured by what we have seen. We are quite prepared to believe that other areas of the philanthropic sector suffer from information gaps, inadequate regulation, and policies which have been poorly thought through. This is precisely the kind of environment in which ill-conceived legislative and administrative proposals flourish.

A longer-range reassessment of basic tax and regulatory policy affecting philanthropic giving and charitable organizations should be undertaken promptly. Some of the issues which deserve careful deliberation have been mentioned in other connections. Stated from a new perspective, they include the following.

Improvement of Tax Incentives for Charitable Giving. This task will require careful and diligent work by experts to design new incentives which will increase charitable giving without doing violence to tax equity and without disrupting the operation of worthwhile charitable organizations by causing a rapid alteration in giving patterns. (We have recommended in chapter 16 the appointment of a task force of tax experts to review tax incentives for philanthropy.) In addition to income tax incentives, consideration should also be given to the effect on charitable bequests of estate tax revision.

It must also be decided what contributions will be eligible for tax incentives. Should an attempt be made to narrow the definition of eligible recipients to exclude those whose activities are considered less deserving? Or, on the contrary, should the definition of contributions eligible for incentives be broadened? For example, should taxpayers be permitted to deduct contributions to citizens, consumer, or public interest lobbying organizations in order to put these groups more on a parity with other organizations which are able to engage in legislative activities with tax-deductible dollars (business expense) or tax-exempt income? Within the group of eligible recipients, should an attempt be made to channel a greater proportion of contributions to certain types of charitable organizations through a differential in incentives?

The Advisory Board on Philanthropic Policy would be an excellent group to review the recommendations of a task force of tax experts dealing with incentives for philanthropy and to make their own independent recommendations. This task force could be established by the board if it is not otherwise in operation.

Improvement of Tax Treatment and Regulation of Charitable Organizations. Some experts in this area contend that the entire structure of federal law respecting charitable organizations is virtually unworkable in its present form. Because the only sanction has been revocation of tax exemption, no attempt is made to enforce many provisions of the law except in blatant cases, and the rules are exposed neither to public attention nor to judicial interpretation. The new law affecting private foundations, which includes more meaningful sanctions, may improve the situation, but it will not solve the basic problems. A thorough reassessment of basic tax and regulatory policy is needed, including the possibility of alternatives to tax exemption as a form of tax-favored treatment for charitable organizations.

Among the questions which should be asked are the following:

1. What is the proper extent of involvement in business by charitable organizations? The problem of unfair competitive advantage of a tax-exempt entity over tax-paying enterprise was the basis for the "unrelated business income tax" initially imposed on charitable organizations in 1950. In addition to technical problems concerning the coverage and meaning of the provisions, there are more basic problems of determining when a business is "unrelated" to the organization's charitable purposes or functions and the proper treatment of business which is "related" but operates in direct competition with nonexempt businesses.

There is an allied question of who should own and profit from work financed with the funds of tax-exempt organizations, including difficult issues of copyright and patent policy.

The problems are extremely thorny ones, especially in view of the complex financial structure and range of activities of modern charitable organizations.

2. What program activities are proper for charitable organizations? Each of the major permissible purposes under present law—"religious," "charitable," "educational," and "scientific"—is difficult to define. To what extent, for example, are the methods utilized by an organization with qualifying "charitable" objectives relevant to its tax status? May a group with the objective of eliminating prejudice and discrimination—a qualifying objective under present law—picket, demonstrate, or

use other confrontation tactics? Similarly, to what extent are the subjects in which an organization with "educational" functions offer instruction relevant to its tax status? How is it determined whether these subjects are beneficial?

To what extent should a charitable organization be permitted to become involved in the legislative process or seek to mold public opinion on public policy issues? This is a subsidiary problem of definition. A British royal commission report (the Nathan report), discussing the role of charitable organizations in a welfare state, concluded in 1952 that

> Some of the most valuable activities of voluntary societies consist . . . in the fact that they are able to stand aside from and criticize state action, or inaction, in the interests of the inarticulate man-in-the-street. This may take the form of helping individuals to know and obtain their rights. It also consists in a more general activity of collecting data about some point where the shoe seems to pinch or a need remains unmet. The general machinery of democratic agitation, deputations, letters to the Press, questions in the House, conferences and the rest of it, may then be put into operation in order to convince a wider public that action is necessary.

Nevertheless, in terms of proper tax policy, there is a strong feeling clearly reflected in the Tax Reform Act that it is inappropriate for government to subsidize attempts to influence legislative action. We have discussed this issue elsewhere in this report with respect to foundations, but the same problems arise with other charitable organizations. In view of the pervasive nature of legislation today, and the wide variety of noncharitable organizations that can and do take positions on a variety of social issues while enjoying favorable tax treatment of such expenditures, is it realistic to exclude from the category of charitable organizations those which have, and advocate, a main objective that "may be attained only by legislation"? Should the present strictures on the activities of educational and charitable organizations be loosened to permit their more active participation in public policy discussion and formulation?

This is only a partial agenda of federal regulatory issues concerning charitable organizations. There are a variety of others, some of an exceptionally technical nature. And there are a number of complex issues concerning state and local tax treatment of charitable organizations, including the delicate balance to be achieved between the proper property-tax treatment of real estate owned by churches and other charitable organizations and the needs of local governmental units for an expanded tax base.

Improvement of the Administration of Regulation of Charitable Orga- nizations. The tasks in this area include the following:

1. The need to devise appropriate methods of meshing federal and state regulatory responsibilities.

2. The need to encourage uniform state laws dealing with founda- tions and other charitable organizations. In analogous situations, top leadership and research have made a decisive contribution. The Advis- ory Board on Philanthropic Policy could initiate and encourage the process in this field to achieve more uniformity.

3. The proper balance between administrative regulation and judicial remedies including the feasibility of federal equity jurisdiction.

4. The appropriate organizational structure within the federal gov- ernment to administer federal regulation of charitable organizations.

5. The responsibilities and potential liabilities of trustees of chari- table organizations. This subject deserves thorough scrutiny, especially in connection with a reassessment of sanctions for violation of regula- tions affecting charitable organizations. Most trustees receive no com- pensation; they join boards in order to perform a public service. There is considerable uncertainty about their legal duties and responsibilities. Standards should be developed for their guidance.

We believe this preliminary agenda of both continuing functions and policy questions for the Advisory Board on Philanthropic Policy illus- trates the need for such a top-level group. We believe this Advisory Board on Philanthropic Policy in no way obviates the need for the foundation organization which is required to focus on the many prob- lems specific to foundations.

Some people oppose the creation of a board to deal with one of the most sensitive areas in the private sector. They fear that a "quasi- governmental" board would not stay "quasi" very long, and that the result would be excessive governmental intrusion into the activities of the charitable section. While we recognize this danger, we believe that the appointment of an exclusively private-citizen membership will mini- mize it.

It is also objected that the functions we have proposed for the board cannot feasibly be combined in a single organization, especially with a hybrid public-private character. Some of these problems, it is said, re- quire a concerted attack by technical people, best handled within the Treasury Department and other government agencies, while others— such as data gathering and informing the public—might best be done through private auspices by expanding the activities of the Foundation

Center and other organizations now serving these functions. The suggestion is made that a single board—especially one intended to be broadly representative of top-level leadership—would not be expected to devote the thorough attention to each of these tasks that is necessary.

This commission understands these concerns but is not persuaded by them. What is clearly lacking in this field is not specialists but involved and informed generalists to coordinate inputs and advise at the strategic or policy level. The extent of the commitment of top-level private citizens to make distinctive public service contributions suggests that they can fulfill this role and give the work of the board visibility and status. We believe, in short, that the Advisory Board on Philanthropic Policy would be a valuable institution to study problems, propose new philanthropic policies in consultation with key government agencies, and inform Congress, the president, and the public.

We again commend the Nixon administration for its efforts to support voluntarism and we believe that the work of the Advisory Board on Philanthropic Policy, given the central importance of philanthropy in the larger world of voluntarism, should be coordinated with and related to that effort. We may hope—and there are encouraging auguries —that the future will see a powerful influence exerted on behalf of independent citizen action. Those in government concerned with education, health, and other aspects of the general welfare must be an official lobby for philanthropy if the merit of voluntarism, as against compulsion, is to get the support it deserves. What is at stake is the survival of private philanthropy. This is important for its own sake. But it is most important because of the contributions that newly invigorated foundations and other philanthropic institutions can make to our troubled society.

We need these contributions—urgently.

Appendixes

I DESCRIPTION OF SURVEYS
Survey of Distinguished Citizens   191
Survey of Chicago Philanthropic Organizations   193
Survey of Foundations   195
Survey of Accountants   197
Tabulation of Sample of 999-A's   199
Survey of Large Private Donors   199

II FINDINGS OF THE SURVEY OF DISTINGUISHED CITIZENS   201

III FINDINGS OF THE SURVEY OF CHICAGO PHILANTHROPIC
ORGANIZATIONS   227

IV TABLES SUMMARIZING THE SURVEY OF FOUNDATIONS   241

V PHILANTHROPY AND THE ECONOMY
By Mary Hamilton   256

VI ENLIGHTENED SELF-INTEREST AND CORPORATE PHILANTHROPY
By William J. Baumol   262

Description of Surveys

SURVEY OF DISTINGUISHED CITIZENS

In the summer of 1969 the Commission on Foundations and Private Philanthropy wrote to a cross-section of America's opinion leaders to obtain their views on the complex subject of philanthropy in the United States. The persons questioned in this study were leaders in many fields of endeavor. They included Nobel Prize laureates, university presidents, business leaders, government officials, labor leaders, physicians, attorneys, and leaders in the arts and sciences. These persons proved to be knowledgeable about one or more fields of philanthropy and they responded fully and frankly to the commission's survey.

In reviewing the response of these distinguished citizens, the field(s) of philanthropy about which they felt most knowledgeable was carefully noted and their opinions and attitudes were tabulated accordingly. The thrust of the commission's questions to these distinguished citizens may be summarized in three categories of inquiry: (1) expected trends in the financial needs of charitable organizations over the next five to ten years; (2) the position of government (public) policy vis-à-vis private philanthropy and foundations; (3) the philanthropic function of foundations and their role in American society.

Survey Method

The commission's information-gathering technique for this study was a mail-interview opinion survey. A sample of 4,016 persons was drawn from 49 different source lists. An interview questionnaire was constructed using both free response and structural questions. This questionnaire was mailed to respondents between 1 August and 30 September 1969, and 885 returns (22 percent) were received prior to final computer tabulation of the response in late November.

The sample selection objective was to reach prominent persons who could comment on the field of philanthropy. The sample was nonrandom in the sense that lists of names were carefully selected to represent leadership of particular fields of endeavor, namely, arts and humanities, education, business, medicine, science, law, government and urban affairs, religion, and labor. The kind of source lists used were, in addition to *Who's Who in America*, directories of the American Psychological Association, the American Sociological Association, the American Medical Association, the American Association for the Advancement of Science, the American Bar Association, and the National Urban League. Also consulted were directories of national arts associations and of national and international labor unions and lists published by *Fortune* magazine and other periodicals. Names chosen were for the most part those of persons in positions of leadership such as directors of associations, chairmen of association chapters, deans of professional schools, museum directors, and theater managers. Large lists were subsampled on an every-"nth"-name basis.

When the survey responses were tabulated, both an "absolute" and a "weighted" response were tabulated. The absolute response was the simple sum of the answers received to each question. The weighted response was the simple sum of answers received, multiplied by a weighting factor. This factor equalized the response value of each field of endeavor from which the sample was drawn. The effect was to give each field an approximately equal "vote" in the final summary tabulation. This weighted response is used in the report.

The persons interviewed were assumed to have knowledge of one or more areas of society in terms of the effect of private philanthropy, including contributions of foundations, as well as the effect of government support. However, the area(s) of society in which the respondents felt most knowledgeable was unknown to the commission at the outset of the survey. Accordingly, each person interviewed selected one field or more to comment upon in his questionnaire. These fields are shown in table A.1 along with the "weighted" and "unweighted" ratio of persons who felt knowledgeable in each area.

Since it was not possible to control the number of individuals in each field of endeavor who responded to the survey mailing, the weighting device was used to equalize the "vote" of doctors, lawyers, educators, government officials, scientists, etc., who returned questionnaires. The

TABLE A.1.

"Which of the following fields or areas of our society do you feel you know the most about . . . in terms of the impact of private philanthropy, including contributions of foundations, as well as government support?" (N = 885)

Field of Philanthropy Known Best	Weighted Response (percent)	Unweighted Response (percent)
Education	34.2	28.2
Medicine and health	17.2	28.5
Religion	9.1	5.1
Science	9.0	10.0
Arts (ballet, symphony, painting, sculpture, etc.)	8.7	10.7
Welfare programs	8.1	5.3
International aid	3.1	2.1
Humanities	2.1	2.9
Other miscellaneous	8.5	7.2
	100.0	100.0

areas of private philanthropy in which these people felt knowledgeable are shown above. It was possible during the analysis of the survey to tabulate answers to the questions by these fields of "knowledgeability" so that results could be compared. The commission shows some of these comparisons in its report for four of the fields (education, medicine and health, science, arts) where actual questionnaire returns equalled 10 percent or more of the total "unweighted" survey response.

SURVEY OF CHICAGO PHILANTHROPIC ORGANIZATIONS

A total of fifty-one charitable organizations in the Chicago metropolitan area were surveyed. The organizations included were:

American Cancer Society (Illinois Division)
American Indian Center
American Red Cross (Mid-America Chapter)
Art Institute of Chicago
Association for Family Living
Boy Scouts of America (Chicago Council)
Catholic Charities of Chicago
Chicago Boys Clubs
Chicago Child Care Society
Chicago Commons Association
Chicago Community Fund
Chicago Council on Alcoholism
Chicago Educational Television Association
Chicago Heart Association
Chicago Public Library
Chicago Symphony Orchestra

Chicago Urban League
Chicago Youth Centers
Community Renewal Society
Ecumenical Institute
Episcopal Diocese of Chicago
Field Museum of Natural History
Girl Scouts of Greater Chicago
Hospital Planning Council for
  Metropolitan Chicago
Hull House Association
Illinois Association of Homes for the
  Aged
Illinois Children's Home and Aid
  Society
Illinois Institute of Technology
John Crerar Library
Lawndale People's Planning and
  Action Conference
Leadership Council for Metropolitan
  Open Communities
Lutheran Charities Federation
Lutheran Welfare Services of
  Illinois
Mental Health Association of
  Greater Chicago
Michael Reese Hospital

Museum of Science and Industry
Open Lands Project
Provident Hospital and Training
  School
Rehabilitation Institute of Chicago
Salvation Army
Scholarship and Guidance
  Association
The Woodlawn Organization
Travelers Aid Society of
  Metropolitan Chicago
Union of American Hebrew
  Congregations
United Cerebral Palsy of Greater
  Chicago
United Charities of Chicago
University of Chicago
Visiting Nurses Association of
  Chicago
Welfare Council of Metropolitan
  Chicago
Young Men's Christian Association
  of Greater Chicago
Young Women's Christian
  Association of Greater Chicago

The fifty-one organizations surveyed are active in the following fields: hospitals and health services (10), education (3), cultural (6), neighborhood service (9), religion (2), family services and assistance (6), services for children (3), services for the aged (2), general community planning and specialized services (10).

The survey was directed to two groups of data: first, the organization's own financial situation, including future needs and the extent to which it relied upon private giving; and, second, the organization's attitudes toward foundations, based on its experience as an applicant for foundation funds and, in many cases, as a grantee.

The survey consisted of a written questionnaire in combination with a taped personal interview. In most cases, the executive director of the organization answered the questions. In a few instances, the chairman of the board of trustees or another high-ranking officer was interviewed.

The questionnaire was divided into two sections. The first part asked for detailed financial information for the years 1963 and 1968 and a projection for 1975. The second part sought the respondent's opinions on a number of subjects, including the future financial need of his institution, his experience with various types of funding, his views on foundations, and his ideas about tax policy relating to philanthropy. The questions were open-ended, permitting the respondents to elaborate on their answers and give supporting examples.

Thirty-nine institutions provided sufficiently detailed and complete financial information on the first part of the questionnaire to permit tabulation. All fifty-one responded to the second part.

Chicago was selected for this survey primarily for logistical reasons. The commission's offices are located in Chicago, and the commission has close ties with this city. For the purposes of this study, Chicago seemed sufficiently representative of American cities. It has the range of charitable institutions which we sought to interview.

The selection of organizations for inclusion in the survey was made by those working for the commission on this project. These individuals are knowledgeable about charitable activities in the Chicago metropolitan area and utilized their own judgment to select representative organizations covering a range of charitable fields. In addition, they received advice from the Welfare Council of Metropolitan Chicago, the Chicago Community Trust, and others with local experience in this area. The sample was not randomly drawn; such factors as the ability to obtain an interview within the relatively brief period during which the survey was conducted influenced the choice of respondents.

While the distribution of respondents among fields of charitable activity is doubtless not proportionate to the distribution of all charitable organizations in the Chicago area, we do not believe that this seriously skews the major trends the survey shows. The respondents cover the range of charitable institutions providing services which most would agree are valuable to the community, contributing to the general quality of life in Chicago. We believe that the data obtained from them are reasonably reliable indicators of trends among all charitable organizations in the area.

SURVEY OF FOUNDATIONS

A stratified sample research technique was used in this project. The entire population of foundations was divided into seven categories. Company foundations and community foundations each comprised a category, while private foundations were divided into five categories depending upon size of assets. A random sample was then drawn from each of these categories. The size of that sample depended upon the

category from which the sample was drawn. For instance, 251 foundations were sampled out of the estimated 16,000 private foundations with
under $200,000 in assets, while 23 were sampled out of the 27 private
foundations with over $100 million in assets. A much higher proportion
of the population was sampled in the latter category, but in absolute
terms the smaller category contained a larger sample. This research design balances the interest in each of the larger foundations with the
diversity (both real and statistical) of the smaller foundations. Thus, the
43 foundations with under $200,000 in assets were weighted to represent
the estimated 16,000 foundations which meet this description. Each returned questionnaire was assumed to represent 372 foundations. Similarly, the 17 foundations with over $100 million in assets were weighted
to represent the expected 27 foundations which actually fall into the
category.

TABLE A.2.

	Population	Sample	Completed		Weight
Private foundations:					
Under $200,000	16,000	251	43	17.1%	372.1
$200,000–$1 million	5,339	74	21	28.4	254.2
$1–10 million	1,227	68	39	57.3	31.5
$10–100 million	210	100	23	23.0	9.1
Over $100 million	27	23	17	73.9	1.6
Company foundations	1,472	100	39	39.0	37.7
Community foundations	225	71	19	26.8	11.8
	24,499	687	201	29.2%	

Two interview techniques were used to collect the data. For the three
categories containing the smallest private foundations (in aggregate,
those with under $10 million in assets) personal interviews were con-
ducted by trained professional personnel. For the other four categories
the questionnaire was mailed following a telephone contact. The questionnaire included a large variety of topics, such as source and type
of contributions, scope and nature of foundation activity (including
geographical focus, type of recipients of grants, and areas of major interest), administrative procedures (including reimbursement and compensation of officers), nature and size of grants as well as grant-making
processes, financial situations and policies, and connections between the
foundation and any parent organizations or major donors. Only a small
portion of the data have been presented in this report, and the remainder
remains as a rich source of information.

The percentage of sampled foundations which completed the questionnaire varied drastically from category to category. For the large private foundations 74 percent of the questionnaires were completed, while for the smallest private foundations only 17 percent were completed.

Several reasons are available for the discrepancy. Many of the smallest foundations did not have any professional staff that could be assigned to the task, while the large foundations contributed many manhours to this research project. The interview technique also affected the completion rate. Personal interviews seemed to produce a much higher return rate, as evidenced by the fact that only 23 percent of the private foundations with assets of $10–100 million completed their questionnaires, while 57 percent of the next smaller category completed theirs.

Some problems arose in the initial classification of foundations. For instance, some foundations which were thought to be private when the sample was drawn turned out to be company foundations. These foundations were moved into the most appropriate category. Some private foundations were found to have actual assets which differed considerably from those reported on the Internal Revenue Service Form 990's. One reason for this is that assets may be carried on the Form 990 at cost, while their market price may now be considerably above that. Some foundations were moved from one category to another for this reason. The number of foundations which had to be moved in this manner was small and in any case should not have affected the validity of the sample.

SURVEY OF ACCOUNTANTS

At the request of the commission, Arthur Andersen and Company conducted a survey of certified public accountants to obtain their impressions of the extent of abuse in small foundations (those with $200,000 or less in assets). The questionnaire was prepared by the commission staff; the sample was selected, questionnaires mailed, and returns compiled by Arthur Andersen and Company.

The four cities in which CPA's were queried were Chicago, Houston, Los Angeles, and New York. Each of the "Big Eight" CPA firms (those national firms known to be largest in size) were included in the sample for each city. Those firms in the "Second Eight" were included if they had an office in the city. (In addition, three other medium-sized firms were included in Los Angeles.) A sample of small CPA firms was selected for each city, including 101 in Chicago, 100 in Houston, 100 in Los Angeles, and 255 in New York.

The accountants responding to the survey were asked to complete it anonymously. In addition, firms were encouraged to duplicate copies of the questionnaire so that more than one member of the firm could reply.

A total of 600 questionnaires were mailed (and not returned as undeliverable). The return is shown on table A.3.

TABLE A.3.

City and type of firm	Questionnaires Mailed	Replies	Recent Exposure to Small Foundations
Chicago			
Big 8	8	31*	25
Second 8	7	4	3
Small firms	101	58	40
Houston			
Big 8	8	12*	9
Second 8	4	1	1
Small firms	99	58	24
Los Angeles			
Big 8	8	17*	12
Second 8	8	4	4
Small firms	98	54	27
New York			
Big 8	8	18*	18
Second 8	8	2	2
Small firms	243	89	56
TOTAL	600	348	221

*Number of replies exceeds number of questionnaires because of duplication of questionnaires by firms.

Recipients of the questionnaires were asked to indicate the extent of their recent exposure to small foundations. Those who had none were asked to indicate that fact and to return the questionnaire without replying to the substantive questions. In some instances, respondents may have failed to comply with this instruction. It seems reasonable to assume that a portion of the nonrespondents consists of accountants who thought it unnecessary to return a questionnaire indicating only that they had no recent exposure to small foundations.

The data reported in the text of this report are based on a simple numerical count of all completed questionnaires returned by respondents with recent exposure to one or more small foundations. We made no attempt to weight the replies to reflect the importance of accounting firms of a particular size or location to the accounting profession. Responses were also tabulated, however, by size and location of accounting firm. In general, these tabulations yielded similar results to those shown in the report. We do not believe that reporting the data in aggregate terms introduces any systematic bias.

TABULATION OF SAMPLE OF FORM 990-A'S

The commission obtained a sample of Form 990-A's for reporting years ending in 1968 (the most recent available) from the Internal Revenue Service for the purpose of its Survey of Foundations.

Because we had this sample, we decided to tabulate some information directly from the form. In particular, we tabulated the responses of foundations to question 14 on the 990-A form, which asks about various types of "self-dealing" transactions.

Our tabulation was based on 488 Form 990-A's. While the sample was randomly selected, for this purpose, we did not attempt to weight foundations by class. Thus, the 488 forms overrepresented large foundations and underrepresented small ones.

Our assumption is that the result of this overemphasis on large foundations is to understate somewhat the percentage of all foundations reporting self-dealing transactions. In addition, this percentage may be understated because some foundations which had engaged in transactions of this type may have failed to report them to the Internal Revenue Service.

SURVEY OF LARGE PRIVATE DONORS

During August and September 1969 the commission surveyed a sampling of individuals throughout the country who were known to be philanthropists of significant import. In total, questionnaires were mailed to some 278 persons. Usable responses were received from 85 (31 percent) of those surveyed.

Since there was no known complete listing of important private donors, the commission obtained names of philanthropists from sources such as the American Association of Fund-Raising Counsel, Inc., individuals, and private universities. The latter, in several cases, provided the names of benefactors who were known to have donated major gifts in recent years.

While there was no minimum amount established to qualify persons as "important private donors," it should be noted that the majority of those contacted had made donations of one million dollars or more during the past three years. The eighty-five individuals who responded to the survey donated an average of $375,000 to philanthropic causes annually over the past five years. Other significant characteristics of those who responded are listed below.

Donors having a foundation	74 percent
Donors who in recent years have reached 30 percent ceiling on charitable gifts	82 percent
Donors qualifying for, or who have qualified for, the unlimited deduction	13 percent
Donors currently giving through a family foundation	69 percent
Donors owning over 20 percent of the stock of a company	54 percent
Donors or their families having a foundation that owns over 20 percent of the stock of a company	16 percent

Each donor was asked to complete a detailed questionnaire that described the nature of his giving. Persons who responded to the survey provided detailed information on the *distribution* of their charitable giving over the past five years, both their direct giving and their giving conducted through their foundations. Thus, it was possible for the commission to estimate the relative emphasis that large private donors placed upon such areas as education, religion, health, art, and other cultural fields.

Respondents also provided information on the proportions of their gifts that were made in various *forms*, such as: tangible personal property, donative "bargain" sales, appreciated property, cash, or unappreciated property. Other questions sought information on respondent attitudes concerning provisions of the proposed Income Tax Reform Bill (1969) as first passed by the United States House of Representatives, and how these provisions might affect their future giving.

In many instances the respondents were assisted in filling out the commission's questionnaire by their accountants or tax counsel.

Findings of the Survey of Distinguished Citizens

Prepared for the commission by Phillips W. Goodell, Jr.

1. EXPECTED TRENDS IN THE FINANCIAL NEEDS OF CHARITABLE
ORGANIZATIONS

The commission asked the respondents to its survey of distinguished citizens to reflect upon the likely financial needs of charitable organizations over the next five to ten years. These needs were the "outside" funds required by universities, churches, hospitals, museums, symphonies, welfare organizations, etc. Respondents were asked what they expected the financial trends to be in two categories: (1) charitable organizations in general, and (2) the field of society (philanthropy) in which they felt most knowledgeable.

In both cases, a sizable majority expected financial needs to rise rapidly over the five- to ten-year period. A large majority expected the rise in needs to exceed the rise in the country's gross national product. Another group felt that the needs of charitable organizations would rise at a more modest pace, perhaps approximating the rise in GNP. Few felt that the needs would stay the same or decline. The ratios of response are shown in table A.4.

Looking at the needs in the various fields where respondents felt most knowledgeable, it is apparent that increased needs are anticipated for all areas, with education felt to be more likely than other fields to rise rapidly and science somewhat less likely than other fields to rise rapidly.

TABLE A.4.

"I expect the financial needs over the next five to ten years . . .

	For Charitable Organizations in General (percent)	In Field or Area of Society I Feel Most Knowledgeable about (percent)
. . . to go up rapidly over this period, significantly more rapidly than GNP, for example."	66.0	72.4
. . . to go up but at a relatively modest rate—about like GNP."	32.7	26.2
. . . to stay the same as they are now."	0.7	1.0
. . . to go down over this period."	0.6	0.4
	100.0 (N=827)	100.0 (N=833)

TABLE A.5.

EXPECTED FINANCIAL NEEDS OVER THE NEXT FIVE TO TEN YEARS

	Medicine and Health	Arts	Science	Education	All Others	Total All Fields
Rapid rise	72.8%	76.4%	66.7%	79.3%	64.7%	72.4%
Modest rise	26.4	23.6	31.6	20.0	32.5	26.2
No change	0.4	0	1.7	0.7	1.8	1.0
Decline	0.4	0.6	0	0	1.0	0.4
	100.0%	100.6%	100.0%	100.0%	100.0%	100.0%
	(N=297)	(N=112)	(N=104)	(N=294)	(N=235)	(N=1,042)*

*Includes multiple response; i.e. responding individuals who felt knowledgeable about two or more fields of philanthropy. Total persons responding to survey: 885.

2. PUBLIC POLICY TOWARD PRIVATE PHILANTHROPY

If indeed the needs of charitable organizations were to increase in the future and be accompanied by growing government expenditures, what should be the public policy toward private philanthropy? Should governmental incentives be designed to stimulate more private giving above and beyond its current level? Should current tax incentives be left as they are? Should disincentives to private giving be instituted?

Those surveyed were asked to respond to these questions in terms of their preference of one of three possible courses federal government tax policy could take. Their preferences are shown in table A.6. Reasons explaining their choices are shown in table A.7.

TABLE A.6.
PREFERRED FEDERAL TAX POLICY TOWARD PRIVATE PHILANTHROPY

	Percentage in Favor
"Tax policy should further encourage private philanthropy with the federal government playing only whatever role is then necessary"	68.3
"Tax policy should remain as is today" (August 1969)	21.9
"Tax policy should give reduced incentives to private philanthropy, and federal government should play a much more important role"	9.8
	100.0 (N = 866)

The overwhelming thrust of the response favored greater public policy encouragement for private philanthropy, or at least maintaining the existing tax incentives in effect in 1969. The primary reason given for this attitude was the belief that private philanthropy is vital to American society. This was expressed in many ways, but the essential thought was that our society requires a multitude of individual approaches conceived and supported by many institutions, *both* private and governmental. The ideas of "pluralism" and individuality were voiced repeatedly.

Table A.7 is an attempt to categorize over 600 free response comments that respondents gave explaining their attitudes on public policy toward philanthropy.

3. ATTITUDES TOWARD PREPONDERANT GOVERNMENT SUPPORT OF CHARITABLE ORGANIZATIONS AT THE EXPENSE OF A LESSER ROLE FOR PRIVATE PHILANTHROPIC SECTOR

The citizens surveyed were asked to consider a situation in which the trend of outside support in the field of philanthropy where they were most knowledgeable moved toward the federal government's accounting for a preponderant percentage while private giving fell and became a very small percentage. Respondents were then asked to express their views toward this situation in terms of one of the five statements shown in table A.8. They then elaborated at length on why they felt as they did.

TABLE A.7.
RATIONALE FOR AND AGAINST INCREASED TAX INCENTIVES FOR
PRIVATE PHILANTHROPY

	Persons Giving Reasons
Support of increased or same tax incentives	
Multiple sources of funds are required due to the sheer volume of philanthropic needs. Pluralistic approach is in the American tradition. Both government and private support are needed.	159
Encourage private philanthropy, but eliminate abuses. Reduce tax dodge aspects, but maintain thrust of private giving (an important proviso).	89
Private philanthropy allows more freedom of action and flexibility and less restricted scope of activities.	79
This is not the time to change or decrease tax incentives. The present system has worked well. Work to improve it.	79
Concern over continued existence of charitable institutions should private support be lost or diminished. Private funds more reliable, not subject to changing public budgets.	60
Private charitable organizations are more efficient, effective, objective, and economical administrators of financial resources.	50
Maintain tax incentives to avoid government control and excessive growth of central government.	47
Encourage the individualism represented by private giving . . . characteristic of American ideals.	25
Support of reduced tax incentives	
Abuses of tax incentives are too great.	13
Private funding of philanthropy can never be adequate; government must assume the responsibility.	11
Private philanthropy gives undue power to the wealthy few.	5
Private administration of philanthropic funds is actually less efficient and effective than public administration.	5

Note: 41 other miscellaneous comments were registered which did not fall into clear-cut categories. The total number of supporting comments analyzed was 663.

TABLE A.8.
ATTITUDES TOWARD PREPONDERANT GOVERNMENT SUPPORT OF CHARITABLE ORGANIZATIONS AT THE EXPENSE OF A LESSER ROLE FOR PRIVATE PHILANTHROPIC SECTOR

	Medicine and Health	Arts	Science	Education	All Others	Total, All Fields
Strong disapproval, "a very bad thing," would change character of field	34.3%	28.2%	21.0%	35.7%	37.6%	34.1%
Disapprove, "quite unfortunate," would go along with it but worry about effects on philanthropy	34.1	39.8	39.9	40.0	33.4	36.9
Neutral, doesn't bother me as long as work is being supported	5.8	15.4	15.8	5.1	12.0	9.2
Prefer government support, more likely to get needed funds	10.0	14.0	15.7	10.7	7.2	10.2
Very good thing, should come from public sources	15.8	2.6	7.6	8.5	9.8	9.6
	100.0% (N=297)	100.0% (N=112)	100.0% (N=104)	100.0% (N=294)	100.0% (N=235)	100.0% (N=1,042)*

*Includes multiple response. Total persons responding to the survey were 885.

A large majority (71 percent) of the citizens disapproved of the proposition that government should become the dominant supporter of charitable organizations at the expense of a lesser role for the private sector. These people stressed the flexibility of the private sector in meeting needs that require innovation and initiative. They felt that government programs would be preoccupied with political effects of public opinion.

TABLE A.9.
RATIONALE OF PERSONS WHO DISAPPROVED OF PREPONDERANT GOVERNMENT SUPPORT AT THE EXPENSE OF A LESSER ROLE FOR THE PRIVATE SECTOR (71 percent of those interviewed; 736 comments)

	Percent of Opinion
Flexibility. Private philanthropy allows more flexibility in areas requiring innovation and initiative; . . . government decisions would be more "timid," following public opinion; want less government control and more independence of action.	40.1
Pluralism, we need both private and government support. Private philanthropy cannot do it alone; government financing already present; need balance of support; all support sources are required to fill the need; private support should be encouraged as a basic strength in the American system; government should only become involved in philanthropy when private sector is not equal to the task.	30.2
Superiority of private philanthropy. Must increase or maintain present proportion of private philanthropic funding; private philanthropy has demonstrated effectiveness in areas neglected by government; private philanthropy more efficient: better evaluator of progress and administrator of funds, better decision-making processes.	17.8
Uncertainty of government funding. Government funding lacks continuity, too short-term; government budgets unpredictable, too dependent upon government already; fear cutbacks on programs presently supported by private philanthropy.	9.1
Other miscellaneous comments by persons who were against preponderant government support of charitable institutions at the expense of a lesser private philanthropic role.	2.8
Total	100.0

There was also the concern that dependence upon government support would put charitable organizations at the mercy of federal budget priorities.

The concept of pluralism was again voiced. There was the feeling that government should move into private sector programs only if private support was inadequate. But, along with these thoughts, those who would disapprove of predominant government support often pointed out that, while private support might be better, government aid (and sometimes *increased* aid) would be needed as well.

On the other hand, 29 percent of the distinguished citizens interviewed were positively inclined or neutral toward the idea of preponderant government support of charitable organizations at the expense of the lesser private-sector role.

Only a few of these individuals chose this viewpoint on philosophical grounds. Nearly three-quarters of them (71 percent) pointed out that the economics of the situation was the controlling factor, that the private sector could not do the job adequately, and that government's role of preponderant support was inevitable. At the same time, many of these individuals stated that existing private support should be maintained and even increased.

The qualitative response to both views are summarized in table A.9.

4. LIKELIHOOD THAT THE FEDERAL GOVERNMENT WOULD, IF NECESSARY, FILL MAJOR FUND GAPS

The distinguished respondents were next asked about the possibility of the federal government's filling the gap of financial needs in charitable fields during the next few years. The question was presented as follows, and the resulting opinion is shown in table A.11. "Let us assume that budgets in this field (field of philanthropy best known to respondent) rise rapidly over the next several years; contributions from other sources simply do not meet its needs, and the field is left with a major gap; a major deficit. In your opinion, how likely is it that the federal government will step in and make up a significant part or all of this deficit?" It is clear from these findings that those knowledgeable in the field of the arts are far less sure these future needs would be met than those knowledgeable in medicine and health felt about future support in their field of society.

The fields of religion and the humanities are not shown separately because an insufficiently large sample of individuals returned questionnaires concerning these fields. However, those who did respond

TABLE A.10.
RATIONALE OF PERSONS WHO APPROVED OF PREPONDERANT GOVERNMENT
SUPPORT AT THE EXPENSE OF A LESSER ROLE FOR THE PRIVATE SECTOR, OR
WHO WERE UNCONCERNED (29 percent of those interviewed; 244 comments)

	Percent of Opinion
Necessity of government support. Government will have to move toward greater subsidy of charitable institutions because private sources cannot provide the sheer masses of funds required. The massiveness of charitable needs precludes a preponderant role for private philanthropy. Private philanthropy has not been able to meet the needs; government is already the primary support of many charitable fields. There can and should be an increase in private support . . . it would be unfortunate if private philanthropy were phased out entirely.	71.0
More equitable disbursement and use of funds. Government financing will assure that all necessary areas are attended to . . . assures that the less "glamorous" areas are not neglected . . . government strikes the proper balance between independence and control . . . insures programs are in the public interest.	20.1
Government funds more reliable. Government support provides continuity and follow-through on programs, less waste of funds, better administration, proven effectiveness.	6.9
Other miscellaneous comments by persons favoring preponderant government support of charitable institutions at expense of lesser private philanthropic role.	2.0
	100.0

TABLE A.11.
LIKELIHOOD OF FEDERAL SUPPORT FILLING MAJOR FUND GAPS IN THE NEXT
FEW YEARS, BY FIELD OF PHILANTHROPY

	Medicine and Health	Arts	Science	Education	All Others	All Fields
Very likely	49.0%	7.4%	19.4%	34.0%	20.0%	28.7%
Uncertain	33.7	48.9	63.5	48.1	37.6	44.0
Unlikely	17.3	43.7	17.1	17.9	42.4	27.3
	100.0%	100.0%	100.0%	100.0%	100.0%	100.0%
	(N=297)	(N=112)	(N=104)	(N=294)	(N=235)	(N=1,042)*

*Includes multiple response. Total persons responding to the survey were 885.

in these two fields were quite pessimistic that the federal government would fill the gaps in their charitable needs. On the other hand, respondents thought the international and domestic welfare deficits probably would be met by government. These categories, (along with religion) and the humanities, are grouped together in table A.10 under "All Others."

5. OPINION OF THE "TRACK RECORD" OF GRANT-MAKING FOUNDATIONS

Individuals were asked to state their opinions on the *role of foundations;* the impact and significance of foundations in the fields of philanthropy that they knew best. The first of several questions regarding foundations is presented in table A.12. Five categories of response were offered concerning the role of foundations: (1) Foundations have played a *very significant* role in this field—without them, some of the significant developments perhaps would not have taken place at all, or at least would have been delayed. (2) On balance, foundations have played a positive role—they have tended to support *worthwhile* projects—but on the whole they have been worthwhile. (3) My overall reaction to the contribution of foundations is a mixed one—the record is a *spotty* one, good some of the time, but insignificant, nonexistent and even negative at other times. (4) Foundations have contributed *very little* of *significance* in this field. (5) Foundations have played a *negative role* in this field—I believe the field would have been better off without them.

TABLE A.12.
OPINION OF THE SIGNIFICANCE OF FOUNDATIONS IN VARIOUS FIELDS

	Medicine and Health	Arts	Science	Education	All Others	Total, All Fields
Significant role in field	60.0%	53.5%	50.5%	60.0%	45.0%	54.0%
On balance worthwhile	24.6	28.5	31.0	25.8	25.2	26.2
"Spotty" record	15.2	16.1	15.3	12.6	19.4	15.7
Little significant impact	0.2	1.9	3.2	1.0	9.6	3.7
Negative role	0	0	0	0.6	0.8	0.4
	100.0%	100.0%	100.0%	100.0%	100.0%	100.0%
	(N=297)	(N=112)	(N=104)	(N=294)	(N=235)	(N=1,042)*

*Includes multiple response. Total persons responding to the survey were 885.

In the areas of education and medicine and health, 60 percent of the respondents felt that foundations had played a truly significant role; that without foundation participation, significant developments in these fields might not have happened or at least would have been delayed. A high regard for the role of foundations was also reported for other fields. In all, 80 percent of those interviewed thought that the role of foundations in the fields of philanthropy that they knew best had been either worthwhile (positive) or very significant.

In the fields of religion and welfare (combined with others in the "all others" category) some reservations were expressed concerning the significance of foundation participation. However, even in these two fields a majority of those interviewed thought that foundation contribution had been at least occasionally significant.

6. AWARENESS OF FOUNDATIONS' SUCCESSES AND FAILURES IN PHILANTHROPIC ENDEAVORS

In addition to questions on their general attitude toward the role of foundations, the commission asked respondents if they were actually aware of significant "achievements" or anything they would consider "failures" of foundations. The questions asked were as follows: (1) Are you aware of any significant developments, achievements or innovations in this field or area of society (one about which respondent was most knowledgeable) in which foundations made a contribution? (2) If "yes," could you briefly list some specific examples of foundation contributions in this field? (3) Are you aware of what you would consider to be failures of foundations in this field? (4) If "yes," could you briefly list some specific examples of foundation failures in this field?

TABLE A.13.
AWARENESS OF FOUNDATION SUCCESSES AND FAILURES

	Successes	Failures
Yes	90.2%	48.3%
No	9.8	51.7
	100.0% (N = 1,042)	100.0% (N = 1,042)

The overwhelming majority of distinguished citizens were aware of foundation successes and slightly less than half said they were aware of what they would consider foundation failures (see table A.13).

In describing the specific successes and achievements of foundations, respondents mentioned many diverse programs. Since one purpose of the inquiry was to test the depth of citizens' awareness, the response was divided into four degrees of familiarity with foundation programs: (1) specific awareness of successful programs or projects, (2) general awareness of foundation activities in the field, but no indication of specific programs, (3) comments showing little awareness of foundation activities in the field, and (4) statements that indicated the respondent was unaware of any examples of foundation activities in the field.

Of those who said they were aware of significant foundation achievements (90 percent), seven out of ten fell into the first category and could name specific achievements or successful projects. Another 20 percent had some general awareness of programs in their fields. Only 11 percent indicated little or no actual knowledge of specific foundation successes.

TABLE A.14.
FOUNDATION SHORTCOMINGS

	Percent
Program selection. Poor priorities, failure to recognize real needs, pet projects.	24.3
Administrative failures. Poor coordination, direction, and planning, merit of grantee not properly evaluated, short-term program where longer term requirement existed.	19.9
Lack of innovation. Too often support only of proved institutions and programs. Support confined to local area, too narrow.	14.0
Poor program results. Examples of shortsighted or "meaningless" programs, some "negative" results.	9.9
"Tax dodge" criticism. Abuses of tax privilege status for self-dealing or tax relief.	6.2
Political motivations. Participation in programs designed to lend assistance to political causes.	5.2
Inadequate financing. Failure to provide enough money to fund program.	3.6
Other miscellaneous criticism. Excessive control over grantee, lack of public reporting, etc.	12.2
No examples known of failures.	4.7
Total	100.0*

*Represents the 48.3 percent of all persons interviewed who said that they were aware of some failures or shortcomings of foundations. Nearly two-thirds of these persons also gave specific examples of what they considered achievements or innovations that foundations had contributed to the fields of philanthropy about which they were most knowledgeable.

Quite obviously, many persons who knew of foundation successes also knew of examples of their shortcomings. Of persons who reported that they were aware of what they would consider failures of foundations (48 percent), only two out of ten could name specific failures.

While respondents described foundation achievements with particular examples, they were more general in their description of what they considered to be foundation failures or shortcomings. These criticisms are shown in table A.14. They deal primarily with areas of judgment (program selection), and adequacy of foundation administration and resources.

TABLE A.15.
Subsample Cross-tabulation (Survey of distinguished citizens)

The following cross-tabulation is a subsample of 246 respondents taken from the original total of 885. The purpose of the cross-tabulation is to determine: (a) What proportion of those persons who said they were aware of foundation failures (48.3 percent) could actually cite *specific cases or examples* of failures; (b) Of those who said they were aware of foundation failures, what proportion *also* were aware of and mentioned *specific foundation achievements*.

	Number	Percent	
	246	100	Total subsample picked for purposes of the cross tabulation.
	112	46	Persons aware of foundation failures.
(a)	23	21	Persons aware of foundation failures—who *could cite specific cases* or examples.
(b)	71	63	Persons aware of foundation failures—who *also* were aware of *and mentioned specific foundation achievements*.

7. Characteristics of Foundation Support

Those who favor foundations have made a number of statements concerning the advantages of foundations as opposed to federal government support. Among these are the propositions that: (1) foundations are able to respond to charitable needs more quickly and flexibly, (2) foundations are willing to support unusual, innovative, or unpopular projects, and (3) foundations are less likely to try to impose their own thoughts and policies on grantees.

The commission asked the distinguished citizens interviewed to reflect upon their own experience and react to these statements. The response is shown in table A.16. Respondents were able to accept or reject each statement by choosing from a range of answers the one that best fit their opinions.

TABLE A.16.
ATTITUDES TOWARD STATEMENTS CONCERNING FOUNDATION ADVANTAGES

Statement "A"—Response: "Foundations, because they often have independent endowments, can respond more quickly and flexibly than many other sources."

Statement "B"—Innovation: "Foundations are willing to support unusual or innovative or unpopular projects that others such as the federal government are unable or unwilling to support."

Statement "C"—Less control: "Foundations are less likely to try to impose their own thoughts and policies (criteria) on grantees, and this is a danger when the federal government becomes dominant."

	Statement "A"	Statement "B"	Statement "C"
True in all or most respects	31.7%	21.6%	17.3%
More often true than not	41.4	40.4	34.6
Sometimes true, sometimes false	22.0	30.9	29.7
More often false than not	2.1	4.8	7.4
False in all or most respects	0.4	0.9	5.1
Don't know	2.4	1.4	5.9
	100.0% (N = 1,042)	100.0% (N = 1,042)	100.0% (N = 1,042)

The distinguished citizens strongly agreed with the first two statements; that foundations can, in fact, respond more quickly and flexibly and that they are willing to support innovative or unusual (sometimes unpopular) projects. A majority also agreed with the proposition that foundations are less likely to impose their own thoughts on grantees than the federal government would be. However, some 10 percent of the respondents took exception to this statement and noted that "it depends upon the situation" or that "there is little difference between foundations and the federal government in this regard."

8. IS SOCIETY BETTER OFF WITH, OR WITHOUT, FOUNDATIONS?

When given the "choice" of keeping or abolishing foundations, the distinguished citizens overwhelmingly voiced the opinion that society is better off with foundations than without them.

TABLE A.17.
"In your view, is society better off with foundations, or would it be better off
if they did not exist and all private charity went directly from the giver to the
recipient?"

	Percentage of Reponse
Society would be	
better off with foundations	94.5
better off without them	2.7
No opinion	2.8
	100.0 (N = 1,042)

In explaining their views on why society would be better off with or
without foundations, the citizens brought out a strong list of advantages
that they saw in this source of philanthropy. They emphasized the administrative superiority of foundations in awarding grants, the likelihood of stability of funds, the independence from political pressures,
and the need for multiple sources of philanthropic funds in American
society (see table A.18).

TABLE A.18.
REASONS GIVEN WHY SOCIETY WOULD BE BETTER
OFF WITH, OR WITHOUT, FOUNDATIONS

	Percentage of Response
Administrative advantages. Foundations provide efficient and effective means to plan and evaluate programs, channel and administer money. Foundations assure flexibility, proper balance between control and independence.	34.9
Continuity and sufficiency of funds. Reliability of funds lends stability to programs. Programs have added impetus, more long-run follow-through. Funds not subject to changes in government tax policies. Foundations have sufficient funds to finance significant programs.	12.3
Initiative and innovation. Foundations operate in areas that would be neglected by individual donors. Assure that the "unknowns" can get money, too. Provide funds to less "glamorous" programs. Initiative and innovations are prime characteristics of foundations.	11.8
Act as "catalyst" for philanthropy. Mobilize support for pro-grams. Provide philanthropy sense of direction, a place to give money. Give sense of coordinated individualism, pro-mote personal pride in giving. Cause people to donate who otherwise might not.	9.0

TABLE A.18.—*Continued*
REASONS GIVEN WHY SOCIETY WOULD BE BETTER
OFF WITH, OR WITHOUT, FOUNDATIONS

	Percentage of Response
Pluralism. Essential role of private philanthropy is to provide a balance between the public and private sectors. Foundations a necessary element of society, assist in making private decisions. Help to avoid further government control of society.	7.1
Cannot generalize. Some foundation programs not worthy, but each should be judged on its own merits. On balance, society is better off with foundations. Improve foundations, eliminate abuses.	6.2
Objective action. Foundations can be free of personal obligations and political interest. More objective in decision making.	6.1
Demonstrated worth. Specific works or programs mentioned that demonstrate foundation value. General experience or opinion that foundations worthwhile.	4.8
*Negative comments.** Excessive controls on grantees, poor administration of funds, need for more public reporting of foundation activities, "tax dodges," administrative costs reduce amount for charity (vs. direct giving).	3.5
Miscellaneous comments. Difficult to generalize. Foundations are necessary, sheer massiveness of philanthropic administration has created them, etc.	4.3
Total comment	100.0 (N = 1,042)

*Negative comments were received from persons who thought that society would be better off without foundations and a few who, while favoring foundations, noted what they considered deficiencies that should be eliminated.

9. ATTITUDES TOWARD FOUNDATION PARTICIPATION IN CONTROVERSIAL ACTIVITIES

The commission questionnaire pointed out that at times foundation activities have aroused some controversy, particularly in areas related to social/political actions. In order to establish some parameters for what might be considered permissible and nonpermissible activities, the commission listed a number of "sensitive" areas of activity and asked the distinguished citizens if they thought foundations should participate.

Table A.19 indicates whether or not the respondents favored foundation participation in each "sensitive" area listed. While in general the distinguished citizens studied favored foundation support of most of these controversial activities, this was clearly not the case with grants to government employees.

TABLE A.19.
FOUNDATION PARTICIPATION IN CONTROVERSIAL ACTIVITIES (N = 1,042)

	Favor (Percent)	Do Not Favor (Percent)	No Opinion (Percent)
Support to community organizations which might include a variety of youth groups, such as gangs.	71.7	19.5	8.8
International grants	70.1	18.9	11.0
Grants to study public policy issues and influence public opinion or government action through dissemination of the study.	69.2	22.1	8.7
Voter registration activities	63.4	29.1	7.5
Grants to government employees	27.6	56.7	15.7

10. APPROPRIATE ROLES OF FOUNDATIONS AS THEY RELATE TO GOVERNMENT ACTIVITIES

The commission's questionnaire pointed out that, as the scope of government activities continues to expand rapidly into many areas in which private philanthropic foundations were previously active, it becomes increasingly important to think through the possible roles of foundations as they relate to government activities.

The respondents were asked to look ahead and tell what roles, if any, foundations should fill in our society. For example:

Should foundations work closely with government or operate independently? Should foundations act as partners, or evaluators, or initiators of programs that, if successful, might later receive public support? Should foundations carve out new areas?

The distinguished citizens' recommendations for what they consider to be proper future roles of foundations vis-à-vis the federal government are shown in table A-20.

TABLE A.20.

ATTITUDES REGARDING THE PROPER ROLES OF FOUNDATIONS
AS THEY RELATE TO GOVERNMENT ACTIVITIES

	Percentage of Response
Foundations should innovate, carve out new areas that might later receive public support.	41.7
Foundations should be completely independent of government financing and/or influence.	15.7
Foundations must continue to be an important supporter of private philanthropy (values of pluralism, decentralization, etc.).	7.3
Foundations should cooperate with government, yet remain autonomous.	14.4
Foundations should act as evaluators and objective analysts of philanthropic programs; should criticize and influence government programs.	8.6
Foundations should be a partner with government.	8.1
Other recommendations.	4.2
	100.0 (N = 1,888)*

*Includes multiple response.

EXHIBIT 1:
ILLUSTRATIVE COMMENTS BY DISTINGUISHED CITIZENS

The Survey of Distinguished Citizens yielded considerable written comment on the part of those who responded. The commentary occurred throughout the questionnaire in many cases. Three of the questions which elicited the most frequent and articulate comments are sampled in this section. Quotations have been reproduced verbatim, followed by a general identification of the respondent's position or field of endeavor.

1. FEDERAL TAX POLICY TOWARD PRIVATE PHILANTHROPY

Question: "Assuming growing needs of charitable organizations and growing government expenditures, what should be the public policy toward private philanthropy? Should governmental incentives be designed to stimulate more private giving above and beyond its current level; should current tax incentives be left as they are; should some disincentives to private giving be instituted? How do you feel about this, and why?"

Verbatim Comments:

"Our system of private philanthropy which has been encouraged up until the present has produced many important and worthy institutions in many fields and which have no peers throughout the world. These could not have flourished under a less liberal system.

"Politically dominated government-supported institutions have never produced institutions the equal to the superb schools, museums, research organizations, etc., that have been developed through private philanthropy and which make important contributions to our way of life.

"Tax incentives should be maintained with proper policing policies established to eliminate the abuses that a small minority of individuals are guilty of. The idea that those who avail themselves of provisions of the law in order to increase charitable giving are numerous and should be corrected. Correction in existing law to eliminate making a profit on gifts to charities should be enacted, but to otherwise disincentive private philanthropy could produce a serious and possibly disastrous effect on our fine institutions of learning, culture, and research."

Chairman of the board, business corporation

"Increasing funding from the private sector is badly needed to restore a better balance between government and private funding. More dollars from the private sector are needed to provide the vital factor of protection from an overdependence on a single source of financial support."

President, school of health sciences

"Probably tax policy should encourage more support of recognized and accredited ongoing educational institutions and discourage some of the fringe or less responsible types of so-called educational enterprises."

State university president

"The fallacy here is the assumption that a significant portion of the funds lost by the federal government in tax incentives is actually used for the best philanthropic purposes."

Professor of mathematics, institute of technology

"A countervailing set of institutions is one of our best guarantees against centralized waste, inefficiency, and insensitivity."

President of private company

"The spirit of the Golden Rule among human beings should be cherished and cultivated. Those who have been most successful and are generously endowed with worldly goods and who feel an urgent desire to correct or improve a deficiency of our social order should be encouraged to apply their talents, leadership, and resources to the problem by stimulating their private initiative."

Managing director (scientist), private institute

"There is a growing awareness that we do not know how effective private and government philanthropy are. There seems to be a need, then, to assess the managerial capability of present program management and to develop standards against which to assess them."

Director, computer sciences company

"I think that private philanthropy can and must meet the needs of society. I think that they can best do this by providing the 'risk capital' for educational change. Private philanthropy is much better suited to do this than any governmental unit since it is much more flexible and, thus, better able to meet new situations as they arise."

University president

"The unique value of private philanthropy is pecularly American. It has historically provided unencumbered support to both education and charity, thus encouraging innovation."

Doctor of medicine

"Despite 200 years, nearly, of public education, the majority of the people in this republic are electing to public office more and more men who are willing to raid the public treasury for the benefit of the welfare cancer instead of trying to preserve the future of the working members of society."

Practicing urologist

"Foundations offer, particularly by encouraging individual gifts, an effective means for the citizen to express concern at a time when big government threatens to drown his voice."

Professor of conservation (biology)

"The rapid growth in the size and number of foundations makes it clear that they are not primarily philanthropic institutions. Rather, they serve as tax shelters, sources of low-cost loans, and through their activities are able to support and lobby on behalf of political candidates and issues."

Union research director

"Some instances of private philanthropy to avoid federal and state taxes should be curbed to a much greater degree."

Union regional director

"The abuses of our present tax incentives by private philanthropy and foundations are such that I think it important that we reduce these incentives in a number of areas until such time as the abuses are eliminated. Obviously the federal government, and particularly the Internal Revenue Service, should have a strong say-so on what tax modifications are necessary."

Union regional director

"There is too much evidence that 'so-called' foundations have abused their tax privileges."

Union research director

"Since foundations use taxpayers' money, elected officials and representatives should be responsible for the use of it."

Union official

"There are certain areas where private philanthropies can tread that government cannot. These should be the future arena. However, many of the areas previously dependent upon private philanthropy are now quite properly a matter of right, not a matter of largess. As we explore further the social problems facing our society, I would expect more recognition of this enlightenment."

Union official

"Government cannot—and should not—take the risks and adventures which private philanthropy can undertake. Yet those risks must be taken if our society is to progress. Tax incentives help induce private citizens to take those risks."

Former federal regulatory commission chairman

"Present tax policy encourages some $15 billion of private philanthropy in this country each year. If tax laws remain the same, this figure will increase as gross national product increases."

Former Cabinet Member, federal government

2. PREPONDERANT GOVERNMENT SUPPORT OF CHARITABLE ORGANIZATIONS AT THE EXPENSE OF A LESSER ROLE FOR PRIVATE PHILANTHROPIC SECTOR.

Question: "We'd like to find out your views on what difference it makes what the sources of outside contributions are in this field. Let us assume the trend of outside support in this field (the one you selected in the answer to question 1) moved toward the *federal government's* accounting for a *preponderant* percentage of outside funds in this field, and *private giving fell* and became a very small percentage. What would you think about this?"

Verbatim Comments:
"The private philanthropic programs have been more responsive, flexible, and innovative. We need this approach plus the larger dollar amounts coming from government."

Dean, state university medical center

"Science now requires very substantial support from government and industry and on a *continuing* scale which private foundations cannot possibly meet. Yet the amount available from government, including the states, and industry is inadequate today to pursue all of the important investigations desirable. More important, however, is the need for support in new fields, of younger investigations, and of certain international activities which have *relatively* little appeal to the government."

Executive officer of national science academy

"Government support would be too dependent on whims of political power."

Physician-surgeon

"Tax policy should further encourage private philanthropy, but the federal government *should also* play a much more important role. These two mechanisms of support are *not* incompatible."

Dean, school of medicine

"I may be responding out of inertia. I know the problems and the opportunities that exist under the present situation . . . I'm not sure about what they might be if the government was the preponderant source of funds. I have been in a state system and was appalled at how long (and it wasn't ill will, indifference, or incapacity on the part of the state bureaucrat either—or not entirely) to put a new idea into operation. Like most, I have been overwhelmed by the paperwork accompanying government grants (even as I eagerly sought them)—a work load which is probably essential if monies are to be spent properly. I am impressed, too, by the level of interest shown by extremely capable members of the private sector in the workings of the college —many of them invest their time and their gifts in a charity as carefully as they do in their business—and their 'whys' can force some very healthy reappraisals of what is being done."

President, private college

"I am a firm believer in the freedom-of-enterprise principle (with proper controls) on which our country has been built and under which private philanthropy has been encouraged, and accordingly produced the fine institutions we now have. This method has attracted the ablest professional talent to manage and operate these organizations relatively free of political dominance. While many areas that are government-supported have also flourished, the tremendous waste and cost incurred in these areas makes the entire cost of the private philanthropic program trivial in relation to what it would cost under a government-supported system versus our present private philanthropic method.

"The tremendous gains achieved through freedom of expression and development of ideas that has been fostered and supported by private philanthropy has never been matched by a system of government-supported institutions with all if its red tape, protocol, and stifling of initiative and waste inherent in such a system.

"Under a government-supported program the individual resourcefulness of the professional technician would be more likely to be muffled and stifled from full expression and initiative in developing his ideas and concepts by the politically appointed supervisor, because of his personal limitations and political motivations, than under a private philanthropic program."

Chairman of the board, business corporation

"We need sources of funds for other than totally 'safe' projects, i.e., for projects the government cannot support."

Professor of sociology

"Too few people have a real working concern with charity now—it's so easy to say 'That's up to government,'—and I do believe that private colleges and private hospitals (public charitable though they are) have much to contribute in fighting uniformity and conformity, so that I think there would be a great social loss if more load than is necessary is put on the government sector."

Lawyer

"In the end the resources required will be so vast (e.g., for urban development) that only massive federal expenditure will fill the bill—foundations can only assist and illustrate methods of innovation."

Professor of political science

"Foundations, owned and operated by the wealthy, have not, and will not, with few exceptions, ever serve in the best interests of the working class."

Union research director

"We need more federal aid to education. Local tax rates are unable to support improved quality education at the local level or state universities via state taxes."

Union regional director

"In the area of medicine and health, the federal government should accept a major role. Regretfully, private medicine ignored the public interest and private philanthropy made little impact. In my opinion, competent medical scientists in the employment of the government can state our needs and goals after objective study, and I am hopeful that Congress would respond with the proper legislation and financial resources to meet these goals. To my way of thinking, private insurance that now serves as the vehicle for paying much inflated medical costs does little to point out and eliminate the abuses."

Union regional director

"In either case, the public pays the bill—increased government responsibility through directly increased taxes or increased private contribution through tax revenue lost. Government participation over private is preferable because control of the various programs is through legislative process and not through arbitrary decisions of foundation presidents. It is possible to determine the future political climate of this country. In the area of welfare, the urgency of the demands and the lack of alternatives require increased government participation."

Union official

"The material needs, real and created, of all segments of society leave private charity a matter of conscience and concern. I'm not overly optimistic about any increase in awareness of need, and I have seen private concerns fluctuate too much to depend on."

Union official

"I am a firm believer in the private support of charities, and hopefully we will not become dependent upon the federal government; however, I would prefer to see a much wider area of participation and an increased deduction as opposed to the unlimited deductions by some and government support."

Union president

"Having been in government, I believe a greater government role would inevitably mean more bureaucracy, less initiative, less venturesomeness; more blandness and mediocrity."

Former federal regulatory commission chairman

"Education is already heavily dependent on public funds—local, state, and federal—and will become more so. Federal government will play increasing role. But every decrease in relative role of private sector financing is unfortunate. We need pluralism in this field."

Former cabinet member, federal government

"The restrictions placed upon the spending of federal funds stultifies creativity and imagination—at a time when they are most needed."

Social worker

3. THE ROLE OF PRIVATE FOUNDATIONS IN AMERICAN SOCIETY.

Question: "As the scope of government activities continues to expand rapidly into many areas in which private philanthropic foundations were previously active, it becomes increasingly important to think through possible roles of foundations as they relate to government activities.

"Should foundations work closely with government or operate independently? Should foundations act as partners, or evaluators, or initiators of programs that, if successful, might later receive public support? Should foundations carve out new areas? Looking ahead, what important roles, if any, do you feel foundations should fill in our society?"

Verbatim Comments:

"[Foundations] should act primarily as funders of pilot project–type programs. Social needs are too great to be funded by private contributions, but as pacesetters and innovators they can be very constructive.

"[They] should not work as a partner or in collaboration with government, as it would destroy their independence and objectivity. If the programs are good the government will soon pick them up.

"[They] should constantly be seeking new areas for support and should always be well out in front of public policy."

Chairman and president, insurance company

"Foundations should act as evaluators or initiators of programs which might later receive public support."

Physician

"They should be entirely independent of [government support] and as much as possible operate in fields where government support is not furnished."

Lawyer

"Foundations should work independently or they will soon lose their independence. They should avoid competition with or duplication of governmental activities, except when their approach to a problem might have dimensions not normally available through government sponsorship. On the other hand . . . they should not automatically bow out of a legitimate area of service merely because a governmental agency makes signs of its preemption.

"For selfish reasons I hope an increasing number of foundations will support higher education. Curtailments in governmental support programs and the rather hostile attitude of so many private citizens can only accentuate the difficulties so many of our academic institutions are experiencing.

"The foundations which tend to think in longer range can be of inestimable help in this period of stress and strain."

State college president

"Foundations should be encouraged to remain independent and to *innovate*. Government can support the good ideas after they are proven."

Professor of political science

"I feel that foundations can indeed initiate and experiment in a way which might be prohibitive to the government. If successful, such programs could then be taken on as legitimate governmental activities.

"They can also assist artists whom federal critics might find too avant-garde, the artist being usually ahead of his time. The foundation can help support him in his experimental years, and the government reward him for his achievement."

President, academy of poets

"I believe that foundations should in the beginning work on their own projects and initiate new programs, for in this way many things will be done that public opinion might not allow our legislators to approve at this time. When a project becomes successful and it looks like more money will be needed to work out problems for the good of society, then I think the foundation should work closely with the government, but not necessarily as partners.

"I believe [foundations] should remain independent to the point of being able to state their own opinions, to increase the support or decrease support depending upon the development of events. There is no doubt that foundations will be able to get into many fields of medicine and of social problems that the government cannot properly initiate at this time."

Physician, large private clinic

"Foundations should be encouraged to plow their own furrows. When foundation objectives correspond to current government emphasis, close cooperation is in order. When government policy is opposed to a foundation emphasis, freedom of the foundation is essential. Only in a totalitarian state can government justifiably dictate or determine the legitimacy of private (including foundation) effort.

"To the degree that government attempts to control and direct the activities of foundations, the nation moves away from freedom toward totalitarianism."

President, large city public college

"Foundations should be independent of government. This is the only way to achieve real pluralism: let the foundations use initiative and imagination. "Foundations . . . the more the better . . . make sure that diversity exists. There needs to be diversity among the foundations; some will be interested in one thing, some another. The foundations help make sure that nothing is overlooked . . . they help prevent us going down a single road."

Executive director, political science association

"I feel that, due to the resources available to foundations, they should function as innovators, even in areas covered by government programs. However, where obvious duplication of efforts exists, cooperative efforts should be developed. I see no reason for the two not developing full coordination and planning efforts. Of utmost importance is the need to meet problems, rather than conflict in roles.

"I feel that the foundations should assume a larger role in society and should also enter into more social action areas."

Executive director metropolitan area urban league

"The collective wisdom of Congress, as determined through the elective and the deliberative process, in spite of all its shortcomings, is preferable to arbitrary control of a few wealthy individuals. I do not believe the government should subsidize foundations and, thus, somewhat lessen the need for government regulation of foundation activities. A foundation should be free to participate in any area of interest it feels will benefit society. The roles of government and foundation should complement each other. The foundation's advantage is, given an imaginative board of trustees, quick response, flexibility, courage, and, hopefully, the propensity to undertake innovative and imaginative activities. Foundations should move where the politically motivated representatives are hesitant to do so. The government is responsible for the more massive, costly, and far-reaching programs. However, any institution which directly affects society should be required to submit detailed public reports and a full disclosure of financial interests. The same logic which was applied to labor unions in the enactment of the Labor-Management Reporting and Disclosure Act applies also in the case of foundations. While the federal government's influence on foundations should be minimized, it is obvious some system of financial disclosure and activity reporting is essential."

Union official

"Foundations should feel free to work closely with government if it enhances their effectiveness and does not compromise their independence.

"One of the most important roles for any private-sector nonprofit organization to consider is the Ombudsman role. Closely related is the role of appraiser and evaluator.

"Yes, foundations should carve out new areas.

"Foundations have played a distinguished role in innovation, but may have squandered their resources on bits and pieces of innovation that never added up to anything."

Former cabinet member, federal government

"I think that the government will increasingly and inevitably move into areas with funds and programs where heretofore it has fallen to private tources, including foundations, to sustain them. Specifically, I am thinking of she arts, medical research, health care, etc.

"I think foundations have already been helpful in plowing new ground and should continue by finding more new areas. Federal funding is not so likely to come for brand-new ventures. It is only after some initial success or public knowledge of the existence of a program is established that the necessary momentum can begin to generate, leading to possible federal action."

Union president

"They should work closely with government. Initiating programs would be desirable. In general, their role should be to improve the lot of all Americans in various fields."

Union regional director

"Foundations should operate independently of government. I see no conflict in their evaluating government programs on the basis of research or initiating programs as a testing agency which might later receive public support. There are new legitimate areas of research for foundations to carve out."

Union regional director

"It is my opinion that foundations can readily serve the entire nation in a social, economic area; they could do constructive theorizing in the field of health, education, and welfare. I am somewhat fearful of their activities in the political field, although, with several stringent restrictions, I would not be opposed to such activity."

Union president

"In general, foundations do not have the massive resources to care for "consumer needs"; foundations can work at root causes and can experiment with seed money to devise better solutions than have thus far been found. Government funds are massive; foundation funds are scarce; thus the latter might best be used at the cutting edge of problems. Further, government is reluctant to become heavily involved in certain fields, such as the humanities and the arts."

Former cabinet member, federal government

"Due to the resources available to foundations, they should function as innovators, even in areas covered by government programs. However, where obvious duplication of efforts exists, cooperative efforts should be developed. I see no reason for the two not developing full coordination and planning efforts. Of utmost importance is the need to meet problems, rather than conflict in roles."

Urban league director

Findings of the Survey of Chicago Philanthropic Organizations

Prepared for the commission by Richard H. Chandler

1. OVERALL FINANCIAL REQUIREMENTS

The Survey of Chicago Philanthropic Organizations showed that these institutions are currently facing a severe budget crisis. Fifty-four percent of the organizations replying to the questionnaire experienced a deficit during 1968; for them, total expenditures exceeded total income from all sources.

Part of the explanation for the current critical situation can be found in the rapid growth in these organizations' financial requirements over the past five years. Total annual expenditures increased at a rate of 55 percent for the organizations surveyed, as compared to 47 percent for the United States economy as a whole. Moreover, between 1968 and 1975 this pace is expected to accelerate (see table A.21). It is no wonder that the heads of these institutions, when questioned on the financial outlook for 1975, responded as follows: 55 percent believed their organizations will face a real budget crisis unless some major new sources of funds are developed; 28 percent felt that some cutbacks in programs will be necessary to make ends meet in 1975; only 17 percent

TABLE A.21.

	1963–68 (N = 37)	1968–75 (estimated) (N = 26)
Growth in GNP	+47%	+54%*
Chicago charitable organizations (median increase)	+55%	+68%

*Estimated by the National Industrial Conference Board, *The Conference Board Record*, May 1968.

were confident that income will rise fast enough to meet their needs in 1975. (Forty-seven institutions reported out of fifty-one questioned.)

2. THE COST OF PEOPLE

Part of the explanation for the financial difficulties of the institutions surveyed can be found in the relatively large portion of their operating budgets spent on salaries and related "people" expenses. People accounted for 58 percent of their operating expenses in 1963. By 1968, this figure had risen to 66 percent for these same organizations—as contrasted with 23 percent and 24 percent respectively for typical manufacturing organizations.

Rapidly escalating salaries explain this increase in relative share of the institutional budgets. Between 1963 and 1968, virtually every category of employee in the charitable field received a salary increase above that achieved by the average U.S. production worker (see table A.22). Whereas U.S. industry in 1968 paid 28 percent higher annual wages for its production workers than in 1963, the comparable increase for nurses in Chicago was 49 percent, for social workers 38 percent, for university teachers 34 percent, and for musicians 55 percent.

This can be partially accounted for by the abnormally low salaries paid in many of these fields in 1963. For example, caseworkers for one family service agency earned $5,700 that year; the program director for a youth organization earned $5,800; the office manager for a large charity was paid $5,720; the average intern and nurse salaries were $3,300 and $5,040, respectively; and the average librarian earned $4,944 that year. With clerical and unskilled salaries averaging $4,500–$5,000, these examples for professional workers were certainly abnormally low.

TABLE A.22
COMPARATIVE SALARY INCREASES FOR CHICAGO PHILANTHROPIC INSTITUTIONS, 1963–68

Average U.S. production worker, manufacturing	+23%
Chicago philanthropic institution employees	
Hospital intern	+81%
Musician	+55%
Nurse	+49%
Social caseworker	+38%
University professor	+37%
General administrative	+33%
Executive director	+32%
Librarian	+28%

3. THE IMPROVED QUALITY OF CHARITABLE SERVICES

Another reason for the financial squeeze felt by Chicago's charitable organizations over the 1963–68 period was the increasing breadth and quality of the services provided. In a hospital this is illustrated by improvements in biomedical technology and the increased sophistication of instrumentation in use. In the universities, faculty and student access to computers exemplifies how the educational process has become more complex and more expensive. Museums today are providing improved public services as well as expanded educational programs. In the case of one welfare agency, problems formerly handled by a single nurse are now referred to teams which include a nurse, a social worker, a physical therapist, an occupational therapist, a nutritionist, and a psychologist. A similar trend was cited by other family service agencies. An added dimension to the health and education fields is found in the increased dollars allocated to research. For youth organizations, today's emphasis on the inner city has raised costs by reducing the number of children served per fieldworker. For example, a Girl Scout staff member who can work with 75 girls in a middle-class area can work effectively (by today's standards) with only 15 to 25 girls in the inner city. Boys clubs formerly concerned only with recreation now provide services encompassing health, counseling, job training, and remedial education as well. The trend toward expanded programs and improved technologies cut across almost all institutions surveyed. Along with rising salary costs, this trend was almost universally cited as one of the two main factors contributing to the institutions' increasing need for funds. It seems clear that each unit of charitable service provided is worth more today than ever before.

4. THE RISING COST OF CHARITABLE SERVICES

The other side of this coin is that each unit of charitable service is more expensive than ever before. Labor "productivity," in terms of persons served per employee, has been stable or declining over recent years for the Chicago institutions surveyed. Concurrently, the cost of providing each unit of service has risen sharply (see table A.23). For example, during the period 1963–68, when the consumer price index rose 14 percent, the cost of providing one day of foster-child care rose 69 percent; the cost of educating a university student rose 51 percent; the cost of providing one hospital day for a rehabilitation patient rose 52 percent; and the cost of serving one member of the YWCA rose 55 percent.

5. INCREASE IN USER FEES.

In view of the financial difficulties of Chicago's charitable institutions, one might question to what extent fees charged to the general public can be raised to cover increasing costs. The survey results indicated that the median percentage of total operating expenses covered by these user fees is 14 percent. Only the hospitals are able to charge the public for the major portion of their costs. For many institutions, such as museums and libraries, the services provided are generally free of charge. Most neighborhood service and welfare organizations would go out of existence if they had to depend on user fees. Indeed, it is often inherently impossible for nonprofit, charitable institutions to charge members of the community who benefit *indirectly* from their services; yet to place the entire burden of support upon the *direct* beneficiaries would preclude their using the service entirely. In general, nonprofit institutions arise naturally in fields where the price mechanism has not permitted profit-making entrepreneurs to earn a satisfactory return. If prices were completely flexible, charitable institutions would not be necessary.

TABLE A.23.
RISING COSTS PER UNIT OF CHICAGO CHARITABLE SERVICE 1963–68

Service	
Hull House: cost of serving one person in a variety of community services	+162%
Visiting Nurses Association of Chicago: cost per patient-visit	+108%
YWCA: costs of supporting one member	+ 55%
Girl Scouts: cost of supporting one member	+ 59%
Chicago Rehabilitation Institute: cost of one patient-day	+ 52%
Chicago Boys Clubs: cost of one youth participating in a program	+ 37%
University of Chicago: cost of educating one undergraduate student for an academic year	+ 51%
Michael Reese Hospital: cost of one in-patient day	+113%
Child and Family Services: cost of one day of foster-child care	+ 69%
Consumer price index	+ 13.6%

Despite these limitations, a number of the Chicago institutions surveyed have raised prices dramatically in response to escalating costs (see table A.24). For example, during the 1963–68 period, when the consumer price index rose 13.6 percent, tuition fees at one university increased by 44 percent, the day rate at one hospital by 109 percent, and the charge for a nurse's home visit by 121 percent. Despite these efforts, those surveyed do not expect that user fees will account for a much larger share of total expenditures by 1975 than they did in 1968.

TABLE A.24.
INCREASES IN FEES CHARGED TO PUBLIC FOR SERVICES OF CHICAGO INSTITUTIONS 1963–68

Item	
Michael Reese Hospital: price of one in-patient day	+109%
University of Chicago: undergraduate tuition fee	+ 44%
Chicago Symphony Orchestra: price of balcony tickets	+ 35%
Visiting Nurses Association: price of home nurse's visit	+121%
YWCA: class fees	+ 53%
Chicago Youth Centers: camp fees	+ 43%
Chicago Art Institute: tuition fees	+ 38%
Illinois Institute of Technology: tuition fees	+ 29%
Consumer Price Index	+ 13.6%

6. IMPORTANCE OF VOLUNTEER LABOR

The study showed that Chicago institutions rely heavily on volunteer labor to carry out their programs. Without these contributions of time and energy by interested citizens, many of the organizations could not exist. The head of each institution was asked to estimate the number of volunteers and actual volunteer hours contributed each year. Every organization surveyed reported it benefited from some volunteer labor. For 71 percent, the number of volunteers exceeded paid employees in 1968.

If an arbitrary value of three dollars is placed on each volunteer hour, the total value of contributed labor can be compared to actual payroll expenses. For one out of five institutions, this figure exceeded payroll expenses (see table A.25). For one out of four, it fell between 20 and 100 percent of personnel costs. Organizations which estimated over twenty thousand volunteer hours contributed per year include, in addition to those listed in table A.25, Chicago Educational Television, Travelers' Aid Society, Lutheran Welfare Services, Michael Reese Hospital, Chicago Boys Clubs, the Woodlawn Organization, the Salvation Army, the Hull House Association, and many others.

Were it not for the contribution of services by dedicated citizens, the financial problems of Chicago's philanthropic institutions would be substantially more acute.

TABLE A.25.
VALUE OF VOLUNTEER LABOR COMPARED TO ACTUAL PAYROLL EXPENSES
1963–68

	Dollar Value of Volunteer Labor	Actual Payroll Costs	Volunteer Value as Percentage of Payroll
Mental Health Association	$150,000	$139,000	108
United Cerebral Palsy	$435,000	$263,000	165
American Red Cross	$2,610,000	$1,100,000	238
YWCA	$1,500,000	$1,059,000	142
Chicago Girl Scouts	$1,800,000	$499,000	365
American Cancer Society	$1,200,000	$849,000	142

7. DEPENDENCE ON GOVERNMENT FINANCING

In recent years, our survey showed, the various levels of government have gained importance as a source of funds for Chicago's charitable institutions. In 1963, the median share of total operating budgets paid for by the government amounted to 7 percent for the organizations surveyed. By 1968, the median government share had risen to 23 percent. This trend is viewed with some trepidation by the heads of these institutions. Eighty-four percent felt it would be "quite unfortunate" or "a very bad thing" if the federal government's share ever amounted to a preponderant proportion of their total budgets (see table A.26). And 24 percent said their concerns would be *increased* if the state rather than the federal government assumed a dominant role as a source of funds.

TABLE A.26.
"If the trend of your outside support moved toward the federal government's amounting to a preponderant percentage of your outside funds, which statement would best express your views?"

	Percent
Very good thing.	0
I'd prefer preponderant government support.	7
Doesn't bother or affect me one way or the other.	9
It would be quite unfortunate.	53
It would be a very bad thing.	31
	100 (N = 45)

The most common reasons for these concerns about government financing were (1) it would undermine their ability to attract contributions of both money and time from private individuals; (2) it would involve a sacrifice of local autonomy and control; (3) It would subject the organization to the whims of the political process—annual appropriations, political pressures, sudden cutbacks—making coherent planning much more difficult; (4) It would get the organization hopelessly entangled in red tape, detracting time and energy from programs.

Despite the increasing share of government support their institutions received, 69 percent of the survey respondents felt that it was "very unlikely" the government would make up the deficit if their existence was threatened by a major financing gap. Another 20 percent thought it was very "uncertain" whether the government would come to their rescue. Only 11 percent felt it "very likely" the government would make up a significant part or all of the deficit. From this, one can conclude that the directors of these organizations do not feel government financing provides the kind of solid foundation upon which they could build their future plans.

8. IMPORTANCE OF PRIVATE PHILANTHROPY TO CHICAGO CHARITABLE ORGANIZATIONS

In 1968, the Chicago institutions surveyed raised a median of 23 percent of their operating funds from the government, 14 percent from user fees, and the remaining 63 percent from various kinds of private philanthropic sources—individuals, foundations, corporations, community funds, and affiliate organizations.

In raising endowment funds, these institutions were dependent almost entirely on individual private giving. Of the 69 percent of the institutions which had endowments, most cited individual contributions as accounting for over 95 percent of the funds. Only universities were able to attract broader endowment support. In general, one can say that, without individual philanthropy, the Chicago institutions studied would have precious little in the way of reserves to fall back on to finance operating deficits, provide funds for capital expansion, or yield a steady flow of income.

One measure of the Chicago institutions' reliance on private philanthropy was their response to the question as shown in table A.27.

For 83 percent of institutions surveyed, the results of a 25 percent curtailment would be grave indeed. The general public, who benefit from their programs, would ultimately be the ones to suffer.

TABLE A.27.
"Let us assume that all private giving were reduced 25 percent, including individuals, companies, foundations, etc. How would this effect your organization?"

	Percent
"It would cease to exist"	13
"We would face a very serious budget problem and would have to curtail significant programs."	70
"We would have to tighten the purse strings and perhaps not expand the way we'd like."	11
"It would have very little or no effect."	6
	100 (N = 46)

It was perhaps predictable that 90 percent of those surveyed felt that public tax policy should be changed to further encourage private philanthropy. Ten percent felt tax policy should remain as it is today, while none felt incentives for charity should be reduced.

9. Dependence on Foundations

For the Chicago institutions submitting detailed financial data, the median share of operating expenses coming from foundations amounted to 10 percent in 1968. The range was from 68 percent for the Open Lands Project and 44 percent for the Chicago Council on Alcoholism to zero for the Girl Scouts, the Chicago Boys Clubs, and the YMCA. While not generally preponderant in dollar terms, foundation grants were widespread. Over the past ten years, 94 percent of the institutions surveyed had received foundation support of one kind or another. The only three exceptions in the survey were the Chicago Community Fund, the Mid-America Chapter of the American Red Cross (whose funds come primarily from the Community Fund), and the Episcopal Diocese of Chicago.

For another measure of the institution's reliance on foundations, see table A.28.

While not generally critical to the existence of the Chicago institutions, foundation support is important in the case of specific projects and programs—generally those that are new and innovative. Cutbacks in foundation giving would mean elimination of significant programs and curtailment of expansion into new areas. It would also hinder the Chicago institutions' efforts to attract monies from other sources for which a foundation grant will often act as a catalyst.

TABLE A.28.
"Let us assume that total foundation giving were reduced by 25 percent.
How do you believe this would affect your institution?"

	Percent
"It would cease to exist."	2
"We would face a very serious budget problem and would have to curtail significant programs."	51
"We'd have to tighten the purse strings and perhaps not expand the way we'd like."	27
"It would have little or no effect."	20
	100 (N=45)

10. ATTITUDES TOWARD FOUNDATIONS

The directors of the Chicago institutions had some definite ideas about philanthropic foundations. Based on their experiences as recipients, they overwhelmingly agreed (95 percent) that foundations had done a good and usually excellent job of handling and supervising the grants. They also agreed that foundations have some definite advantages over other types of donors. Seventy percent felt that foundations respond more quickly and flexibly than many other sources of funds. Seventy-six percent agreed that foundations are generally willing to support unusual, innovative, or unpopular projects that others, such as the federal government, will not support. Seventy-three percent felt that foundations are less likely to try to impose their own thoughts, policies, or criteria on the recipients.

The primary complaint, cited consistently by the survey respondents, was that foundations are too often unwilling to support ongoing operating expenses. The penchant for "seed money" projects—innovation—offers a temptation to present old programs as new departures in order to secure foundation attention and backing. This criticism appears to be exaggerated, however, when one looks at the record over the past decade. Of the forty-six organizations surveyed receiving foundation grants, 89 percent received grants in support of specific projects; 67 percent received sustaining operating grants; 46 percent received capital grants. While this breakdown does not indicate the dollar magnitude contributed in each category, it does dispel the contention that foundations always shy away from sustaining support.

11. THE IMPORTANCE OF BUILDING A BROAD BASE OF FINANCIAL
SUPPORT

The Chicago survey questioned an executive of each institution on his
views of each major source of funds: individuals, foundations, companies, and government (see table A.29). The emerging picture, supported rather consistently, is that it is important to maintain multiple
sources of support.

1. Predominance by a single channel will tend to shut off the other
sources entirely. This could be harmful for the future if the situation
should change suddenly.

2. Government support has one major advantage—the large amounts
of dollars available—but many overriding disadvantages. The respondents indicated they will fight to keep as independent of government as
possible—but they will turn to this avenue if they have to in order to
guarantee their survival and growth.

3. Foundations provide an ideal source of funds—few strings, easy to
apply for—but there are simply not enough available for the organization to meet its basic operating requirements. This source is best counted
on for financing new programs.

4. Direct company grants—like foundation grants—are nice if you can
get them but are simply not plentiful enough to be anything beyond an
occasional supplementary source. They have the added disadvantage
that they are more difficult to develop. Company money is more likely
to come through a community fund.

5. It is on individual giving that most of the organizations surveyed
have come to depend for their existence. The advantages of this source—
unrestricted funds, involvement of volunteers, large potential, predicta-
bility, local community identification—add up to making it the strong
base required for any organization to build its future plans.

Fund raising is the one recurring nightmare from which the executive
directors of Chicago's charitable institutions cannot escape. In their
eyes, the continued existence of a strong and independent philanthropic
sector hinges on a public policy which offers increased tax incentives for
private contributors of all kinds—individuals, companies, foundations.
Without those incentives, their rapidly rising costs can push them in only
two directions—toward either a gradual reduction in quality and
breadth of programs or an increased reliance on government support.
To the charitable institutions surveyed, neither alternative is very
satisfactory.

TABLE A.29.
ALTERNATIVE SOURCE OF FUNDS: ADVANTAGES AND DISADVANTAGES

The heads of Chicago philanthropic organizations agreed generally on the following "pros" and "cons" of each source of funds.

1. INDIVIDUALS
   Advantages
   Freedom to use funds without restriction
   Donors have local identification with problem
   Involves volunteers in organization
   Contributions likely to continue in future years
   Large potential of funds available
   Disadvantages
   Great deal of effort required to cultivate; competition increasing
   Gifts are often small
   Capriciousness of some individuals

2. COMPANIES
   Advantages
   Size of gifts
   Support tends to be consistent over time
   Helps develop community understanding
   Disadvantages
   Difficult to approach; requires personal contact
   Frequent turnover of top executives

3. FOUNDATIONS
   Advantages
   Freedom from political pressure
   Competence of professional staffs
   Willingness to support unusually innovative or unpopular projects
   Ability to act quickly
   Disadvantages
   Unwillingness to support ongoing operating costs
   Occasional interference or too much supervision

4. GOVERNMENT
   Advantages
   Large amount of dollars available
   Competence of Washington personnel at upper levels
   Disadvantages
   Red tape
   Unreliability of congressional action
   Annual time horizon too short for planning
   Lack of local community and volunteer involvement
   Political pressures
   Loss of autonomy

EXHIBIT 2: ILLUSTRATIVE COMMENTS BY EXECUTIVES OF CHICAGO PHILANTHROPIC ORGANIZATIONS

1. THE CURRENT SITUATION

"The biggest concern is to generate a sufficient amount of income from private sources—Community Fund, individual contributions, foundations—on a sustaining basis, a nonproject basis, to allow the organization as a voluntary organization to maintain an independence from control by governmental funds. Without governmental funds we will not grow sufficiently to be significant; but if we grow only with governmental funds we reach a point before long in which we become simply a creature of government and cease to fulfill an independent function."

Planning council

"We're concerned about our autonomy so we try to rely on individual donors as much as possible. They like what we're doing and they give us money and they leave us alone. I don't believe that we can increase the present number enough to meet the increase of cost. We will have a real budget crisis unless we find some new sources of funds."

Small specialized service agency

"By 1975 I think you're going to find very many less agencies unless something drastic is done."

Federation of agencies

2. ARE GOVERNMENT FUNDS THE ANSWER?

"It would be a very bad thing for most of our outside funds to come from government. For one thing, It's tremendously important that people who use services of an agency like this are not made to feel that they are being manipulated by some expert for their own good. . . . The autonomy that you get by raising your own funds means that people that get the services feel that they are raising the money for them. It gives people a way to be effective in their own behalf. To lose that is to lose most everything."

Community service agency

"Obviously, you're not going to have private philanthropy if it becomes 60, 70, or 90 percent financed by various forms of government funds. It seems to us that our job is to try to remain a private group in order to exert influence on these political groups."

Health association

"I don't feel that there's anything that's tainted about government money. My feeling that it's a very bad thing stems very largely from the fact that when you accept government funds in an agency, they are always allocated on an annual basis; appropriations are rarely made by the Congress for longer than one year's period of time. And an agency is constantly faced, then, with the cutbacks or the change in direction or the whim of the Congress in allocation processes."

Neighborhood center

"There are some very sharp professional people in Washington working for some kinds of social improvement and social change. This level of awareness is a very decided advantage. . . . But again, if you do get funded, you're going to have to deal with the middleman and his forms."

Community neighborhood organization

3. THE PROS AND CONS OF FOUNDATION GRANTS

"The problem I see with foundations—and I could almost make a generalization—is that this old bugaboo, "innovation," is a strangler, And I think that this is one of the most serious problems that affects the nonprofit sector today. Foundations should think very carefully about responsibility for innovation and later support—not just beget the baby."

Major museum

"One of the saddest things that's happened to foundations over the years has been the gradual transference of its monies into research projects or to so confine its purposes that they're not open to the general mine run of agencies."

Federation of agencies

"It's peachy to have a fancy new experimental class for disadvantaged kids—you might get a grant for that—but the fact that you have to have the grounds cleaned and heat the building and pay for the lights. . . . Very few foundations I've come across are willing to pay for the overhead or ongoing program."

Neighborhood center

"Too frequently foundations are only interested in contributing to special projects for which "seed" money is needed, or to capital fund drives. What agencies like ours require are funds for the everyday operation of services which are crucial to the community quite on their own merit."

Community service organization

"They should be more concerned with the ongoing support of the private agency structure if it is to survive."

Welfare agency

4. PRIVATE DONORS

"Private donors are usually local. They are quite flexible, sensitive. The people served and the contributors have a sense of common enterprise to some degree. You don't have to design something that will fit preexisting categories so that you apply to the categorical source of that money. That kind of independence is very important. The response is much more immediate."

Neighborhood center

5. COMPANIES

"Companies are more aware than they used to be about their responsibilities to the local scene and their dependence on the wellbeing of the less fortunate. They have a stake in the community in which they are operating. They can be spoken to in those terms. . . . The disadvantage is that they are hard to handle. It almost always takes a personal contact."

Welfare agency

6. IF PRIVATE PHILANTHROPY DROPPED BY 25 PERCENT . . .

"We could almost cease to exist. Our agency has extensive facilities for the delivery of services, and these facilities would be drastically underused if there were a 25 percent cut across the board in voluntary giving. It would be a great waste."

Neighborhood center

"There's a compound effect in there. We could be talking about a half million dollars a year and that would hurt. It would mean deferring some construction, would mean not going forward on some programs, would certainly mean cutting back on some things we do. . . . Would have a very significant impact on what we do in a given year."

Major teaching hospital

7. IF FOUNDATION GIVING DROPPED BY 25 PERCENT . . .

"It would be equal to the elimination of both assistant executive directors from our organization, *or* three program directors, *or* the entire bookkeeping staff, *or* three out of three of our day care program directors plus the cooks who feed the kids in our day care program.

"In considering the vital help which private foundation funds have provided to the agencies serving our community, one cannot help but be concerned at the prospect that the availability of these private foundation funds might be reduced as a result of taxes being leveled on the financial resources of foundations. From our experience, it appears that a reduction of funds presently available from foundations would result in a loss far greater than the amount paid in taxes, since foundation monies often act as a catalyst to help attract other financial support."

Welfare agency

"A lot of that money would be missed in the community. If you take off the tax incentive, you're going to hurt many of us who are trying to do something in the community because the money isn't going to be available."

National youth organization

Tables Summarizing the Survey of Foundations

TABLE A.30.
GEOGRAPHICAL FOCUS OF FOUNDATION ACTIVITIES

	"Family" Foundations by Asset Size					Company Foundations	Community Foundations
	Under $200,000	$200,000–$1 million	$1–10 million	$10–100 million	Over $100 million		
City wide	49%	43%	56%	44%	6%	31%	84%
Statewide	9	5	8	9	6	15	5
Regional	9	10	13	9	12	5	11
National	14	33	8	13	29	41	.....
International only	7	5	3	4	.....	.....	.....
National and international	12	5	13	22	47	8	.....
	100%	101%	101%	101%	100%	100%	100%
	(N=43)	(N=21)	(N=39)	(N=23)	(N=17)	(N=19)	(N=39)

TABLE A.31.
CONTRIBUTIONS TO FOUNDATIONS AS A PERCENTAGE OF FOUNDATION ASSETS
END OF 1968

	Assets (Weighted) Including Ford	Assets (Weighted) Excluding Ford
Appreciated tangible personal property	1%	1%
Appreciated real property	3	4
Stock in a company in which a donor and his family owned a controlling interest (20% or more)	41	30
Other appreciated intangible property	30	36
Cash or unappreciated property	21	25
Charitable trust income or remainder	4	5
	100% (N = 193)	101% (N = 192)

TABLE A.32.
CONTRIBUTIONS TO FOUNDATIONS AS A PERCENTAGE OF FOUNDATION ASSETS, BY TYPE AND SIZE OF FOUNDATIONS, END OF 1968

	Foundations by Asset Size							Company Foundations	Community Foundations
	Under $200,000	$200,000–$1 million	$1–10 million	$10–100 million	Over $100 million Total	Over $100 million Excluding Ford	Ford		
Appreciated tangible personal property	.....	.....	7%	†	†	.....	†	.....	.....
Appreciated real property	4%	7%	5	3%	2%	1%	3%	6%	2%
Appreciated intangible property									
Stock in a company in which donor and his family owned a controlling interest (20% or more)	19	20	21	26	70	56	90	10	†
Other intangible property	23	37	28	39	18	30	1	47	62
Cash or unappreciated property	44	24	31	23	10	12	6	37	36
Charitable trust income or remainder	10	12	9	9	†	†	.....	†	†
	100% (N=42)	100% (N=19)	101% (N=39)	100% (N=22)	100% (N=17)	99% (N=16)	100% (N=1)	100% (N=16)	100% (N=38)

†Less than 0.5 percent

TABLE A.33.
FOUNDATIONS RECEIVING HALF OR MORE OF THEIR CONTRIBUTIONS IN SPECIFIED FORMS (N = 193)

Form of Contributions	Percentage of Foundations	Percentage of Total Foundation Assets Held, End of 1968 by Foundations Including Ford	by Foundations Excluding Ford
Stock in a company in which the donor and his family owned a controlling interest (20% or more)	14	42	30
Other appreciated intangible property (stocks, bonds, mortgages, etc.)	35	32	39
All appreciated intangible property	49	76	71
Cash or unappreciated property	45	19	23

TABLE A.34.
FOUNDATION OWNERSHIP OF CORPORATE CONTROL STOCK (N = 197)

	Percentage of Foundations	Percentage of Total Foundation Assets Held, End of 1968
Control stock		
Foundations ever owning more than 20% of the voting stock of any corporation	7	43
Foundations now owning more than 20% of the voting stock of any corporation	4	29
Attributed control stock		
Foundations ever owning stock in a company in which its holdings of voting stock, combined with those of a substantial donor* and his family, added up to 20% or more	8	49
Foundations now owning stock in a company in which the combined holdings are more than 20% of the voting stock	6	39

*In our questionnaire, we defined a "substantial donor" as anyone who, by himself or with his spouse, contributed more than $5,000 to the foundation in any one year or contributed the greatest amount to the foundation in any one year.

TABLE A.35. PERCENTAGE OF FOUNDATION ASSETS DERIVED FROM SPECIFIED SOURCES, END OF 1968

| | "Family" Foundations by Asset Size | | | | | | Company Foundations | Community Foundations | Weighted Total, All Foundations |
| | Under $200,000 | $200,000–$1 million | $1–10 million | $10–100 million | Over $100 million | | | | |
					Total	Excluding Ford			
Contributions by donors during their lifetimes and gains from them	66%	65%	38%	49%	63%	76%	†	14%	47%
Contributions from estates and gains from them	28	14	54	46	14	24	†	81	23
Company contributions and other	6	20	8	5	23	1	100	5	31
	100%	100%	100%	100%	100%	100%	100%	100%	100%
	(N=42)	(N=19)	(N=34)	(N=21)	(N=16)	(N=15)	(N=16)	(N=38)	(N=186)

†Less than 0.5 percent.

248

TABLE A.36.

FOUNDATIONS EXPECTING TO RECEIVE SUBSTANTIAL CONTRIBUTIONS IN THE FUTURE (N=196)

	Percentage of Foundations
"Family" foundations with assets	
under $200,000	49
$200,000–$1 million	67
$1–10 million	32
$10–100 million	35
over $100 million	43
Company foundations	76
Community foundations	94
All foundations	54

TABLE A.37.

FUTURE CONTRIBUTIONS TO EXISTING FOUNDATIONS

	Percentage of Foundations Expecting Future Contributions
Source of Contributions	
Living Donors	64
Bequests	9
Both	27
	100 (N=83)
Form of contributions	
Property	27
Cash	40
Both	33
	100 (N=98)
Are any contributions expected in the form of stock in a corporation controlled by the expected donor or his family?	
Yes	11
No	89
	100 (N=96)

TABLE A.38.
FOUNDATIONS WITH PAID STAFF

	No Paid Staff (%)	Paid Staff (%)	Part-time Only (%)	Full-time Only (%)	Part-time and Full-time (%)
"Family" Foundations with assets					
under $200,000	84	16	14	2	0
$200,000–$1 million	81	19	14	0	5
$1–10 million	41	59	36	15	8
$10–100 million	17	83	30	31	22
over $100 million	0	100	6	41	53
Company foundations	85	15	3	13	0
Community foundations	53	47	21	15	11
Weighted average, all foundations (N = 201)	80	20	15	4	1

TABLE A.39.
FREQUENCY OF FOUNDATION BOARD MEETINGS

	Percentage of Foundations	Percentage of Total Assets Held, End of 1968
Never	9	1
Once every few years	†	†
Annually	32	6
Biennially	20	20
Quarterly	22	45
Monthly	6	24
Whenever necessary	11	5
	100 (N = 188)	100

†Less than 0.5 percent

TABLE A.40.
LENGTH OF AVERAGE FOUNDATION BOARD MEETING

	Percentage of Foundations	Percentage of Total Assets Held, End of 1968
Less than 15 minutes	14	†
15–30 minutes	11	1
30 minutes to 1 hour	16	8
1–2 hours	41	30
2–4 hours	14	29
4–6 hours	2	5
6–8 hours	2	1
8 hours or longer	†	25
	100 (N=178)	100
†Less than 0.5 percent		

TABLE A.41.
DISTRIBUTION OF 1968 FOUNDATION GRANTS

			Foundations by Asset Size						
	Under $200,000	$200,000–$1 million	$1–10 million	$10–100 million	Total	Over $100 million Excluding Ford	Ford	Company Foundations	Community Foundations
Qualified charitable organizations									
Public charities	89%	75%	70%	77%	67%	63%	70%	66%	64%
Other	9	13	22	22	17	22	13	33	23
Noncharitable tax-exempt or nonprofit organizations	†	...	†	†	...	...	...	†	9
Foreign organizations (and profit-making organizations)	...	...	1	1	11	7	14	†	...
Individuals	2	11	7	†	4	6	3	†	4
	100%	99%	100%	100%	99%	98%	100%	99%	100%
	(N=42)	(N=19)	(N=39)	(N=22)	(N=17)	(N=16)	(N=1)	(N=18)	(N=38)

†Less than 0.5 percent.

TABLE A.42.
FOUNDATIONS MAKING ALL GRANTS TO SPECIFIED TYPE OF RECIPIENT, AND
AMOUNT OF GRANTS, 1968 (N = 196)

	Percentage of Foundations	Percentage of Total 1968 Grants Including Ford	Excluding Ford
Public charities	54	29	33
Qualified charitable organizations	80	74	84
Individuals	12	2	2

TABLE A.43.
PURPOSE OF FOUNDATION GRANTS, 1968

| | Foundations by Asset Size | | | | | | | Company Foundations | Community Foundations |
| | | | | | Over $100 million | | | | |
	Under $200,000	$200,000–$1 million	$1–10 million	$10–100 million	Total	Excluding Ford	Ford		
	55%	35%	15%	27%	14%	20%	9%	5%	18%
Health and medicine	1	1	5	2	†	1	0	†	5
Individual and family services	30	16	4	7	1	2	0	20	9
Education	7	19	48	33	40	43	37	35	13
Manpower and vocational training	0	†	1	1	3	2	4	†	2
Housing	†	0	2	†	2	†	3	†	2
Community action and services	2	6	5	8	5	4	5	2	17
Community, racial, or ethnic relations	1	5	†	†	2	2	3	5	6
Political-process related activities	†	†	†	0	1	†	1	†	†
Conservation and recreation	†	1	1	1	3	2	3	†	3
Religion	3	15	11	2	1	2	0	†	1
Science and technology	†	†	1	11	4	7	1	†	0
Cultural institutions	1	2	8	5	9	5	12	23	19
Arts and humanities	1	1	†	†	7	3	10	1	3
Social sciences	†	0	†	1	7	3	9	1	†
Other	0	†	†	1	2	1	3	8	1
	100%	100%	100%	100%	100%	100%	100%	100%	100%
	(N=42)	(N=20)	(N=39)	(N=21)	(N=17)	(N=16)	(N=1)	(N=19)	(N=37)

†Less than 0.5 percent.

TABLE A.44.
FOUNDATIONS MAKING GRANTS ONLY FOR DOMESTIC PROGRAMS OR PROJECTS
IN 1968 (N = 195)

	Percent
Foundations with assets:	
under $200,000	69
$200,000–$1 million	90
$1–10 million	76
$10–100 million	71
over $100 million	29
Company foundations	79
Community foundations	100
All foundations	75
Total 1968 foundation grants made by these foundations	63

TABLE A.45.
"Have field visits or other periodic personal checks been made by foundation personnel or consultants?"

	Percentage of Foundations	Percentage of Foundation Grants, 1968
Never	52	35
Rarely	9	4
Sometimes	19	16
Generally or often	7	39
Always	13	6
	100 (N = 188)	100

TABLE A.46.
"Does the foundation require periodic reports by the recipient as a requirement for payment of installments of the grant?"

	Percentage of Foundations	Percentage of Foundation Grants, 1968
Never	71	37
Rarely	5	4
Sometimes	9	14
Generally or often	4	14
Always	12	31
	100 (N = 189)	100

TABLE A.47.
"Does the foundation require independent auditing of expenditures by the grantee?"

	Percentage of Foundations	Percentage of Foundation Grants, 1968
Never	91	64
Rarely	1	8
Sometimes	2	15
Generally or often	3	6
Always	4	7
	100 (N = 184)	100

Philanthropy and the Economy

by Mary Hamilton

Traditionally, philanthropy has been a way of life in the United States. Health and educational institutions, churches, and the arts have relied heavily on private contributions as a source of funds. In recent years, expanded activities, particularly in the fields of health and education, have necessitated increased dependence on government funds. Despite this additional support, many institutions and organizations are now facing a financial crisis that is likely to persist. In fact, cost increases—generally larger than those in the overall economy—together with increasing demands for services virtually guarantee that it will worsen. The purpose of this report is to examine facts that may shed some light on the magnitude of the philanthropic gap by 1975 under certain assumptions with respect to the economy.

A word of caution is in order. Data in the area of philanthropy are fragmentary and come from a variety of sources. It is therefore difficult, at best, to establish relationships between philanthropy and related economic variables. The only official figures are those published by the Internal Revenue Service in the *Statistics of Income* series. These include: total contributions by individuals reported on tax returns with *itemized* deductions, available only for even-numbered years; bequests reported in estate tax returns, published at two- to three-year intervals; and contributions reported by corporations in tax returns, available with a lag of about three years. Contributions by individuals not itemizing deductions, bequests not reported in estate tax returns, and foundation giving (including corporations) must be estimated from a variety of sources. Any findings suggested in this report should be viewed in this light.

Total Philanthropy and Gross National Product

In 1968, it is estimated[1] that philanthropic giving totaled $15.8 billion. Living individuals contributed $12.1 billion, or 77 percent of the total. The remainder was in the form of bequests or foundation and corporate giving. The 1968 total of $15.8 billion represents an increase of 155 percent over that in 1955. Over the same period gross national product in current dollars increased by a somewhat smaller 118 percent.

The historical relationship between philanthropy and gross national product is shown in table A.48. Since 1960, philanthropy has averaged 1.8 percent of product. No clear pattern is obvious, but the figures do suggest a range within which giving might be expected to fluctuate. It should be mentioned that table A.48 is based on estimates of giving from AAFRC; these are the only available published figures. Unpublished estimates from another source suggest that the percentage, particularly in 1955, may be somewhat low. More important, they suggest a slight downtrend since 1960. It is difficult to draw any firm conclusions, but it is important to bear in mind that small changes in the percentage imply a dollar impact on philanthropy which is not negligible.

TABLE A.48.
PHILANTHROPY AND GROSS NATIONAL PRODUCT

Year	Philanthropy[a] (Millions)	GNP[b] (Billions)	Philanthropy as a Percentage of GNP
1955	$ 6,202	$398.0	1.56
1960	8,919	503.7	1.77
1961	9,708	520.1	1.87
1962	10,111	560.3	1.80
1963	10,668	590.5	1.81
1964	11,439	632.4	1.81
1965	12,210	684.9	1.78
1966	12,894	749.9	1.72
1967	14,549	793.5	1.83
1968	15,800	865.7	1.82

[a]Source: American Association of Fund-Raising Counsel, Inc.
[b]Source: U.S. Department of Commerce.

1. Estimates made by the American Association of Fund-Raising Counsel, Inc.

Giving by Living Individuals and Income

Giving by living individuals constitutes the major portion of philanthropy, although there is some suggestion in table A.49 that the percentage is declining. Table A.49 also presents individual giving as a percentage of personal income. In the years 1960–68, the percentage averages 1.785, and in 1968, 1.759.

TABLE A.49.
GIVING OF LIVING INDIVIDUALS

Year	Amount[a] (Millions)	Percentage of Philanthropy	Percentage of Personal Income
1955	$ 5,100	82.23	1.64
1960	7,150	80.23	1.78
1961	7,620	78.49	1.83
1962	8,116	80.27	1.83
1963	8,316	77.95	1.79
1964	8,926	78.03	1.79
1965	9,276	75.97	1.72
1966	10,530	81.67	1.79
1967	11,144	76.60	1.77
1968	12,100	76.58	1.76

[a]Source: American Association of Fund-Raising Counsel, Inc.

A somewhat different picture emerges from an examination of contributions reported on tax returns with itemized deductions. Contributions as a percentage of adjusted gross income by income class appear in table A.50. The downward trend is pronounced and consistent for most income groups. The exceptions are the classes over $1 million and under $5,000. Of relevance is the fact that the income distribution has been shifting upward, particularly at the lower end. This together with the greater relative stability of giving by those in top income brackets has resulted in an increasing importance of large donors. In 1966, the latest year for which data are available, contributions reported in returns with adjusted gross income of $100,000 and over were 8.9 percent of the total reported, as compared with 7.1 percent in 1960. For returns with adjusted gross income of $50,000 and over, the comparable figures are 14.1 and 11.2 percent respectively. This finding could be of importance in any consideration of tax proposals.

TABLE A.50.
CONTRIBUTIONS AS A PERCENTAGE OF ADJUSTED GROSS INCOME, BY INCOME
CLASSES

Income Class	1958	1960	1962	1964	1966
Under $5,000	4.61%	4.58%	4.34%	4.54%	4.56%
$ 5,000– 9,999	3.51	3.35	3.18	3.13	2.97
$ 10,000–14,999		3.22	3.03	2.90	2.66
$ 15,000–19,999		3.26	3.14	2.96	2.70
$ 20,000–49,999	4.06	3.42	3.30	3.18	2.83
$ 50,000–99,999		4.24	4.15	3.98	3.39
$100,000 and over		9.81	9.83	9.13	7.66
All classes	3.92	3.73	3.53	3.41	3.13
Addendum					
$ 100,000–499,999		7.87	8.04	7.33	6.02
$ 500,000–999,999		16.14	11.74	10.82	10.17
$1,000,000 and over		16.79	18.79	17.94	15.36

Source: Internal Revenue Service, Statistics of Income

Contributions reported on itemized deduction returns are about
86–90 percent of the estimated total giving by living individuals. Unless individuals taking the standard deduction behave quite differently,
the relative downtrend in giving is likely to become evident in the
relation between personal income and giving by all individuals. This
is an important consideration in assessing estimates of future total
philanthropy.

Corporate Contributions and Corporate Profits

Corporate contributions reported on income tax returns are estimated
by AAFRC at $925 million in 1968. Since 1954, these show a fairly
steady pattern of increase reflecting the rise in corporate profits. As a
percentage of profits, contributions in the 1960s have ranged between
0.97 and 1.12 percent. Part of the fluctuation in the percentage may be
a result of budgeting contributions a year in advance of the expenditure.
For example, in 1967 the percentage rose to 1.12, reflecting not only
the increase in contributions but also the decline in profits. These
figures appear in table A.51.

The Outlook for Philanthropy in 1975

The difficulties inherent in estimating a philanthropic gap in 1975 are
overwhelming. Estimates of needs are highly tentative, with the pos-

sible exception of expenditures for health and education. In general, however, expenditures are of necessity over the long run geared to income. At the same time, it seems clear that needs, if measured by society's demand for services, can only increase. In addition, cost advances are apt to outrun those in the overall economy.[2] Similarly, on the giving side, the lack of data and the looseness of relationships to economic variables suggest that any estimates may be subject to fairly substantial margins of error.

TABLE A.51.
CORPORATE GIVING AND CORPORATE PROFITS BEFORE TAX

Year	Giving (Millions)	Profits (Billions)	Giving as a Percentage of Profits
1954	$314	$38.0	0.826%
1955	415	46.9	0.895
1956	418	46.1	0.907
1957	417	45.6	0.914
1958	395	41.1	0.961
1959	482	51.7	0.932
1960	482	49.9	0.966
1961	512	50.3	1.018
1962	595	55.7	1.068
1963	657	58.9	1.115
1964	729	66.3	1.100
1965	785	76.1	1.032
1966	805	82.4	0.977
1967	890	79.2	1.124
1968	925*	87.9	1.052

Sources: Internal Revenue Service (for corporate giving). Department of Commerce (for corporate profits); includes inventory valuation adjustment.
*Estimate from American Association of Fund-Raising Counsel, Inc.

Given these limitations, a reasonable approach would seem to be to estimate a range of potential giving in 1975 based on assumed levels of gross national product. This approximation has implications for relations between components of total giving and income, for example, which can be compared with those existing in the past.

2. By way of illustration, in health and education wages and salaries have advanced rapidly, in part, because of historic low levels. Moreover, increasing sophistication of knowledge and methods requires increasingly costly equipment. Finally, these are areas in which increases in productivity are difficult to achieve.

A variety of estimates of gross national product in 1975 suggest a level in the neighborhood of $1,150 billion in 1968 dollars. This level is suggested by the Report of the Council of Economic Advisors (January 1969) and forecasts made by the National Planning Association (January 1969) and by the Morgan Guaranty Bank (November 1969). The implied annual growth rate is approximately 4.3 percent. If, in addition, prices increase at an annual rate of 2.6 percent, gross national product in current dollars would be approximately $1,367 billion. The latter estimate was made by the NPA and is associated with a current dollar personal income of $1,063 billion. Using these estimates, the past relationship between output and philanthropy suggests the following levels of giving.

	Gross National Product			Philanthropy	
	Billions of 1968 Dollars	Billions of Current Dollars	Billions of 1968 Dollars	Billions of Current Dollars	Percent of GNP
1968	865.7	865.7	15.8	15.8	1.825
1975	1,150.0	1,367.0	20.4–21.2	24.2–25.2	1.77–1.84

If the 1968 percentage of 1.825 is applied, the estimates of philanthropy in 1975 are $21.0 billion in 1968 dollars and $24.9 billion in current dollars. For simplification, the latter figure is used in the comparisons which follow.

Assuming that contributions of living individuals are maintained as a percentage of philanthropy at the 1968 level (76.58 percent), in 1975 they would total $19.1 billion in current dollars. However, this is 1.8 percent of personal income (NPA estimate), which seems high in the light of the earlier discussion. If, alternatively, individuals contributed $18.6 billion (1.75 percent of personal income), their contributions would be 74.6 percent of the total. This is probably more reasonable, but it does imply that other sources of philanthropy must increase relative to the total.

In conclusion, it is obvious that the possible range of estimates of philanthropy in 1975 is extremely broad. Limited information on past trends lends some support to an estimated giving level of $20–21 billion in 1968 dollars ($24–25 in current dollars) by 1975. This implies total giving (using the estimates based on 1968 relation to gross national product) of $131 billion in 1968 dollars ($147 billion in current dollars) over the years 1969–75. Clearly, this is a considerable amount and figures importantly in the ability to provide needed services.

Enlightened Self-Interest and Corporate Philanthropy

by W. J Baumol

1. *Corporate Giving and Self-Interest*

Giving by corporations is in at least one respect a paradoxical phenomenon. The corporation owes its existence and its continued prosperity to the successful operation of the economy and the viability of the social arrangements. Since a significant subset of the institutions vital for the functioning of that society are financed largely on an eleemosynary basis, it is surely appropriate for the corporations to help to support the operations of these nonprofit groups. Gifts by private firms are justified not merely as a matter of their indebtedness to the nonprofit institutions for their past accomplishments, but also as a matter of self-interest, for the deterioration of such institutions as universities and hospitals would no doubt have serious consequences for private enterprise. Yet it is also arguable that the business of the corporation *is* just business, and, therefore, philanthropy has no legitimate role in its operations. Rather, it might well be suggested, the corporation should pass the funds in question on to its stockholders, who would then decide for themselves the amounts they wish to give and the groups to which they desire to make their contributions.

It should be emphasized that reservations about the legitimacy of corporate philanthropy are not expressed only by extreme conservatives or by the greediest of stockholders. Among those who consider themselves nineteenth-century liberals, and even in the ranks of the more radical, one finds individuals who fear the intrusion of the business firm into areas of social activity which do not concern it. Anyone to whom the "industrial-military complex" is suspect may well view with concern any growth in dependence upon the nation's business firms of its arts and its educational system. Reservations have been expressed about management's power to allocate society's resources among such institutions, an activity for which they have no mandate from, nor any obligation of formal responsibility to, the general public.

More vociferous, however, are stockholder groups who have been known to hold that management has no right to give away funds that belong legitimately to themselves, the holders of the company's equity. It is no doubt the pressures from this source which have succeeded in holding average corporate giving to little more than 1 percent of company profits.[1]

The solution to the dilemma posed by such reservations, and one that has the sanction of the courts, is that corporate giving is appropriate only so long as it serves the interests of the firm, broadly defined. Surely, the argument runs, a gift to a department of engineering which will help to provide trained personnel to the company in the future is no less appropriate than a payment to a supplier of raw materials for the inputs which he provides to the firm. Neither of these involves an intrusion of management into an area beyond its legitimate concern, and neither is in any sense a giveaway of the stockholders' resources.

Once this argument is granted it can be stretched considerably. One can maintain, for example, that a company much of whose operation must unavoidably take place in urban locations has a legitimate reason to invest in the prosperity and viability of the nation's cities. If without better ghetto housing and ghetto education our cities cannot survive, then such a firm must, for its own sake, be prepared to contribute toward their improvement.

Later in this paper it will be shown that even this resolution of the paradox is not without its difficulties. An understanding of the problem is important not simply as a theoretical matter but as an essential element in the practicalities of corporate philanthropy. Until it is understood, and means to deal with it are devised and implemented, it may not be possible to expand materially the rate of corporate giving, which, at least in some quarters, is considered rather disappointing.

1. Though the group of stockholders opposed to corporate contributions is vociferous it is apparently not very strong. Watson reports that resolutions designed to restrict corporate giving generally draw no more than 5 per cent of the shares voted. In the years investigated by Watson, all such resolutions were defeated. See John H. Watson III, "Corporate Contributions Policy," *The Conference Board Record,* June 1967, p. 13.

2. *Some Background on Corporate Contributions*

Before the Second World War corporate contributions ran considerably below their current levels, both relatively and in absolute terms. During the 1930s giving by the nation's corporations usually amounted to some 0.04 percent of net profits. The total sum involved ran between thirty and forty million dollars. By 1966 philanthropic outlays be corporations had reached some $800 million.

Toward the end of the war giving for the first time exceeded 1 percent of net profits—its approximate current rate. It is plausible that this rather dramatic upsurge can be ascribed in large part to the excess profits tax, under whose provisions 95 percent of marginal company earnings went to the government. At such tax rates giving clearly became very inexpensive to the stockholder, who lost only $5 for every $100 given away. This observation is significant because it suggests that the magnitude of corporate giving can be influenced significantly by government policy.

However, not all policy measures designed for the purpose are equally effective. There is, for example, no evidence of a corresponding upsurge in the period following the 1935 amendment in the Internal Revenue Code, which for the first time permitted the deduction of charitable contributions by corporations up to a maximum of 5 percent.[2]

After the end of the war the rate of corporate giving fell from its peak of 1.25 percent in 1945–46 to a range between 0.6 and 0.8 percent toward the beginning of the next decade (table A.52). In more recent years, presumably because of increased social concern on the part of corporate management, corporate donations have once again risen to slightly more than 1 percent of profits or about 0.1 percent of GNP. In absolute dollars they have increased more than twentyfold from their levels in the 1930s,[3] and have now achieved a significant role in the operations of the nation's nonprofit institutions.

It has been estimated[4] that, by the middle of the 1960's, corporations supplied approximately 4–5 percent of total private philanthropy, with

2. It is interesting that this measure seems to have been opposed by President Roosevelt, who was, however, persuaded by those engaged in philanthropic work to refrain from vetoing the Act.

3. These figures are derived from U.S. Treasury Department Internal Revenue Service, *Statistics of Income, Corporate Tax Returns*, for various years.

4. See W. J. Baumol and W. G. Bowen, *Performing Arts: The Economic Dilemma*, Twentieth Century Fund, New York, 1966, Chapters 13 and 14.

TABLE A.52.
PHILANTHROPIC CONTRIBUTIONS OF CORPORATIONS, 1936–69

Year*	Net Profit before Deductions for Contributions (Millions)	Contributions Deducted (Millions)	Contributions as Percentage of Net Profit (col. 2 ÷ col. 1)
	(1)	(2)	(3)
1936–37	$ 7,771	$ 30	0.39
1937–38	7,830	33	0.42
1938–39	4,131	27	0.65
1939–40	7,178	31	0.43
1940–41	9,348	38	0.41
1941–42	16,675	58	0.35
1942–43	23,389	98	0.42
1943–44	28,126	159	0.57
1944–45	26,454	234	0.88
1945–46	21,345	266	1.25
1946–47	25,399	214	0.84
1947–48	31,615	241	0.76
1948–49	34,588	239	0.69
1949–50	28,387	223	0.79
1950–51	42,831	252	0.59
1951–52	43,800	343	0.78
1952–53	38,735	399	1.03
1953–54	39,801	495	1.24
1954–55	36,721	314	0.86
1955–56	47,949	415	0.87
1956–57	47,412	418	0.88
1957–58	45,073	417	0.93
1958–59	39,224	395	1.01
1959–60	47,655	482	1.01
1960–61	44,499	482	1.08
1961–62	47,034	512	1.09
1962–63	50,842	595	1.11
1963–64	55,737	657	1.18
1964–65	74,741	785	1.05

Source: U.S. Treasury Department, Internal Revenue Service, *Statistics of Income, Corporate Tax Returns,* various years. For 1964–65: *Statistics of Business Taxes.*

*The figures given here for, say, 1936–37 are for accounting periods which ended *between* 1 July and 30 June 1937. That is, corporate returns are partly on a fiscal year basis and partly on a calendar year basis.

6–8 percent coming from foundations and the remainder being given by individuals, either directly or in the form of bequests (which themselves constituted 8–10 percent of the total). While corporations, then, are the smallest of the three major philanthropic sources, they are by no means negligible. Moreover, there seems to be a feeling among those engaged in the raising of philanthropic funds that there is considerable room for expansion of giving from this source relative to the potential flow to be derived from other private donors.

The legal status of corporate contributions has not always been as clear as it is today. It has already been reported that tax deductability of corporate contributions was first instituted in 1935. Since then various court decisions have dealt with the legalities of corporate giving, notably with the legitimacy of philanthropic donations for purposes providing no *direct* benefits to the firms, under the terms of their corporate charters. Perhaps the most noteworthy decision in this area was that in the Smith case of 1956, in which the New Jersey Superior Court affirmed the right of the company to provide funds to the university. In this case it was arranged for a friendly stockholder to challenge a gift to Princeton University by a manufacturing company located in New Jersey. The decision, favoring the university, was subsequently upheld by the state Supreme Court.

The decision was noteworthy on at least two counts. The first was the justification for the donative powers on the ground that the company could not hope to operate effectively in a society which is not functioning well. Second, the decision was important because it based itself on the common law, consequently offering a legal basis for giving to corporations throughout the country. Some sorts of gifts by corporations are now explicitly authorized by law in most states of the Union, and national banks are also authorized to make contributions by an amendment to the National Banking Act.

A survey of patterns of giving by 540 corporations conducted in 1965 indicated that slightly more than 40 percent of their gifts went to education; a slightly smaller proportion was devoted to united funds, hospitals, and organizations collecting for health and welfare; about 6 percent of the total was devoted to civic causes; about 3 percent to cultural activities; and the remainder going to miscellaneous groups. The results are reproduced in table A.53.[5]

5. See John H. Watson III, "Report on Company Contributions for 1965", *The Conference Board Record*, October 1966, pp. 45–54. It should be noted that Watson's work and, in particular, his careful surveys are the most illuminating and reliable

This pattern of giving fits in well with the doctrine that corporations should provide funds only to organizations which serve the firm's interests, broadly conceived. Support of education (which nearly trebled its share of corporate contributions over the decade 1955–65) can be justified in terms of the quality of life in the communities in which the companies are located and, more important, because it is to the educational institutions that the business firms look for their supply of trained personnel.

Gifts related to health and welfare can also be rationalized directly. In trying to attract persons of high quality to their employment, business firms find that they must offer candidates a community in which facilities such as hospitals are well run and readily available. The same is true of cultural activities. Increasingly, companies making heavy use of scientists, engineers, programmers, and other technical personnel have emphasized in their advertising the availability of cultural activities in their communities. For such organizations the local theatrical group and the symphony orchestra has become an asset of marked economic value. Here, then, are clear-cut examples of corporate giving following the patterns of enlightened self-interest recommended by the courts and by what appears to be general good judgment.

3. *Evaluation of Corporate Philanthropic Performance*

Despite all this, an air of disappointment in the extent of corporate support is to be discerned among many of those who look to these companies for a substantial portion of their funding. It is noted that while the internal revenue code provisions seem to suggest that 5 percent of net profits is an appropriate standard, corporate giving has so far hardly exceeded one-fifth of this amount.[6]

By way of comparison it may be observed that individual itemized contributions have run as high as 4 percent of adjusted gross income,

---

source of information on corporate contributions, their magnitude, their trends, their distribution, and the amounts coming from firms of different types. Some of the most thoughtful work on the rationale of corporate contribution has been contributed by Professor Richard Eells. For a recent discussion by this author see "A Philosophy for Corporate Giving," *The Conference Board Record*, January 1968, pp. 14–18.

6. Eells does point out (*loc. cit.*) that the figures omit such contributions as gifts-in-kind, the lending of company personnel and good will expenditures for local causes. He notes that while business contributions amount to about 6 percent of total private philanthropy, if religious causes are omitted, corporate giving jumps to perhaps one-fourth or even one-third of the total.

TABLE A.53.
THE COMPANY CONTRIBUTIONS DOLLAR, 1965

	540 Companies		313 Companies without Foundations		227 Companies with Foundations	
	Thousands of Dollars	Percentage of Total	Thousands of Dollars	Percentage of Total	Thousands of Dollars	Percentage of Total
Health and Welfare						
Federated drives: United Funds and the like	50,558	24.2	24,446	26.5	26,112	22.2
National health agencies (not included above)	3,176	1.5	1,238	1.3	1,938	1.7
National welfare agencies (not included above)	4,043	1.9	2,067	2.2	1,976	1.7
Hospitals						
Capital grants	17,172	8.2	9,130	9.9	8,042	6.8
Operating grants	2,018	1.0	1,265	1.4	753	0.6
Other local health and welfare agencies	5,301	2.5	2,274	2.5	3,027	2.6
Capital grants (excluding hospitals)	4,653	2.2	1,997	2.2	2,656	2.3
Total health and welfare	86,921	41.5	42,417	46.0	44,504	38.0
Education						
Higher education						
Scholarships	10,569	5.0	4,800	5.2	5,769	4.9
Fellowships	4,715	2.3	2,300	2.5	2,415	2.1
Research grants (not treated as a business expense)	5,073	2.4	3,501	3.8	1,572	1.3
Capital funds	15,180	7.3	6,245	6.8	8,935	7.6
Direct unrestricted grants	20,487	9.8	8,306	9.0	12,181	10.4
Grants to state, area and na-						

Education-related agencies	3,741	1.8	887	…	…	2.0
Other	8,513	4.1	2,717	3.0	5,706	4.9
Secondary Education						
Capital grants	765	0.4	231	0.3	534	0.5
Other	4,233	2.0	802	0.9	3,431	2.9
Total education	80,344	38.4	32,094	34.8	48,250	41.2
Cultural (cultural centers, performing arts, museums, etc.)						
Operating funds	3,332	1.6	1,702	1.9	1,630	1.4
Capital grants	2,501	1.2	863	0.9	1,638	1.4
Total cultural	5,833	2.8	2,565	2.6	3,268	2.8
Civic causes (municipal and community improvement, good government, and the like)						
Total civic	12,099	5.8	5,658	6.1	6,441	5.5
Other						
Religious causes	1,053	0.5	307	0.3	746	0.6
Groups devoted solely to economic education	1,788	0.9	713	0.8	1,075	0.9
Groups in U.S. whose principal objective is aid to other countries	7,868	3.8	3,779	4.1	4,089	3.5
Causes other than above	8,474	4.0	3,719	4.0	4,755	4.1
Total "other"	19,183	9.2	8,518	9.2	10,665	9.1
Dollars not identifiable because donee is unknown	4,916	2.3	977	1.1	3,939	3.4
Grand total	209,296	100.00	92,229	100.0	117,067	100.0

Source: John H. Watson III, "Report on Company Contributions for 1965," *Conference Board Record*, October 1966, pp. 45–54.

while all taxpayers (whether their returns are itemized or not) have been estimated to devote some 2.5 percent of their adjusted gross income to philanthropy.

It is sometimes suggested that national corporations are particularly remiss in this respect. When a local firm is merged into a company national or international in its scope, it is reported that the amount given to local nonprofit institutions typically suffers a sharp decline. Watson (see footnote 5, above) reports that recent data still support this observation (see table A.54), but that the variation in giving patterns between local and national companies is declining. Generosity also seems to vary inversely with size of corporations. Until recently smaller companies tended to be the most liberal in their giving, but in the past decade an increasing number of medium-sized companies have become relatively open-handed in their contributions policy. This again has raised some questions about the relative niggardliness of the largest firms.

TABLE A.54.
PERCENTAGE OF CONTRIBUTIONS TO NET INCOME, BEFORE TAXES, OF COMPANIES GROUPED ACCORDING TO NUMBER OF EMPLOYEES
(Insurance companies excluded)

Company Size by Number of Employees	Number of Companies	Net Income before Taxes in Thousands	Contributions in Thousands	Percentage of Contributions to Net Income
0–249	11	$ 10,712	$ 163	1.52
250–499	27	49,961	640	1.31
500–999	47	157,421	1,959	1.24
1,000–4,999	152	2,108,554	16,170	0.77
5,000–9,999	79	2,397,911	24,750	1.03
10,000 and over	132	21,707,096	136,558	0.63
Total	448	26,430,655	180,240	0.68

Source: John H. Watson III (see table A.52).

Whether or not one accepts the view that corporate giving is disappointing, it may nevertheless be agreed that the financial needs of the activities of the nonprofit organizations are growing precipitously. With costs per student in elementary and higher education rising at nearly 7 percent per year, compounded even before the recent inflationary upsurge, with medical costs and costs in the performing arts increasing at comparable rates, it is hardly surprising that these organizations have been looking anxiously to the corporations, as to other donors, for increased support. One naturally asks what limits the extent of corporate giving to these groups. If corporations provide support for them only in response to the donors' own interests, why is there a scarcity of funds supplied by the nation's business firms?

4. *Self-Interest and Public Goods*

To analyze the structure of the problem it is necessary to digress into a subject which may at first appear to be irrelevant—the nature of public goods. The point, in brief, is that, while under the free enterprise system the pursuit of self-interest will assure the supply of adequate amounts of most goods and services, there exists an important class of services which economists refer to as public goods, whose quantity when supplied by private enterprise is likely to fall far short of the amount desired by the public. It will be shown that the supply of such goods serves the interests of consumers in exactly the same way as the services of many nonprofit activities serve the interests of corporations. Yet in either case, because both are public goods, the activity level in question is likely, unless special arrangements are made, to fall far short of that which is appropriate in terms of the interests of those concerned. The following pages undertake to show precisely how such problems can arise, why they apply in particular to the issue of corporate giving, and what can be done to overcome them.

As already indicated, for a very substantial proportion of the goods and services provided by our economy, the profit system is an adequate device to assure the supply of quantities at least approximately equal to the amounts demanded by consumers. If potential purchasers increase the number of pairs of shoes or shirts that they desire, and are willing to pay for them, the supply will be forthcoming. This is so because the supplier can normally earn a profit if, and only if, he follows the patterns of consumer demand in the manner just described. A critical element in this process, as we will see in a moment, is what economists have labeled "the excludability property" that characterizes such items. If the consumer does not pay for the item he can be excluded from its use—no payment, no shirt.

There do in fact exist a substantial number of products which do not have the excludability property. Compare the cleaning of an office with the cleaning of the air in a city. The suppliers of the former service can exclude from its benefits anyone who does not pay the fee—if you don't pay, we won't clean your office. But the suppliers of clean air, that is, the manufacturers of filtering devices, etc., once having purified the atmosphere, cannot prevent any inhabitant, or for that matter any visitor, from enjoying the improvement. Clean air is not a salable commodity because once it is supplied to anyone it is automatically available, *without payment*, to everyone else. The supplier has no way to exclude anyone from using it because of failure to pay a price for it.

This is the fundamental property of any public good. Its benefits cannot be provided to one purchaser without automatically being provided to many other individuals. In some cases the number of persons benefitted will be very large (e.g., in the provision of national defense). In other cases, as in the elimination of air pollution in a single city, a more restricted set of individuals will gain. Sometimes (as in snow removal from a dead-end street) the number of persons benefiting will be very small. But in all these cases, once the job is done for one person it will be accomplished for everyone in the pertinent group.

Consider now the position of an individual in such a group, one whose self-interest will be served by the provision of the service in question. If he were to undertake to contract for the job, he would be providing benefits to the other members of the group: he would be offering to the group what are called "external benefits.") He would be in the position of bearing all of the costs by himself while reaping only a proportion of the benefits, and clearly this may not be a reasonable proposition. While it might well be worth his while if he could arrange to pay his pro rata share of the costs, it might be quite undesirable for him when he had to bear the expense entirely by himself. Even where the individual does undertake to pay for the service, he will frequently be prepared to undertake far less of it than he would if the group were acting together.

Where such goods are in question, there are two ways in which their supply is usually handled. The first is for the government to supply them and to assign to each of the beneficiaries a share of the cost in the form of taxation. Where the number of individuals affected is relatively large this may be the only practical way to assure the production of the good or service. That is why such items are called "public goods," and why pollution control and national defense are normally handled by legislation.

A second way of arranging for the supply of public services works typically where the number of persons affected is relatively small. For in such circumstances it is administratively feasible to organize a cooperating group—a consortium. A neighborhood association in a private street may assess each of the (say, ten) resident homeowners one-tenth of the costs of snow removal, and then arrange for the job to be done. The voluntary group works because it is able to "internalize the externalities." The benefits, while in part external to any one individual, are internal to the association. The entire group that benefits is involved in payment of the costs. Taking the group rather than the individual as the relevant decision unit, the excludability property holds as effectively as it does in the sale of a shirt to a single customer.

5. *Practical Application: Oil Exploration*

The notions that have been described in the preceding section are not mere abstractions. They are extremely practical in their import, and the growing seriousness of problems such as pollution, road crowding, and urban decay are at least in part manifestations of these relationships.

Similar problems affect the operations of practical businessmen, and at least in some cases they have developed means of the sort discussed in order to deal with them. A particularly clear example is provided by oil exploration. This activity is characterized by fragmentation in the ownership of real estate which is suspected to be oil-bearing. If four persons own portions of a field that may contain oil, it is only necessary for one of them to test for its presence. One test boring can suffice to determine for all four property owners whether they should construct their own wells.

However, the individual who undertakes the test boring obviously supplies a public good, because he bears all the cost by himself. Whether or not he turns out to have produced a dry hole, the others will have obtained, absolutely free, some extremely valuable information. In such cases the consortium is the obvious way to make sure that such explorations take place and to guarantee that each beneficiary bears a share of the costs. This is apparently the pattern that has emerged. Exploration does in fact take place under the joint sponsorship of those who stand to gain thereby.

However, the industry has not left these matters to chance. It does not rely on the good will of each of the individual property owners to assure the formation of such consortia. The courts are prepared to enforce their formation. Under current arrangements, the owner of such a property need merely propose a set of reasonable offers to the others who stand to benefit. This may involve a cost-sharing agreement which compensates him by a stake in the profits in the other wells, or some other equivalent scheme, and, if the courts find the terms to be acceptable, the others involved may be required to agree to some one of the offers. In this way a quasi-voluntary association principle has been institutionalized as a matter of good business policy, a means to assure that the public good in question is in fact supplied.

6. Application to Corporate Philanthropy

After this long digression we may return to the basic subject, the volume of corporate philanthropy. We began with the proposition that such funds can normally be expected to flow to activities which serve the enlightened self-interest of the firm. But we have just seen that self-interest may not be enough to assure the supply of a desired service, and that even where some is supplied, its volume will be less than the amount that is optimal from the point of view of the beneficiaries.

The objects of corporate philanthropy typically bear all of these characteristics. A grant to an educational institution, even if restricted, say, to a chemistry department, does not guarantee that the increased supply of chemists will flow exclusively to the donor. More trained individuals will also become available to other companies, including perhaps the direct competitors of the donor firm. Similarly, a gift to a symphony orchestra may make the company's community more attractive to engineers who come to work for it, but it will inevitably help other firms in the area in a similar way. A contribution to an outdoor recreation project which makes the city a safer place for the corporation to operate also simultaneously contributes to the safety of other activities.

Indeed, it is difficult to think of a significant class of beneficiary of corporate philanthropy whose activity cannot be described as the supply of a public good. Nor is this purely accidental. If it were otherwise, it would simply be incorrect to describe the company's payment as a gift. If, as an object of company self-interest, the activity could be supplied to our firm all by itself, the activity would have the exclusion characteristic which permits its supply on a profit-making basis by some private enterprise. Nonprofit enterprises do not operate in such fields because there is no need for them.

The consequence is another difficulty that characterizes the supply of all public goods. The company that makes a contribution toward their provision is, strictly speaking, not acting in accord with its own interests. The term *enlightened self-interest* is a euphemism which refers to a compound of facts: the public pressures for a "socially responsible" stance on the part of the firm, the social conscience of management, and its hope that its own contribution will serve as an example to others. Yet as with other public goods, the output of these philanthropic services is likely to be well below what is optimal from the point of view of all companies taken together. Each one of them by itself will finance far fewer of such activities than it would wish to do if all other enterprises were to undertake to match its contributions.

In this the firm is the victim of what has been described as "the tyranny of the small decision." Each company knows that its own contribution can make little difference to, for example, the overall future of higher education. If others fail to contribute, our firm alone cannot save the private universities, while if others do provide sufficient funding, our company's benefaction will not add very much. The net result is that education will not receive as much from industry as it is in the interests of private enterprise as a whole to contribute.

The resolution to the dilemma may perhaps be found by taking a lesson from other public-good cases. The consortium of business donors may go far in dealing with the difficulty. Consider a group of firms which benefit from the presence of a regional theater in their community. If those companies form an association in which each pledges to bear its share of the deficit of the theater, provided all other members also do so, then the connection between the outlay and the return will become a direct one. The externalities will have been internalized. Each management will indeed be able to say to its stockholders that the outlay is a simple matter of economics and self-interest. Moreover, the cost incurred by each will be small, but the effectiveness of its contribution in preserving the activities of the theater will be very substantial. Similarly, consortia may be formed to sustain a private college or a hospital or any other nonprofit enterprise whose welfare is essential for the interests of the group. The initiative for such an association may appropriately come from the contributor corporations or from the organizations they are designed to support. In some cases one might consider utilization of industry or trade organizations that are already in operation—here corporate executives can bring their proposed contribution programs, decide on an appropriate apportionment of the cost, and work out a detailed plan and time schedule.

In any event, this organizational innovation seems well worth trying, for it may succeed in providing a far more direct connection between the firm's contribution and the benefits it receives from the social activity in question. If one is not to be bound by tradition in the area of corporate philanthropy, one must seek for precisely that sort of development— for novel means that can make more immediate the element of self-interest involved in the firm's contribution. Only in this way can stockholders be reassured and management induced to increase its contributions to a level commensurate with the social returns to the supported activity. The analogy with the provision of other public goods suggests that the consortium of firms, all bound together in the support of one or a set of nonprofit institutions, may prove an effective instrument to provide the enlightenment on the self-interest of the contributor which currently seems in somewhat short supply.

7. *Activities That Can Be Undertaken by Individual Firms*

A number of firms have been attempting on their own to systematize and facilitate their contributions programs. The means they have adopted are of some interest as measures that might be considered by others who desire to act on these issues by themselves.

A number of corporations have undertaken to formalize their contribution procedures in a variety of ways. Some have established contribution committees, some have assigned the task of contribution administration and planning to full-time employees, hired specifically for the task. Many firms now have specific budgets devoted exclusively to their program of gifts. A survey conducted in 1963 indicated that 29 percent of the respondents prepare an annual contributions budget, a 15 percent increase over the 1956 figure.[7] A somewhat more recent study reported that some 15–20 percent of the companies surveyed employed a formula determining how much they give.[8]

Perhaps the most important development in this category has been the advent of the company foundation. From a mere twenty such organizations in existence before 1939, by 1962 their number had grown to over fifteen hundred. More than 60 percent of these were established during World War II and the Korean War, when tax rates were extraordinarily high. Aside from any tax advantages they may offer, such foundations are useful because they can impart stability to the donation process. By cutting the tie between the volume of company philanthropy and the level of current profits, the foundation protects the beneficiary from the year-to-year vicissitudes in company earnings.

All of these innovations have obviously facilitated corporate philanthropy. But corporate giving will no doubt be stimulated most effec-

7. American Society of Corporate Secretaries, *Corporate Contributions Report*, 3rd ed., March 1965.
8. "139 Companies Report on Corporate Philanthropy," *Business Management*, December 1965, pp. 14–20.

tively by continued managerial reassessment of the firm's stake in the functioning of society. As businessmen see more clearly and are able to show more effectively to their stockholders that the company's prosperity depends on the health of the community in which it operates, it will become clearer that self-interest is indeed served by corporate contributions. The company pays a high price for operating in a region where education is poor, where living conditions are reprehensible, where health is poorly protected, where property is unsafe, and where cultural activity is all but dead. As it grows clear to stockholders and the others immediately concerned that these circumstances are all more expensive than is corporate giving, the rationality of business philanthropy must become obvious.

It will also be recognized that for business firms this is often a matter which can only be dealt with collectively, by voluntary groupings of firms rather than by the individual enterprises. For it is only such groupings of firms that can provide resources sufficient to make the difference. Groups of firms have long known how to band together when their narrower interests are concerned. In a society in which education, health facilities, and social services generally are beset by precipitously mounting costs, the long-run dangers to the business community may be far greater than the threats against which firms have stood together in the past.

Index

AAFRC. *See* American
Association of Fund-raising
Counsel
ABC. *See* Americans Building
Constitutionally
Acadia National Park, 110
Accountants, survey of, 197–99
Addams, Jane, 63
Administrative abuses of
foundations, 59–60
Administrative expenditures of
foundations, 87
limitation on, 156–57
Advisory Board on Philanthropic
Policy, proposals for, 139–44,
169–70, 181–88
AICPA. *See* American Institute of
Certified Public Accountants
American Association for the
Advancement of Science, 192
American Association of
Fund-Raising Counsel
(AAFRC), 199, 257, 259
American Bar Association, 192
American Dilemma (Myrdal), 130
American Film Institute, 106, 107
American Institute of Certified
Public Accountants, 152–53
American Literary Anthology, 106
American Medical Association, 192
American Psychological Association,
192
American Red Cross, Mid-America
Chapter of, 18, 234
American Sociological Association,
192

Americans Building
Constitutionally (ABC), 54
Andrew W. Mellon Foundation,
109
Appreciated property, 35, 45, 56, 72
Arthur Andersen and Company, 5,
56, 58–60, 197
Arts programs, 104–8
Austin, J. Paul, on foundation
payout requirement, 158–59
Avalon Foundation, 107, 109, 110

Baumol, W. J., on corporate
philanthropy and self-interest,
262–77
Berelson, Bernard, 99n
Boards of trustees. *See* Trustees,
foundation
Bolton, Frances P., 108
Brandeis, Louis D., 124
Bricker Amendment, 65
Bruce, Ailsa Mellon, 109
Bundy, McGeorge, 114
Burke, Edmund, 90

Cape Cod National Seashore, 109
Cape Hatteras National Seashore,
110
Cape Lookout National Seashore,
110
Carnegie, Andrew, 94
Carnegie Commission on Higher
Education, 103
Carnegie Corporation, 103
and noncommercial television,
112–15, 128

Carnegie Endowment for
    International Peace, 66
Carnegie Foundation for the
    Advancement of Teaching, 103
Centers for International Studies, 99
Central Intelligence Agency (CIA),
    69
Chaban-Delmas, Jacques, 19–20
Chandler, Richard H., on survey of
    Chicago philanthropic
    organizations, 227–40
Charitable organizations:
    fee increases of, 25
    financial crisis of, 21–29
        dissenting view of (Kirkland),
            178
        views of distinguished citizens
            on 201–2
    and foundations, interaction of,
        43, 77, 115–16, 234–35,
        239–40
    legislative activities by,
        prohibition of, 186
    operating costs of, 27–28
    personnel expenses of, 23–24
    regulation of, 185–88
    See also Chicago philanthropic
        organizations, survey of;
        Contributions, charitable;
        Corporate giving;
        Foundations; Philanthropy
Chicago Boys Clubs, 231, 234
Chicago Community Fund, 234
Chicago Community Trust, 51, 111,
    195
Chicago Council on Alcoholism, 234
Chicago Educational Television, 231
Chicago philanthropic organizations,
    survey of, 193–94, 227–40
    and cost of services, 229–30
    and fee increases, 230–31
    and foundations, 234–35, 239–40
    and government financing, 232–33,
        238–39
    and importance of broad financial
        base, 236–37
    and improved quality of services,
        229

and overall financial
    requirements, 227–28, 238
and personnel expenses, 228–29
and private philanthropy, 233–34,
    239–40
and volunteer workers, 231–32
See also Charitable organizations
CIA. See Central Intelligence
    Agency
"Clay Brown" transactions, 59
Cleveland Foundation, 51
Colonial National Historical Park,
    109
Committee for Research on
    Problems of Sex, 101
Commonwealth Fund, 96
Community foundations, 51–52
Company foundations, 52, 276
Contributions, charitable, 72–73,
    243–45
    estimated reduction of, without
        tax incentives, 34
    expected future, 248
    and GNP, 22, 28, 227, 257, 261
    trends in, 258–59
    See also Charitable
        organizations; Corporate
        giving; Foundations,
        contributions to
Controversial programs, 82–84,
    101, 127–28
    attitudes of distinguished citizens
        toward, 215–16
Cornell University, department of
    computer science, 98–99
Corporate control stock,
    foundation ownership of, 44,
    246
Corporate giving, 262–77
    background on, 264–67
    evaluation of, 267–71
    patterns of, 266, 268–69
    and profits, 259–60, 263, 265, 270
    and public goods, 271–76
    and self-interest, 262–77
Corporation for Public
    Broadcasting, 113, 114, 128
Council of Economic Advisors, 261

Council on Foundations, 142
Cousins, Norman, 104
Cox, Edward E., congressional
    investigation of foundations
    headed by, 65–67

Devine, Edward T., 63
Digests of foundation-supported
    programs, 136
Distinguished citizens, survey of,
    191–93, 201–26
  and controversial programs,
    215–16
  and financial needs of charitable
    organizations, 201–2
  and foundations' achievements
    and failures, 210–12
  and foundations' roles vis-à-vis
    government, 216–17
  and foundations' significance,
    209–10
  and foundations' social value,
    213–15
  and foundations' support,
    characteristics of, 212–13
  and government vs. private
    philanthropy, 203, 205–9,
    220–26
  and tax incentives, 202–4, 217–20
Duke Endowment, 94
Dulles, John Foster, 65

Ebb, Carmel P., 152n
Economy and philanthropy, 256–61
Educational Facilities Act, 114
Educational programs, 99, 101–4, 128
    See also National Educational
    Television
Eells, Richard, 267n
Eisenhower, Dwight D., 65
Elas U. Pardee Fund, 110–11
Election activities, prohibition of,
    by foundations, 43, 163–64,
    176
Episcopal Diocese of Chicago, 234
Esso Education Foundation, 103–4
Excise tax on foundation income,
    45, 167

Federal Communications
    Commission (FCC), 113–14
Federal Laboratory Theatre
    Project, 107
Financial reporting by foundations,
    45, 152–56
Financial restrictions on
    foundations, 44–45, 57–61,
    167–68, 176
  dissenting view of (Kirkland),
    179–80
Flexner, Abraham, 95, 112, 130
Ford Foundation, 47, 51, 62, 65,
    68, 74, 77–78, 94
  and arts programs, 107
  and domestic vs. international
    programs, 81
  and educational programs, 99,
    103
  and hospital grants, 96
  and national parklands, 110
  and noncommercial television,
    112–15, 128
  and population studies, 100, 101
  and purpose of grants, 79–80
  and social action programs,
    68–69, 82
Fortas, Abe, 69
Fortune, 192
Foundation Center, 4n, 48, 49, 81,
    110, 112, 142, 155, 187–88
Foundation Directory, 155
Foundation grants, 77–86
  abuses of, 60–62
  administration of, 87–92
  controversial, 82–84, 101, 127–28
  distribution of, 251
  for domestic programs only, 254
  evaluation of, 135
  guidelines for, 164–65
  to individuals, 43, 60–61, 77, 99,
    164
  innovative, 84–85
  for international programs, 69,
    80–82, 97, 110
  monitoring of use of, 43, 90–92,
    132–34, 254–55
  purposes of, 78–80, 253

and trustees, role of, 88–90
and types of recipient, 77–78, 252
See also Payout of foundation funds
Foundations:
abuses of, 54–62, 124
achievements of, 95–115, 210–12
administrative expenditures of, 87, 156–57
assessment of, 117–19
assets of, 72–73
    derived from specified sources, percentage of, 247
basic characteristics of, 39–41
board meetings of, 249–50
and charitable organizations, interaction of, 43, 77, 115–16, 234–35, 239–40
classification of, for regulatory purposes, 174–75
contributions to, 72–73, 243–45
    discouragement of, by Tax Reform Act, 165–66
    expected future, 248
and controversial programs, 82–84, 101, 127–28, 215–16
and corporate control stock, 44, 246
digests of programs supported by, 136
and dissemination of research results, 136–37
dissenting views on, 158–59, 177–80
election activities by, prohibition of, 43, 163–64, 176
European vs. U.S., 53
excise tax payable by, 45, 167
failures of, 115, 135, 210–12
federal and state regulation of, 171–72
financial restrictions of, 44–45, 57–61, 167–68, 175–76, 179–80
geographical focus of, 52–53, 242

and government agencies, 216–17
    areas of superiority to, 127–29
    evaluation of, 129
government investigations of, 63–67
government regulation of, 124, 147–59
history of, 93–94
investment performance of, 73–76, 137
IRS auditing of, 62, 170
IRS regulation of, 169–70, 176–77
legal framework for, 41–45
legislative activities by, prohibition of, 43, 160–63, 176
new, discouragement of, 166–68
and nongovernmental institutions, 130–31
with paid staff, 249
and payout of funds, 43, 44, 76, 147–51, 158–59, 172, 175–76
perpetual life of, 172–74
planning and staff of, suggested improvements in, 131–32
politically motivated attacks on, 63–71
proposed organization to improve performance and support of, 139–44, 169–70, 181–88
and public interest, 70, 126
public reporting of activities of, 45, 124, 130–31, 134, 151–56, 165
reasons for establishing, 45–47
small, accomplishments of, 110–11
and social action programs, 26, 68–69, 82–83, 97
support of, characteristics of, 212–13
survey of, 195–97, 199, 241–55
Treasury Department study of, 54–56, 59, 144
trustees of, 89–90, 137–39
types and distribution of, 47–53
views of distinguished citizens on, 209–17, 219, 222–26
Friedman, Martin, 95
Fund for Adult Education, 114

Fund for the Advancement of Education, 114

General Education Board, 64
George Peabody Education Fund, 93
Girl Scouts of Greater Chicago, 18, 234
GNP. *See* Gross national product
Goodell, Phillips W., Jr., on survey of distinguished citizens, 201–26
Gore, Albert, 67
Government agencies:
  as ally of philanthropic organizations, 13–16, 109–10
  areas of foundation superiority to, 127–29
  evaluation of, by foundations, 129
  foundations' roles vis-à-vis, 216–17
  vs. philanthropic organizations, 203, 205–9, 220–26
Government investigations of foundations, 63–67
Government regulation of foundations, 124, 147–59
  and limitation on administrative expenditures, 156–57
  and payout requirement, 147–51, 158–59
  and reporting and disclosure, 124, 130–31, 134, 151–56
  and sanctions for violations, 157–58
  and state regulation, 171–72
Grand Teton National Park, 110
Grant Foundation, 110
Gray, Gordon, 109
Great Smoky Mountains National Park, 110
Gross national product (GNP), 22, 28, 227, 257, 261
Guggenheim Foundation. *See* John Simon Guggenheim Memorial Foundation; Solomon R. Guggenheim Foundation

Hamilton, Mary, on philanthropy and economy, 256–61
Health Insurance Plan of Greater New York, 96
Hiss, Alger, 66
Historical sites, preservation of, 108–9
Historic Sites Act (1935), 109
Hoffman, Paul, 65
Hull House Association (Chicago), 231
Hunterdon Medical Center (New Jersey), 96
Hutchins, Robert Maynard, 65

Institutions, nongovernmental, foundation evaluation of, 130–31
Internal Revenue Service (IRS):
  data on philanthropy provided by, 256
  regulation of foundation operations by, 169–70, 176–77
  and survey of foundations, 199
International Health Board, 97
International programs, 69, 80–82, 97, 110
Investment abuses of foundations, 56–59
Investment performance of foundations, 73–76, 137
IRS. *See* Internal Revenue Service
Irvine Foundation, 49
Ittleson Foundation, 110

J. M. Kaplan Fund, 106
John F. Slater Fund, 93
John Hay Whitney Foundation, 101, 102
John Simon Guggenheim Memorial Foundation, 94, 107
  fellowship program of, 102
Johns Hopkins University School of Hygiene and Public Health, 95
Joint Council on Educational Television, 113

Josiah Macy Junior Foundation,
    96, 110
Juilliard Music Foundation, 94, 108
Juilliard Music School, 108

Kaiser Health Plan, 96
Kansas City Association of Trusts
    and Foundations, 103
Kaplan Fund. *See* J. M. Kaplan
    Fund
Keele, Harold M., 65–66
Kellogg Foundation. *See* W. K.
    Kellogg Foundation
Kennedy, Robert F., 69, 78
Kerr, Clark, 103
Killian, James, 128
King, William L. Mackenzie, 64
Kinsey, Alfred C., 101
Kirkland, Lane, dissent to
    commission recommendations
    by, 177–80
Krause, Arlington C., 111

Laura Spelman Rockefeller
    Memorial, 94
Lee, Philip R., 95
Legislative activities, prohibition
    of, by foundations, 43,
    160–63, 176, 186
Levine Foundation. *See* Samuel Z.
    Levine Foundation for
    International Child Health
Library of Congress, 106
Lilly Foundation, 94
Lincoln, Abraham, 71, 123
Long, Franklin A., 95
Lutheran Welfare Services
    (Chicago), 231

Macaulay, Thomas Babington, 82
McKinsey and Company, 107
Macy Foundation. *See* Josiah Macy
    Junior Foundation
Market Facts, Inc., 5
Mayo Clinic, 96
Mayo Foundation, 96
Medical programs, 95–98, 110–11
Melbourne, Lord, 11

Mellon, Paul, 109
Mellon Foundation. *See* Andrew
    W. Mellon Foundation;
    Avalon Foundation; Old
    Dominion Foundation;
    Richard King Mellon
    Foundation
Michael Reese Hospital (Chicago),
    231
Milbank Memorial Fund, 94, 100
Montefiore Hospital (New York),
    96
Monticello (Jefferson's home), 108
Morgan Guaranty Bank, 261
Moskin, Morton, 152n
Mount Vernon (Washington's
    home), 108
Myrdal, Gunnar, 130

Nathan report, 186
National Banking Act, 266
National Council on
    Philanthropy, 142
National Educational Television,
    112–15
National Endowment for the Arts,
    106
National Merit Scholarship
    Corporation, 103
National Opinion Research
    Center, 5
National parks, 109–10
National Planning Association
    (NPA), 261
National Research Council, 101
National Scholarship Service for
    Negro Students, 101–2
National Trust for Historic
    Preservation, 108, 109
National Urban League, 192
Nature Conservancy, 110
Negro education, 101–2
NET. *See* National Educational
    Television
New York Academy of Medicine, 96
New York State Arts Council, 107
New York University Medical
    Center, 96

Notestein, Frank W., 99n
NPA. *See* National Planning
    Association

Office of Population Research, 100
Oil exploration, 273–74
Old Dominion Foundation, 107,
    109, 110
Olin Foundation, 99
Omnibus, 113
Open Lands Project (Chicago), 234
"Operating" foundations, 39
Opportunity Fellowship Program
    (John Hay Whitney
    Foundation), 101–2

Pan-American Health Organization,
    97
Pardee Fund. *See* Elas U. Pardee
    Fund
Patman, Wright, 4n, 48, 54, 59,
    67–69, 80–81
Payout of foundation funds, 43, 44,
    147–51, 172, 175–76
    dissenting view of (Austin),
    158–59
    as percentage of assets, 76
Peabody Fund. *See* George
    Peabody Education Fund
Permanent Charities Fund of
    Boston, 51
Peterson, Peter G., 3
Pew Foundation, 94
Phelps-Stokes Fund, 94
Philanthropists, survey of, 199–200
Philanthropy:
    as ally of government, 13–16,
    109–10
    criticisms of, 11–13
    distribution of, 1969, 2
    and economy, 256–61
    European vs. U.S., 19–20
    future of, 259–61
    and GNP, 22, 28, 227, 257, 261
    vs. government financing, 203,
    205–9, 220–26
    as self-serving institution, 11–13
    and social unrest, 16–17

and tax incentives, 12, 30–36,
    145–46, 165–68
    views of distinguished citizens on,
    201–26
    and volunteer work, 18–19
    See also Charitable
    organizations; Contributions,
    charitable; Corporate giving;
    Foundations
Pifer, Alan, 3
Population Council, 100
Population studies, 99–101
Public goods, 271–73
Public health, 95–98
Public interest, 70, 126
Public reporting of foundation
    activities, 45, 124, 130–31,
    134, 151–56
    in sensitive areas, 165
Public Theater (New York), 107

Reece, B. Carroll, congressional
    investigation of foundations
    headed by, 66–67
Reporting and disclosure. *See*
    Public reporting of
    foundation activities
Research results, dissemination of,
    136–37
Richard King Mellon Foundation,
    94
Richmond Foundation, 69
Robinson, Daniel, 152n
Rockefeller, John D., 64, 94
Rockefeller, John D., Jr., 108–10
Rockefeller, John D. III, 2–3, 100
Rockefeller Foundation, 63–64, 94
    and arts programs, 107
    and Kinsey sex studies, 101
    and medicine, 95–97
Rockefeller Memorial. *See* Laura
    Spelman Rockefeller
    Memorial
Rockefeller Sanitary Commission, 97
Roosevelt, Franklin D., 264n
Rosenwald, Julius, 174
Rosenwald Fund, 94, 101, 102
Russell Sage Foundation, 94, 142

Salk, Jonas, 96
Salvation Army (Chicago), 231
Samuel Z. Levine Foundation for
    International Child Health,
    110
Schultze, Charles, 51, 68n
Scientific research, 98–99
    dissemination of results of,
    136–37
Scripps Foundation for Research in
    Population Control, 100
Sensitive areas, guidelines for
    grant making in, 164–65
Sesame Street, 115
Slater Fund. *See* John F. Slater
    Fund
Sloan Foundation, 94, 98–99
Smith, Kline, and French
    Foundation, 103
Smithsonian Institution, 106
Social action programs, 26, 68–69,
    82–83, 97
Solomon R. Guggenheim
    Foundation, 107
Southern Regional Council, 133
Spaeth Foundation, 110
Specialized programs, 128
Spelman Fund, 94
State regulation of foundations,
    171–72
Statistics of Income (IRS), data on
    philanthropy included in, 256

T. B. Walker Foundation, 107–8
Taft, Robert A., 65
Tax on foundation income, 45, 167
Tax incentives, 12, 30–36, 145–46,
    165–68
    dissenting view of (Kirkland),
    177–80
    estimated reduction of charitable
    donations without, 34
    proposals on, 183–85
    views of distinguished citizens on,
    202–4, 217–20
    See also Appreciated property
Tax Reform Act (1969), 4–6,
    32–33, 54–55

definition of "private
    foundations" in, 40, 42–43,
    48
discouragement of contributions
    to foundations by, 165–66
discouragement of establishment
    of new foundations by,
    166–68
and excise tax payable by
    foundations, 45, 167
limitation on foundations'
    administrative expenditures
    by, 156–57
and monitoring of foundation
    grants, 43
and payout of foundation funds,
    43, 44, 147–51, 158–59, 172,
    175–76
and prohibition of election
    activities by foundations, 43,
    163–64, 176
and prohibition of legislative
    activities by foundations, 43,
    160–63, 176, 186
and prohibition of payments to
    government officials by
    foundations, 43
and reporting of foundations'
    financial and program
    activities, 45, 151–56
and restriction of foundations'
    financial activities, 44–45,
    57–61, 167–68
sanctions for violations of, 157–
    58
and state regulation of
    foundations, 171–72
Television, noncommercial. *See*
    National Educational
    Television
Thales (Greek astronomer), 93
Thompson, Warren S., 100
Thoreau, Henry David, 1
Travelers' Aid Society (Chicago),
    231
Trustees, foundation, 87–90,
    137–39
    meetings of, 249–50

United Cerebral Palsy, 18
University of Minnesota Drama
    Program, 107
U.S. Treasury Department, study of
    foundations by, 54–56, 59,
    144

Volunteer workers, 18–19, 231–32

W. K. Kellogg Foundation, 94, 96
Walker Art Center
    (Minneapolis), 108
Walker Foundation. *See* T. B.
    Walker Foundation
Walsh, Frank P., 64
Watson, John H. III, 263n,
    266n–67n, 270
Weaver, Robert C., 101–2

Welch, William, 95
Welfare Council of Metropolitan
    Chicago, 18, 195
Whitney Foundation. *See* John Hay
    Whitney Foundation
Who's Who in America, 192
Wieboldt Foundation, 111
Williamsburg, Va., restoration of, 108
Wirth, Conrad L., 109
Wolfson Foundation, 69
Woodlawn Organization (Chicago),
    231
Woodrow Wilson National
    Fellowship Foundation, 103
Woods Charitable Fund, 111
World Health Organization, 97

YMCA of Greater Chicago, 18, 234